READING THE BIBLE ON TURTLE ISLAND

T. Christopher Hoklotubbe
and H. Daniel Zacharias

Foreword by Shari Russell

An imprint of InterVarsity Press
Downers Grove, Illinois

InterVarsity Press
P.O. Box 1400 | Downers Grove, IL 60515-1426
ivpress.com | email@ivpress.com

©2025 by Thomas Christopher Hoklotubbe and Hermann Daniel Zacharias

All rights reserved. No part of this book may be reproduced in any form without written permission from InterVarsity Press.

InterVarsity Press® is the publishing division of InterVarsity Christian Fellowship/USA®. For more information, visit intervarsity.org.

All Scripture quotations, unless otherwise indicated, are taken from the Common English Bible, copyright 2011. Used by permission. All rights reserved.

While any stories in this book are true, some names and identifying information may have been changed to protect the privacy of individuals.

The publisher cannot verify the accuracy or functionality of website URLs used in this book beyond the date of publication.

Cover design: Faceout Studio, Jeff Miller
Interior design: Jeanna Wiggins
Images: Getty Images: © Raj Kamal / Stockbyte
　　　　　　　　　© fotograzia / Moment
　　　　　　　　　© filo / DigitalVision Vectors
　　　　　　　　　© amtitus / DigitalVision Vectors
　　　　　　　　　© aleksandarvelasevic / DigitalVision Vectors

ISBN 978-1-5140-0756-3 (print) | ISBN 978-1-5140-0757-0 (digital)

Library of Congress Cataloging-in-Publication Data
A catalog record for this book is available from the Library of Congress.

31　30　29　28　27　26　25　　|　　12　11　10　9　8　7　6　5　4　3　2　1

"We have been waiting for a book like this—one that presents indigenous biblical interpretation. T. Christopher Hoklotubbe and H. Daniel Zacharias call their approach to biblical interpretation Turtle Island Hermeneutics. I call it groundbreaking, urgent, and necessary at this present moment. Now students studying the Bible in seminary or college will have a text that will help them do what few books on interpretation can do—take the dirt, the water, the air, our animal kin, and of course, indigenous thought and life seriously. We are now in a new day for biblical scholarship."

Willie James Jennings, Andrew W. Mellon Professor of Systematic Theology and Africana Studies at Yale University Divinity School

"Some years ago, I was told that Indigenous contributions to biblical scholarship would, at best, be superficial. The real work, after all, had already been done by European scholars. *Reading the Bible on Turtle Island* justifies my contention that this was not so. T. Christopher Hoklotubbe and H. Daniel Zacharias unpack Indigenous understandings of the biblical narrative for us in profoundly earthy and culturally complex ways. For the first time ever, many Indigenous people have read themselves into the biblical story and, together with the authors, have answered Lamin Sanneh's 2003 question, 'Whose religion is Christianity?' 'It's ours,' they have said!"

Terry LeBlanc, director emeritus and elder in residence of NAIITS: An Indigenous Learning Community

"*Reading the Bible on Turtle Island* introduces us to the riches of Indigenous interpretation of Scripture and invites us to gather around the council fire and learn from the ongoing discussion Indigenous disciples of Jesus are having about how to 'seek Creator in the Good Medicine Way of Jesus.' T. Christopher Hoklotubbe and H. Daniel Zacharias not only create a dialogue between biblical scholarship, Indigenous history and wisdom, and ongoing debates about how to relate the gospel to culture, they do so in a way that is simultaneously accessible, deeply moving, gracious enough to create room for disagreement and ongoing debate, and occasionally laugh-out-loud funny. Yet the book also offers a challenge, that the path to the healing of the nations and the Western church includes learning from Indigenous disciples who bear witness to the good word of Creator-made-flesh."

Michael J. Rhodes, author of *Just Discipleship* and lecturer in Old Testament at Carey Baptist College

"How we read ourselves into the Bible shapes the theology we develop. This book offers all Christians another reading, a reading that takes our stories seriously and provides an opportunity to develop an Indigenous theology rather than simply reconciling ourselves to a theology rooted in European priorities."

Patty Krawec, author of *Becoming Kin: An Indigenous Call to Unforgetting the Past and Reimagining Our Future* and *Bad Indians Book Club: Reading at the Edge of a Thousand Worlds*

"*Reading the Bible on Turtle Island* is a thought-provoking contribution that invites those shaped by a Western Christian worldview into the circle of Indigenous theological conversation. T. Christopher Hoklotubbe and H. Daniel Zacharias weave a compelling narrative that honors Indigenous insights and engages the Scriptures with depth and integrity. They speak with an authority born of lived experience and careful listening. This book invites readers into a sacred dance of interpretation—one that is deeply communal, rooted in place, and led by the Spirit. It is both a gift and an invitation for the church to do justice, love mercy, and walk humbly on a path toward genuine reconciliation. Highly recommended!"

Terry M. Wildman, lead translator, general editor, and project manager for the *First Nations Version* and *First Nations Version Psalms and Proverbs*

"This book was not written for me, but I was deeply moved by it. Born and raised in Oklahoma, I am a settler who grew up proximate to Indigenous peoples but remained in great need of the education T. Christopher Hoklotubbe and H. Daniel Zacharias provide here. Through honest history, insightful exegesis, and thought-provoking and transformative theology, *Reading the Bible on Turtle Island* drew forth both laughter and tears. I pray Indigenous readers are encouraged by it and settler-readers, like myself, are awakened by it. This book is a must-read for everyone."

Amy Peeler, Kenneth T. Wessner Chair of Biblical Studies at Wheaton College and coeditor of *The New Testament in Color*

"This book will change the way you read the Bible and see the world. It invites readers to learn from creation as we do from Scripture. T. Christopher Hoklotubbe and H. Daniel Zacharias see themselves and their ancestors in Scripture and weave Indigenous stories, ceremonies, and lifeways into their engagement with biblical narratives. In doing so, they confront colonial legacies while offering liberative readings of biblical texts that arise from within the land. This book has expanded my understanding of community and deepened my desire to be in harmonious relationships with Creator and all my creational kin."

Janette H. Ok, associate professor of New Testament at Fuller Theological Seminary

FOR TERRY AND BEV LEBLANC

On behalf of the entire NAIITS community

We are your legacy

CONTENTS

FOREWORD BY SHARI RUSSELL	ix
PROTOCOL	xiii
1 Entering the Circle Dance *An Introduction to Turtle Island Hermeneutics*	1
2 It's All Relative *The Scriptures, Creational Kinship, and "All Our Relations"*	30
3 Reading Along the Bright Path *How Jesus' Jubilee Teachings Can Lead Us Back into Shalom/Harmony with All Our Relations*	55
4 Crying for a Vision of Who We Are *Seeing Our Ancestors and Ourselves in Scripture*	82
5 Naboth's Descendants *Reading the Bible Along a Trail of Broken Treaties*	103
6 From Babylon to Boarding Schools *Reading Scripture and Sharing Truths for Reconciliation and Healing*	131
7 Reading While Red(bone) *Come and Get Your Love and Ceremony*	159
CONCLUSION	
The Call of the Drum *An Invitation to the Circle of Turtle Island Hermeneutics*	185
PRELUDE/APPENDIX	
Smoke Signals from the Trail *Honoring Our Elders Around the Council Fire*	191
GENERAL INDEX	216
SCRIPTURE INDEX	218

FOREWORD

Shari Russell

> *When the drum beats*
> *it resonates beyond your body. It*
> *becomes the heartbeat of Creation as*
> *it was meant to be. To sing with it is*
> *to offer a blessing to all that is and to*
> *receive blessings back. That's why drums*
> *echo. Put your hand on your chest. Close*
> *your eyes. Feel the drum in your chest.*
> *Sing with it and blessings become your*
> *breath, indrawn and expelled, emptying*
> *and filling, all the world at once...*
>
> RICHARD WAGAMESE, *EMBERS:*
> *ONE OJIBWAYS'S MEDITATIONS*, 56.

THE FIRST TIME I REMEMBER HEARING the powwow drum, I was in grade 12. The sound reverberated from the arena and my heart aligned with its pulsating rhythm. I shared my desire to check it out, but the disapproving words *evil* and *demonic* stifled any curiosity for my Indigenous traditions and culture. It would be decades until I found myself reconnecting with my culture and coming home to the soothing sounds of a mother's heartbeat in the cadenced reverberation of the powwow drum. As I breathed in deeply, the assurance and blessing of Creator's gift filled my lungs, my heart, and my whole being. I was home.

This story is not uncommon as the impact of colonial ideology merged with missionary endeavors inculcated Indigenous peoples with the message that their culture, traditions, and spirituality needed to be replaced with Christian dogma and rules. Decades later, after much theological study and discourse, the narrative is changing. Indigenous peoples are coming home to the sound of the drum to reclaim their Creator-given identity and to share this blessing with the body of Christ.

When Danny and Chris approached me about writing this foreword, I was honored and filled with a sense of pride as I reflected on their journey. I appreciated Chris and Danny's use of humor and cheeky jesting that grounds their writing in relationality. It is such a blessing to see these two biblical scholars reclaim their Indigenous heritage and to hear them integrate their Indigenous understandings of land and creation in their writing.

Not too long ago, I was asked to share at the Acadia Divinity College chapel service. I asked Danny if he would play a prayer song on the hand drum. Danny had previously written a song and I assumed he might share that. To my surprise, Danny shared a new song he was gifting for the NAIITS' community for the entry of the NAIITS' Eagle Staff that had been made. As I listened to his son Jack and him singing, I was overwhelmed, thinking of how Indigenous peoples were forbidden to use our songs, our prayers, our languages, and our ceremonies. Tears of joy and pride freely flowed as Danny engaged his whole being in reclaiming his Indigenous heritage; both he and Chris are contributing to the flourishing of theology as Indigenous biblical scholars. I admit, I especially enjoy watching Chris on the drum—he really does make me chuckle and smile with delight. The first time he was invited to join the drum circle at the NAIITS symposium, tears filled my eyes, not just because of his lack of drumming ability, but because of the embrace he received from those around the drum, which signified his welcome back into his Indigenous identity, into tradition and culture, and into family and community.

This book synthesizes the theological dialogue of the NAIITS community since its inception in 2001. I hear the words and thoughts of NAIITS founding members throughout. It is a gift that will bring the healing and restoration necessary for the flourishing of Indigenous peoples and the whole body of Christ. No longer do we have to leave behind our Indigenous ways of thinking and being. No longer do we have to justify how Indigenous traditions fit into Christian faith and practice. In this book, Danny and Chris address difficult passages that have previously been used to limit Indigenous perspectives. They flip upside down conventional ways of understanding Scripture, such as the view of wilderness as a desolate place rather than a sacred place of communion or consecration. Although readers will be challenged and stretched to think beyond the European dominant, Western theological frameworks, Danny and Chris integrate biblical knowledge with Indigenous interpretation of Scripture across Turtle Island. Rather than being restrictive, they expand and enrich our understanding of Creator, humanity, and our place within creation. In all this, they maintain the centrality of Jesus and the gospel story.

This is one of the first books I have read that attempts to bring together the experience of Indigenous followers of Jesus in Canada and the United States. Danny and Chris seek to build bridges between Christian understandings and Indigenous perspectives, showing the breadth, depth, and inclusivity of the gospel's invitation. They have brought together Indigenous voices from diverse demographics: women, men, older and younger generations, varying denominational affiliations, and the spectrum of contextual practices spanning from integration to separation. Chris and Danny seek to maintain the balance of not romanticizing Indigenous experiences and perspectives through their humility in recognizing the tensions encountered. Yet, they call for a reorientation within the Christian faith and practice of aligning the place of humanity within the kinship web of all creation. They have heard the heartbeat of the drum calling us to receive the blessing and then to share it. They are sharing this blessing as they share the insights of Indigenous peoples who have listened and heard God speaking through the generations and have embraced the whole person of Jesus. As they invite us to learn to dance, to sing a new song, and to embrace the flourishing of all humanity as Creator desires, may we walk gently and with humility.

PROTOCOL

LAND ACKNOWLEDGMENT

Land acknowledgments may be new to you. They are statements that recognize the importance of the local land and especially the First Peoples of that land and their ancestral connection to it. They range from being beautiful to deeply contested. We have been in entertainment venues where a canned, prerecorded land acknowledgment played on repeat overhead to a distracted and inattentive crowd. We have been in professional settings where the land acknowledgment has been done to check off a box, read by the person who happened to be opening a meeting, sprung on them at the last minute. But we have also been to events where the land acknowledgment was written for the moment and deeply thoughtful. And we have been at or taken part in land acknowledgments that are themselves the ceremonial opening to a gathering. There are many who see a land acknowledgment as part of the "woke" agenda and get angry and roll their eyes. There are others for whom a land acknowledgment must begin any formal gathering, and not to do so is a sign of disrespect that may taint the remainder of the gathering.

You can probably guess where we land as authors. While we recognize that land acknowledgments can frequently feel rote and perfunctory, we could as Christians say the same thing about calls to worship, about the Lord's Prayer said together, and any other number of things that become regular parts of our collective gathering. It is the work of individuals and communities to continue to imbue importance into these aspects of communal life. Land acknowledgments remind us of the community of creation that we are a part of. They are reminders that every place we are, whether at home or in travel, is a storied place, full of history, life, and relationships. In colonized spaces such as Turtle Island (the Indigenous designation for

North America), it is a reminder for Indigenous peoples that our stories and histories matter and that our ancestors have known, shaped, and been shaped by the land we are in. For some non-Indigenous folks, it may serve as a reminder that they know very little of the history of the lands they occupy and hopefully as a moment of gratitude for the way the land takes care of us, as well as gratitude for the original inhabitants who were caretakers of the land prior to colonization.

We, as authors, recognize that stories and wisdom are held by places. Stories, wisdom, and belonging are tied to the land, and we aim to live in a good way in the places we live and the places we visit. And in recognizing land as a storied place, we recognize that Creator apportioned lands to peoples. Indigenous peoples of Turtle Island do not think that the land belongs to them but that we belong to the land. In preparation for this book, we both traveled across our respective countries, separately and together. We beheld the beauty of different territories, heard the stories, met the people, felt the joys and the heartaches. Through all of these travels and in times of sitting together to write face to face, or pixel to pixel, we gave thanks for the goodness of Creator and acknowledged the lands that have welcomed us and continue to sustain us. I (Danny) am grateful for the land of Mi'kma'ki, the ancestral and unceded territory of the Mi'kmaq people, where my little town of Wolfville, Nova Scotia, resides. And I (Chris) honor the many tribes for whom the land of Mount Vernon and Lisbon, Iowa, was and is home, including the Bájoxe (Ioway), the Oceti Ŝakowiŋ ("The Seven Council Fires," including the Lakota, Dakota, and Nakota), the Meskwaki Nation (Sac and Fox of the Mississippi in Iowa), the Kiikaapoi (Kickapoo), and the Ho-Chunk (Winnebago Tribe of Nebraska).

ACKNOWLEDGMENTS

In our preparation to write this book, Chris and Danny traveled across parts of the United States and Canada, interviewing Indigenous Christian ministers and leaders through the generous financial support of the Louisville Institute. We are immensely grateful for the Louisville Institute's investment in this project and in us. We are also thankful to the leadership of our respective academic institutions for their support and encouragement of our research and writing: Shari Russell (NAIITS: An Indigenous Learning

Community), Anna Robbins (Acadia Divinity College), and Ilene Crawford (Cornell College).

No Indigenous project can speak for all Indigenous peoples, especially not ours. As of 2023, the United States recognizes 574 tribes, and Canada recognizes 630 First Nations, the Métis (a distinct cultural group, with mixed Indigenous and settler ancestry), and the Inuit and Innu (Indigenous peoples of the Arctic). Moreover, many tribes remain unrecognized by their respective governments and individuals remain unenrolled. Chris writes from his social location as mixed Indigenous and settler (German, Jewish, Spanish-Mexican), being a proud member of the Choctaw Nation of Oklahoma in the United States. Danny's maternal ancestry encompasses the Indigenous peoples of the lands now called Manitoba, the Nêhiyawak (Cree), the Métis, and the Anishinaabe, and his paternal ancestry is Austrian. His maternal ancestors reside in the territories of treaties 1, 2, 3, and 5.[1] While neither of us was raised in our respective Indigenous communities, over the past number of years we have both sought to reclaim our cultural heritages. The NAIITS Indigenous Learning community in particular has been a life-giving and supportive space to grow among a diverse community of Indigenous followers of Jesus. In many ways, our research, writing, and visits with elders for this project have contributed to this personal, life-giving journey of revitalizing our Indigenous heritage.

We approach this project in all humility, knowing how privileged we are to carry the stories, experiences, and wisdom that have been shared with us by our Indigenous elders and kin in the faith. We have sought to be broad in our representation of voices without presuming to be exhaustive. We can only hope that the examples, stories, and interpretations we present in this work are representative enough for other Indigenous people to see a resemblance of their own heritage and to feel invited to join the dance. Moreover, we recognize that our account does not address our Mexican Indigenous kin at the tail of the turtle. Indeed, Indigenous followers of Jesus in Central and South America have a rich heritage and tradition of engaging with the kinds

---

[1] The numbered treaties refer to the eleven treaties that were signed between 1871 and 1921 between the Canadian monarch and many First Nations across Canada. These treaties were designed to provide the space for the federal government to arrange for western settlement and expanded resource extraction.

of questions and explorations we are engaged with in this book. Every project has its limits, and we hope that you as the reader can graciously forgive whatever gaps you perceive to be in our work. Danny encourages all such concerns to be directed to Chris, who in turn will forward them to our wonderful editor, Rachel Hastings.

In all seriousness, we cannot express enough gratitude for Rachel's fierce support and brilliance. She was an invaluable sounding board for our vision, tolerated our humor, and gave sagacious feedback. Rachel went above and beyond as an editor to attend a NAIITS symposium in South Dakota and to encounter the community from which and to whom we write. We are also grateful to the sharp anonymous reviewers who offered insightful engagement with our work that widened our analysis, tightened our prose, and nuanced our rhetoric to avoid unnecessary arguments.

This work arises from two years of marinating in the stories, wisdom, and relationships with Indigenous ministers, leaders, and practitioners across Turtle Island. Native peoples have been interpreting the Bible from their very first encounters with missionaries, and we knew that to do this project justice we would need to participate in worshiping communities, listen to online sermons, sit in coffee shops, set up tipis, smudge, perspire in sweat lodges, and laugh with Indigenous people across the United States and Canada. We are grateful for the many stories we received permission to share here in this book. Through those many conversations and visits, there was an incredible amount of wisdom shared with us that did not make it into the book—but the wisdom made it into us. It shaped our spirits and our imaginations, inspired what we wrote here, and will continue to shape our work in the future. Thank you all. For Indigenous thinkers who have put their work into print, we provide a fuller acknowledgment to many of these incredible individuals and their contributions to Indigenous interpretations of the Bible in our prelude/appendix.

From both of us, *Mîkwêc, ekosani,* and *yakoke* to Ray Aldred, Amy N. Allan, Sarah Augustine, the Azak family, Hubert Barton, Cheryl Bear, Donnie and Renee Begay, Maka Black Elk, Vance Blackfox, Anna M. V. Bowden, Basil Brave Heart, Martin Brokenleg, Shaneequa Brokenleg, Allen Buck, Jared Byas, Ji-gaabiikwe Campeau, Mark Charles, Casey and Lora Church, George Cote, Mary Crist, Murray Crookes, Christina Dawson, Cameron Eggie, Kelly

Montijo Fink, Wanda Frenchman, J. Goins, Mackenzie Griffin, Bradley S. Hauff, Ted Hernandez, Eddie Hoklotubbe, Courtland Hopkins, Josh Hopping, Adrian Jacobs, Karen and Howard Jolly, Chad Johnson, Chebon Kernell, Patty Krawec, Megan Murdock Krischke, Michelle Oberwise Lacock, Carol Lakota-Eastin, Terry and Bev LeBlanc, Catherine Martin, Willard Martin, Harry Moore, Michelle Nieviadomy, Steven Hunter Oklatubbee, Christopher Peele, Stephanie Perdew, Kenny Pretty On Top Jr., Irv Porter, Christina Quintanilla, Mark Ravenhair, Harold Roscher, Sun Rise Tiger Ross, Tim Ross, Shari Russell, Frances Sampson, Jim Sequeira, Kelly Sherman-Conroy, Dean Shingoose, Dave Skene, Jane Smith, Paul Sneve, Tony Snow, Vincent Solomon, Elona Street-Stewart, Iglahiq Suuqiina, Lenore Three Stars, Tink Tinker, Daniel and Roseanna Tubby, Robert Two Bulls, Kenny Wallace, David Wilson, Larry Wilson, Terry and Darlene Wildman, Wendy Weston, Zelma Wind, Randy and Edith Woodley, Clarence Yarholar, Vincent Yellow Old Woman, and Frankie Young.

Thank you to many of our brilliant family and friends who provided insightful editorial suggestions on early drafts of this book, including Chris's wife, Stephanie Hoklotubbe, Terry LeBlanc, Bobby Outterson-Murphy, and Clare Willrodt. We also thank our students, including Shandy Browett, Dan Christmas, Marla Dunn, Will Krischke, Cheryl Poole, Heaven Scott, and Marlene Wolters. Everyone's honest feedback helped us to make this book readable and maybe even enjoyable. Chris also thanks his students, Elinor Ascher-Handlin from Cornell College and Grant Showalter-Swanson from Garrett-Evangelical Theological Seminary, who assisted him in the early research stages of this project.

I (Chris) deeply appreciate the unconditional love and support of my wife, Stephanie, and my daughters Claire and Emily, whose infectious joy gives my days meaning. I dedicate this book to my Opa (grandfather), Edwin Hoklotubbe, whose stick-figure theology lessons over napkins and gentle encouragement to memorize Bible verses instilled in me a deep love for Scripture. The simplicity of his spirituality as a Choctaw Presbyterian taught me to love God, others, and myself. He still inspires my family today.

I (Danny) thank my wonderful wife, Maria, and children Lex, Jack, Ella-Rose, and our little ball of energy, Hudson. Much thanks also to my colleagues at Acadia Divinity College for their support and encouragement, and the space to travel, study, read, and write. A lot of travel and time went into this project, and Maria and my older children bore the brunt of my travels. My successes are shared with you. Like Chris, I dedicate this to my grandparents, Bert and Dolly. They loved God, loved the Scriptures, and loved their families, and it is a legacy I hope that I embody and pass on to my children and grandchildren.

1

ENTERING THE CIRCLE DANCE

An Introduction to Turtle Island Hermeneutics

NEITHER OF US, CHRIS NOR DANNY, is a particularly good dancer. We are certainly not *fancy* dancers, dressed in colorful regalia at powwows and coordinated in their dramatic movement. But when the drum leader invites the community into the circle dance during our annual NAIITS symposium gatherings, we join.[1] When the round dance takes place, everyone gathers in a wide circle, shoulder to shoulder, and performs a two-step shuffle to the beat of the drum that is simple enough (even for Chris and Danny) to follow along. Historically, there have been disagreements about *which* direction we dance, whether clockwise or counterclockwise. Each Indigenous band and nation has its own protocol, and we defer to the protocol of the people whose ancestral homelands we dance on. Nevertheless, wherever we dance, there are always a few who roll their eyes and make it known that we are dancing the wrong way according to *their* tradition. And we dance as the drummers sing the "Friendship Dance" and "We Dance Before You." "As we rise, our prayer is our dance," intones the solemn voice of Mohawk singer, Jonathan Maracle. "We dance before your holy throne," the song continues, alluding to the image of the "persons from every tribe, language, people, and nation" (Rev 5:9) who encircle the throne of God (Rev 4–5). As our hearts rhythmically align with the vibrations of the drumbeat, our dance may be a foretaste of the sacred round dance that our

---

[1] NAIITS at its origin stood for the North American Institute of Indigenous Theological Studies, but since its founding twenty-five years ago, we have expanded beyond North America, with academic partnerships and students from across the globe. There is now a NAIITS presence in Australia, as well as expanding partnerships in the Philippines, Central and South America, and Aotearoa (New Zealand). So NAIITS now simply goes by NAIITS: An Indigenous Learning Community.

elder in the faith, John of Patmos, envisioned.[2] Here in this dance is Indigenous joy. Here is life at its best.

In this book, we invite you to join us in the round dance of North American Indigenous interpretations of Christian Scripture. Like Indigenous round dances, Indigenous interpretations have recognizable patterns and steps that distinguish one dance from another and characteristics that reflect local customs and histories. There are sometimes disagreements about how things should be done. But we can agree to disagree, recognizing that each tradition is worth preserving. The performance of Indigenous interpretation invites participants to be aware of their bodies, hearts, and minds. It invites them to coordinate their movements in sync with the bodies of those around them, lest they step on others' toes; with the land they all mutually dance on; and with the Spirit, whose rhythm fills and inspires the space. Interpretation, like dance, puts us in the shoes of our grandmothers and ancestors. We dance steps similar to what has been danced before and connect with something much older and larger than ourselves. And like dance, the power of Indigenous interpretation, in part, lies in its art and its beauty, which can move the soul toward spiritual revelations and experiences of belonging, harmony, and peace.

We've titled our book *Reading the Bible on Turtle Island* in order to forefront an Indigenous worldview that privileges an Indigenous name and story for a land that Euroamericans have called North America. The title also emphasizes the importance that place plays in how Indigenous people understand themselves. Granted, not every Indigenous band, tribe, or nation refers to North America as Turtle Island. But it is enough for us that many Indigenous peoples have creation stories that describe the present-day United States, Canada, and Mexico as residing on the back of a turtle, including the Anishinaabe, Haudenosaunee, and Wabanaki/Abenaki peoples. While elements of this story differ among bands, the general creation story begins with Sky Woman, who, as her namesake implies, dwells in the sky but falls or is pushed through a hole and descends to the earth. Birds of the air rescue Sky Woman, catching her on their backs and delivering her onto the back of a hospitable turtle. While the turtle is generous enough to offer his shell as a home for Sky Woman, there is not enough space to host her and the offspring she holds in her belly. And so the

---

[2]See H. Daniel Zacharias, "The Throne and the Round Dance: An Ethno-musicological and Intercultural Look at Revelation 4–5," *Journal of NAIITS* 21 (2023): 146-57.

animals take council and decide to gather mud from the bottom of the sea to spread on the turtle's back to create more livable space. This proves a difficult task, with none but a single animal able to plunge deep enough to retrieve the mud. This animal is variably identified as a muskrat or toad or turtle. In many stories, this animal dies in the process of retrieving the mud, emphasizing the great cost by which we come by this gift of land and the respect we owe our animal kin for our survival. The mud is spread out on the turtle's back, which miraculously expands to form the continent of North America. If you squint just right, you can make out the outline of the turtle, with Baja California, Florida, Labrador/Quebec, and Alaska making up its legs, the Arctic Islands its head, and Mexico and Central America the tail.

TURTLE ISLAND HERMENEUTICS

It is our pleasure and honor to introduce you to Turtle Island hermeneutics. *Hermeneutics* is a fancy word meaning "the process of interpretation" and helps us sound more civilized and sophisticated among biblical scholars. A core assumption of Turtle Island hermeneutics is that Creator, who made a covenant with the Israelite patriarchs and matriarchs, had not ignored the Indigenous peoples of North America until the European colonizers arrived. Rather, Creator has always been present on Turtle Island and made a mark on the stories, ceremonies, lands, worldviews, and lifeways of its Indigenous peoples. This ought to be no surprise for those who hold the Bible as sacred. After all, God indicates that he works with nations outside Israel in passages such as Amos 9:7: "Haven't I brought Israel up from the land of Egypt, and the Philistines from Caphtor and the Arameans from Kir?" Likewise, the apostle Paul while in Athens states, "From one person God created every human nation to live on the whole earth, having determined their appointed times and the boundaries of their lands" (Acts 17:26). God has not been uninvolved in the affairs of world history, as he is the Creator of all and comes to reconcile all things to himself (Col 1:20).

The belief that God cares for the whole world and works with all nations should seem like common sense to believers—but tragically it has not. The Doctrine of Discovery, a legal principle derived from a series of fifteenth-century papal bulls (i.e., public decrees from the pope), declared that any land inhabited by non-Christians could be "discovered" and "owned." This theologically justified the theft of Indigenous lands because Turtle Island was populated by "heathens."³ This meant that the land was considered empty (*terra nullius*). This dehumanization continued and was enshrined in the Declaration of Independence, with its denigration of Indigenous peoples as "merciless Indian Savages."⁴ The theology of the colonizers was put on display in their actions, revealing their belief that God was absent from these lands that were "promised" to them. This belief, as Steven Newcomb (Shawnee, Lenape) argues, has whitewashed how settlers tell stories about their national pasts and their "encounters" with the Indians, justifying their "legal" entitlement to property that was theirs for the taking.⁵ As US Supreme Court Justice John Marshall famously declared in his opening to *Johnson v. McIntosh* (1823): "On the discovery of this immense continent . . . the character and religion of its inhabitants [European colonizers] afforded an apology [i.e., justification] for considering them [Native Americans] as a people over whom the superior genius of Europe might claim an ascendancy."⁶

The belief that God has been most present in settler stories and its Manifest Destiny to hold dominion over Turtle Island haunts us still and reverberates even into theological spaces. For instance, theology is often labeled simply as "theology" when written by a white scholar but requires an adjective when done by others (e.g., African American theology, Asian American theology, etc.). The idea that God is most fully understood and held as the norm in Euroamerican spaces must be firmly rejected in our theology and practice as we do the work of decentering European-descended voices and amplify the voices of the global and multiethnic church—this is part of what it means to decolonize theological spaces. This is why the core assumption that Creator has been present with Indigenous peoples since the beginning needs to be decisively stated at the outset of our description of Turtle Island hermeneutics.

Turtle Island hermeneutics reads biblical narratives according to frameworks and categories that align with and arise from our Indigenous heritage and lands. Such interpretations take seriously how our *social locations*

---

³See Mark Charles and Soong-Chan Rah, *Unsettling Truths: The Ongoing, Dehumanizing Legacy of the Doctrine of Discovery* (Downers Grove, IL: InterVarsity Press, 2019), 14-23.
⁴On this see especially chap. 6 of Charles and Rah, *Unsettling Truths*.
⁵See Steven T. Newcomb, *Pagans in the Promised Land: Decoding the Doctrine of Christian Discovery* (Golden, CO: Fulcrum, 2008).
⁶*Johnson v. McIntosh*, 21 U.S. (8 Wheat.) 543 (1823); see Newcomb, *Pagans in the Promised Land*, 73-87.

influence the questions and concerns we bring to Scripture. Social location is an important component of any interpretive process, since, as readers, we always bring ourselves to a text. What we bring to the text inevitably shapes what broader patterns and meanings we both discover from and impose on the text. Particular aspects of our lives not only shape our questions but also provide us with a set of glasses, as it were, which can often bring into focus aspects of the text that are blurry to others because their social locations or glasses are different. We do not pretend that we can achieve a disconnected objectivity when we encounter Scripture. Truth be told, even those biblical scholars and pastors who frame their research and sermons as recovering "what the Bible actually says" are at the same time still reconstructing the biblical contexts and texts to make the Bible speak to their present moment in ways that are inherently informed by their social location. This is not to be a cultural relativist; it is to be a humble realist. That said, as biblical scholars, we are constantly teaching our students about the importance of the historical and cultural context of Scriptures for interpreting the Bible well.

Western biblical scholars have often framed hermeneutics with a universal frame of reference, assuming that the methods and approaches would be equally applicable at all times and places. This is markedly different from socially located hermeneutical approaches. We as Indigenous Christians are individuals and communities grounded in and formed by the "community of creation," with our distinct histories, stories, and theologies.[7] We belong to our families, we belong to our communities, and we belong to the land. These circles of relationship form us and inform our encounter with the scriptural text. Turtle Island hermeneutics expressly does not seek a universal frame of reference that comes from nowhere yet is everywhere. Rather, we try to take seriously all those things in our lives and history that have shaped us to be who we are and the goodness within our cultural heritages. From there, we ask what assets we bring with us as we encounter the text. This emphasis on social location in biblical interpretation has resulted in insightful and helpful volumes

---

[7]"Community of creation" is a phrase we will use throughout the book. The description can be traced back to Jürgen Moltmann and has been used by Richard Bauckham and Randy Woodley. See Richard Bauckham, *Living with Other Creatures: Green Exegesis and Theology* (Waco, TX: Baylor University Press, 2011); Jürgen Moltmann, *God in Creation: A New Theology of Creation and the Spirit of God*, The Gifford Lectures (San Francisco: Harper & Row, 1985); Randy S. Woodley, *Shalom and the Community of Creation: An Indigenous Vision*, Prophetic Christianity (Grand Rapids, MI: Eerdmans, 2012).

from scholars of African, Latino/a, Asian, and European descent.[8] Interpreters who fully understand and embrace their social location can offer unique insight and assets that aid in arriving at a reasonable approximation of what the authors of Scripture meant, as well as what the scriptural text now means for a community of faith. Our encounter with the Scriptures is a dynamic process that involves not only sincere and concerted effort to understand the communicative intent of the author but also continually asking the question of how Scripture shapes and guides our lives in the circumstances we find ourselves in.[9]

We also live within the reality of colonization and the brutal legacy of the Doctrine of Discovery.[10] We do not leave these historical realities behind as we encounter Scripture. Indeed, it was this sacred text that was often used to justify the theft of Indigenous lands and the practice of cultural genocide. These are realities that Indigenous peoples live with every day. North America is still divided as the colonially governed nation states of Canada, the United States, and Mexico. These are recent dividing lines along our landscapes, lines that

---

[8] The biblical scholarship arising from different social locations is growing rapidly. See, for example, Amy Lindeman Allen, Francisco Lozada Jr., and Yak-hwee Tan, eds., *The Critic in the World: Essays in Honor of Fernando F. Segovia*, Resources for Biblical Study 108 (Atlanta: SBL Press, 2024); Mary F. Foskett and Jeffrey K. Kuan, eds., *Ways of Being, Ways of Reading: Asian American Biblical Interpretation* (St. Louis: Chalice, 2006); Lisa M. Bowens, *African American Readings of Paul: Reception, Resistance, and Transformation* (Grand Rapids, MI: Eerdmans, 2020); Beverley Moana Hall-Smith, "Whakapapa (Genealogy), a Hermeneutical Framework for Reading Biblical Texts: A Māori Woman Encounters Rape and Violence in Judges 19–21" (PhD diss., Flinders University, 2017); Jerry Hwang, *Contextualization and the Old Testament: Between Asian and Western Perspectives*, Logia Series (Cumbria, CA: Langham, 2022); Francisco Lozada and Fernando F. Segovia, eds., *Latino/a Biblical Hermeneutics: Problematics, Objectives, Strategies* (Atlanta: SBL Press, 2014); Esau McCaulley, *Reading While Black: African American Biblical Interpretation as an Exercise in Hope* (Downers Grove, IL: InterVarsity Press, 2020); R. S. Sugirtharajah, *Voices from the Margin: Interpreting the Bible in the Third World*, 3rd ed. (Maryknoll, NY: Orbis Books, 2006).
[9] On the paradigm of Scripture as a communicative act and the implications for interpretation, see Jeannine K. Brown, *Scripture as Communication: Introducing Biblical Hermeneutics*, 2nd ed. (Grand Rapids, MI: Baker Academic, 2021).
[10] "The Doctrine of Discovery was set out in a series of declarations by popes in the 15th century. These declarations (known as 'papal bulls') provided religious authority for Christian empires to invade and subjugate non-Christian lands, peoples and sovereign nations, impose Christianity on these populations, and claim their resources. These papal bulls were written at a time when European empires were embarking on widescale colonial expansion." Travis Tomchuk, "The Doctrine of Discovery," Canadian Museum of Human Rights, updated May 11, 2023, https://humanrights.ca/story/doctrine-discovery. For theological engagement on the Doctrine of Discovery, see Sarah Augustine, *The Land Is Not Empty: Following Jesus in Dismantling the Doctrine of Discovery* (Harrisonburg, VA: Herald, 2021); Charles and Rah, *Unsettling Truths*; Steve Heinrichs, ed., *Yours, Mine, Ours: Unraveling the Doctrine of Discovery*, Intotemak (Altona, MB: Mennonite Church Canada, 2016); Newcomb, *Pagans in the Promised Land*.

ignored Indigenous sovereignty, traditional territories and communities, and even natural land barriers. European colonization of countries happened around the globe, not simply in North America. But for many of these countries, the colonizing power eventually retreated from the land, and the country has returned to the people. This is not the case on Turtle Island. For this reason, Turtle Island hermeneutics is not a *post*colonial hermeneutic but is rather an ongoing work of decolonizing.[11] All these historical realities we bring in ourselves as we encounter the Scriptures. And this grounded framework can often emphasize previously unnoticed elements within biblical prose and narratives or resignify the meaning of technical terms or narrative elements and figures.

DANCING THROUGH THE MEDICINE WHEEL

The medicine wheel is a common symbol and paradigm for organizing teachings in many North American Indigenous nations. Its symbolism is used in many different aspects of life and for our purposes helps to orient the approach of Turtle Island hermeneutics. Returning to the image of the dance, communal dances draw people together, strengthen bonds, and bring people in sync. The relational aspect of dance is especially important as we talk about Turtle Island hermeneutics, because it is relationships that order Indigenous worldviews and lifeways. As we encounter the Scriptures, we do so in recognition that we have a particular relationship to the Scriptures. We also do so in recognition that we have other relationships from which we derive teaching, wisdom, meaning, identity, and belonging. All these relationships come to bear on us as we seek Creator in the good medicine Way of Jesus.[12] The circle

---

[11]*Postcolonial* interpretations critically examine the influence of colonial, European values and culture on how Scripture is interpreted among those living in lands *once* (post-) colonized but are now independent from colonial rule (e.g., much of Africa and the Indian subcontinent). It also amplifies marginalized voices within those contexts, whose experiences and concerns frame their interpretation of Scripture. The project of *decolonization* is complex and shares similarities with *postcolonial* analyses. Within the scope of our project, *decolonizing* biblical interpretation is about critically examining the influence of colonial, Euroamerican values and culture on how we interpret Scripture on Turtle Island (North America). Moreover, our work of "decolonizing" is a (re)constructive project that celebrates the revitalization of Indigenous values and culture, recognizing our rich ancestral traditions and wisdom as assets for living in harmony with Creator. For an approachable introduction to these concepts, see Randy S. Woodley and Bo C. Sanders, *Decolonizing Evangelicalism: An 11:59 p.m. Conversation* (Eugene, OR: Cascade Books, 2020).

[12]"Good medicine" is a term common among many North American Indigenous peoples to describe divine or supernatural power or presence that can dwell within a person, plant, place, or ritual and that brings wholistic healing in some way to a person and/or community.

is a prized shape in Indigenous communities because it places things into nonhierarchical relationships with one another. "You will notice," as Black Elk (Lakota) observes, "that everything the Indian does is in a circle . . . the power from the sacred hoop."[13] Each portion of the wheel has a measure of unique authority depending on the circumstances in which we find ourselves. As we journey through life, different aspects of this wheel come to bear, shedding light on our choices and giving us wisdom for the journey. Creator does and will speak to us through these relationships.

What is crucial as we describe Turtle Island hermeneutics is the inner circle of arrows in figure 1.1—the dance arrows of continual dynamic movement. Each segment in some ways does stand alone; however, because these are domains of authority and guiding wisdom in which Indigenous readers dance, these segments intersect, engage with, and cross-pollinate one another as they come to shape the believer. These domains of wisdom and teaching dynamically influence our encounter with the Christian Scriptures. Turtle Island hermeneutics recognizes and celebrates this dynamic communal dance, an approach that is different from those that assume a hierarchical relationship of the Scriptures over against any other source of truth and wisdom.

Scripture. Scripture holds a unique position of authority for Indigenous followers of Christ, and indeed for all believers, because it is the primary witness to the life, teachings, death, and resurrection of the Lord Jesus Christ. While other domains of wisdom and teaching in the circle do at times reveal things about Christ, Scripture is unique and unrivaled in this manner. We have noticed in our conversations with Indigenous Christians throughout Turtle Island a marked preference for the stories of Scripture, and especially a preference for the Gospel stories of Jesus. Even non-Christian Indigenous people respect Jesus and his teachings, seeing him as a powerful ancestor, a powerful medicine man, or a spiritual being.

The relationship we have with Jesus informs and shapes our relationship with Scripture. We recognize Jesus as a brown-skinned Indigenous man whose land was colonized. He was shaped by the stories of his people and the revelations that came from Creator and were written down by the Hebrew prophets. We have been adopted into the global and multiethnic family of Jesus; he is our

---

[13]Raymond J. DeMallie, *The Sixth Grandfather: Black Elk's Teachings Given to John G. Neihardt* (Lincoln: University of Nebraska Press, 1984), 290.

Figure 1.1. Medicine wheel of Turtle Island hermeneutics. For a color version of the medicine wheel, please visit www.ivpress.com/resources/turtle-island-medicine-wheel

elder brother (Mk 3:34-35; Rom 8:15-17; Gal 4:4-7). As we are now adopted into his family as kin, his ancestral stories and histories have now become part of our stories and histories as we join into the faith family of Abraham (Gal 3:7). These stories do not replace our previous stories and histories but join the dance circle. The words of Scripture have become the wisdom of our adoptive elders and ancestors. The desire for the Scriptures to dominate as the sole authority, denigrating and replacing Indigenous cultural traditions, is a colonizing form of Christianity that Indigenous people the world over have encountered.

Indigenous followers of Christ do not enter into this relationship blissfully ignorant and unwilling to reckon with the sometimes harsh realities of the biblical text. As you will read in the forthcoming pages, Indigenous encounters with the biblical text have not shied away from wrestling with and critiquing the biblical text. Jacob/Israel encountered God at Bethel and wrestled through the night with him (Gen 32:22-31). He left the encounter with a blessing but also with a limp. The Scriptures today are like a modern-day Bethel for the family of faith—a place in which we encounter God and can leave the encounter blessed or bruised, sometimes both simultaneously. But in the midst of these encounters, we maintain our hope in the power of the "God-breathed" or "inspired" Scriptures (2 Tim 3:16) to give life to those who hold them as sacred.[14] This understanding of the inspired nature of the Christian Scriptures points primarily to its relational orientation with the reader rather than a claim about its objective uniqueness and origin.

As we move to speak about the other spheres of wisdom and authority that are part of the Turtle Island hermeneutical dance, it is important to recognize that Scripture itself holds an open hand to seeking truth and guidance outside its pages. In this regard, the Wisdom literature of the Hebrew Bible is where we can mostly clearly see this invitation. For example, scholars note how an Egyptian work, the Instruction of Amenemope, was likely reshaped in Proverbs 22:17–23:11.[15] Regarding the Wisdom literature, William P. Brown's insight that the "Bible's wisdom corpus is the open door in an otherwise closed canon" invites us to adopt the posture of Proverbs to appreciate wisdom where it can be found.[16] To this we can add the extraordinary chapters of Job 38–41, where the beauty, mystery, and wisdom in creation is brought forth in God's speech. God traverses the wonders of the heavens and weather, then parades numerous animals (lion, goat, deer, ox, horse, etc.) and the two primordial animals Behemoth (Job 40) and Leviathan (Job 41). The Bible itself offers us a model for seeking wisdom and guidance outside pages of Scripture. These observations contrast with how some church cultures have discouraged Christians, Indigenous or otherwise, from appreciating and exploring the wisdom traditions of their own cultures or the wisdom given by the community of creation.

Cultural traditions. Cultural heritage and traditions of Indigenous peoples encompass the teachings, stories, dances, prayers, songs, dress, food, arts, language, protocols, and ceremonies that shape and characterize nations and unite them as a people. These cultural traditions are living and tied to

---

[14]In a thorough and detailed analysis of 2 Tim 3:16, John Poirier convincingly argues that an understanding of the Scriptures as God-breathed/inspired is about its function to revive a reader, to give life. See Poirier, *The Invention of the Inspired Text: Philological Windows on the Theopneustia of Scripture*, Library of New Testament Studies 640 (London: T&T Clark, 2020).

[15]Ernest Lucas, *Proverbs*, Two Horizons Old Testament Commentary (Grand Rapids, MI: Eerdmans, 2015), 32-33; Michael V. Fox, *Proverbs 10–31: A New Translation with Introduction and Commentary*, Anchor Bible 18B (New Haven, CT: Yale University Press, 2009), 482.

[16]William P. Brown, *Wisdom's Wonder: Character, Creation, and Crisis in the Bible's Wisdom Literature* (Grand Rapids, MI: Eerdmans, 2014), 3.

the lands of the people and to the more-than-human inhabitants with which they share those territories. These cultural traditions dynamically shape and reinforce the worldviews and lifeways of the people. By passing on their cultural traditions, Indigenous nations preserve their heritage in perpetuity. In the case of some Indigenous people, such as the two of us, who did not have their cultural traditions passed on (a legacy of colonialism and assimilation policies), the work of cultural reclamation is about being introduced to these aspects of our cultural traditions and allowing them to shape us as we connect with the traditions of our ancestors. These cultural traditions themselves hold memory and knowledge, and as dances are learned or songs are sung, this traditional knowledge is enacted, absorbed, and passed on.

Bodies of traditional knowledge within Indigenous cultures are a domain of wisdom that Indigenous followers of Christ look to and engage with. These traditions may encode knowledge about traditional landscapes, the flora and fauna of a particular territory, Creator, or a given Indigenous people, or may encode wisdom for life's journey. In the past and on into the present, Western missionaries and believers have often denigrated or demonized these traditional teachings in order to dissuade Indigenous peoples from engaging with their cultural heritage. Nisga'a Elder Willard Martin shared with Danny how Methodist missionaries worked among his people on the west coast of Canada. "They worked really hard at separating them [their converts] from their families . . . they relocated all the converts to this village here . . . they gathered all their artifacts like their regalia, drums, rattles, talking sticks. Anything to do with totem poles, they started cutting them down and burning them."[17] The cultural genocide that was so often coupled with colonial missionary work has proved disastrous for the beautiful diversity that the church is to be (Rev 5:9). Part of decolonizing the church and theology is a rejection of cultural hegemony in which the Euroamerican culture is considered the norm and the one that most aligns with and is permissible for Christians.[18] How, then, ought First Nations Christians to relate to their cultural traditions?

In a seminal article on Indigenous interpretations of Scripture and approaches to theology, Episcopal Bishop Steven Charleston (Choctaw) encourages

---

[17]Willard Martin, interview by Danny Zacharias, October 15, 2022.
[18]On this, see Richard Twiss, *Rescuing the Gospel from the Cowboys: A Native American Expression of the Jesus Way* (Downers Grove, IL: InterVarsity Press, 2015).

Indigenous Christians to understand the account of their people's history, teachings, laws, and covenant with the Creator as their own "Old" or, as we might say, "Original" Testament.[19] According to Charleston, these ancestral stories, traditions, and ceremonial rites are Original Instructions that were given by Creator to each Indigenous nation. Indigenous Christians do not need to reject or relegate their traditions in order to accept the Hebrew Bible as Scripture. Indigenous Christians can appreciate how the Hebrew Bible explains Creator's unique dealings with a particular tribe and nation, which culminated in the coming of Christ for all the world. The Hebrew Bible then enters a sacred circle of wisdom that shapes the Indigenous Christian—held as unique and sacred in its own particular way—alongside our own sacred traditions. Native theologians therefore must discern how their own stories, rituals, and lifeways—the Original Instructions to the nations of Turtle Island—can both *inform* and *be informed* by their interpretation of the Christian Scriptures in order to empower, inspire, challenge, and guide Indigenous followers of Christ.

This insight from Charleston has important implications for Indigenous peoples; and indeed for any person, as we are all indigenous to somewhere. Anecdotally, we have observed in some Christians a cultural vacuum that they attempt to fill with foreign cultural practices. Settler people, often disconnected from their ancestral lands for many generations, lose their cultural traditions and practices and adopt modern consumerist culture, which is a mile wide but an inch deep. This lack of cultural rootedness sometimes results in cultural appropriation, something that Indigenous North Americans are acutely aware of, as Indigenous culture is recognized as meaningful and even at times exotic, and so those who feel a cultural vacuum engage in Indigenous cultural practices.[20] Another example of this in Christian spaces is the "Hebrew roots" movement. This nonorganized movement within the church has (usually white) Christians adopting many practices of early Judaism, as this is the culture that they are most exposed to through the Bible. Behind the practice is the (mistaken) assumption that the Jewish culture is one mandated by God. Why might Christians do this

---

[19] Steven Charleston, "The Old Testament of Native America," in *Lift Every Voice: Constructing Christian Theologies from the Underside*, rev. and expanded ed., ed. Susan Brooks Thistlethwaite and Mary Potter Engel (Maryknoll, NY: Orbis Books, 1990), 69-81; reprinted in James Treat, ed., *Native and Christian: Indigenous Voices on Religious Identity in the United States and Canada* (New York: Routledge, 1996).

[20] The extreme result of this has sometimes been the outright claim to Indigeneity, the phenomenon of "pretendians."

today? In the words of Cayuga First Nation theologian Adrian Jacobs, "It is because they do not have their own Old Testament!" Having lost the riches of their own cultural heritage over generations, and unsatisfied with the vacuous nature of American pop culture, they turn to the riches they see in the cultural heritage they are most familiar with. This modern example serves to illustrate the ubiquitous need and longing we all share for rootedness in a cultural heritage.

What do we do when teachings from cultural traditions are seen as contradicting scriptural teaching? This tends to be a question mostly asked by non-Indigenous people. There are several reasons for this. First, Indigenous peoples are often more comfortable with tensions and contradictions. Indeed, there are stories and elements within some Indigenous traditions that expressly highlight and enact contradictions and chaos, because this is part of the reality of life.[21] This tension also exists within Scripture. For example, two contradictory proverbs sit side by side (Prov 26:4-5). Tensions between divergent accounts abound in the New Testament, ranging from how each of the four Gospels depicts events in Jesus' life or how Luke presents Paul in Acts as opposed to how Paul represents himself in his letters (i.e., compare Acts 15 and Gal 2). Second, Western theology is less storied than Indigenous theology. This is likely due in part to the prominence and reception of the apostle Paul in the post-Reformation Western church, which has read Paul analytically—as if his theology could be systematized like math apart from story. When we think of truth as propositionally based, a post-Enlightenment, reason-formed mind begins to weigh claims dialectically or, in words Chris can understand, one against another. This type of analysis, while useful, cannot replicate the learning we gain through truth-bearing stories. Stories invite reflection, wonder, imagination, imitation, and retelling. Stories embrace mystery, paradoxes, and absurdities that resonate with lived experience.

Within the Hebrew Bible, the Israelite scribes and prophets knew and poetically referenced multiple creation stories beyond those preserved in Genesis 1–2. The Hebrew Bible alludes to and adapts Canaanite and Babylonian creation accounts that personified the sea as a monstrous agent of chaos that must be defeated.[22] For example, in Isaiah 51:9-12, the prophetic author in Babylonian

---

[21]See our later discussions on the trickster figure and sacred clowns.
[22]Jon D. Levenson, *Creation and the Persistence of Evil* (Princeton, NJ: Princeton University Press, 1994), 14-25.

exile describes God as having accomplished heroic feats, such as piercing the dragon and drying up the sea, which ancient audiences would have recognized as riffing off the Babylonian work Enuma Elish. In this Babylonian creation story, the divine Marduk defeats Tiamat, the goddess of the sea, and divides up her body to structure the heavens and the earth. Consider also the many references to God setting the boundaries of the sea (e.g., Job 38:8-11; Ps 104:6-9) or taming the ancient sea beast Leviathan (e.g., Job 41:1-34; Ps 104:26). These themes come together especially in Psalm 74:12-14:

> Yet God has been my king from ancient days—
> > God, who makes salvation happen in the heart of the earth!
> > > You split the sea with your power.
> > > You shattered the heads of sea monsters on the water.
> > > You crushed Leviathan's heads.
> > > You gave it to the desert dwellers for food.

Where in Genesis, in the days of old, did the God of Israel defeat sea monsters and use their bodies to nourish desert creatures? The biblical scribes responsible for these passages seem to have found local—and might we say, Indigenous—creation stories helpful to *think with* as they sought to poignantly describe God's inspiring might and creating power.

Given that ancient Israelite scribes and prophets could creatively adopt and adapt creation stories of other cultures and not simply dismiss them outright, we see this as an invitation to do the same.[23] Indigenous followers of Christ hold complementary creation stories. Some Indigenous nations have multiple creation stories already, and the addition of the biblical creation story (or stories) adds to the richness of the traditions from which they draw. Indeed, creation stories within Indigenous worldviews are not solely about origins but how to *think with* the story and its implications. Creation stories are often *creating stories*—creating in us the recognition of our belonging, our roles and responsibilities, and how the world is ordered. They cause us to live in certain ways, they create in us a worldview, and they call us forth to be creators and contributors in the world.

---

[23]Of course, some scribal adaptations were critical of the original ancient stories. The description in Ps 104:6-9 of Creator as setting the boundaries of the sea can be interpreted as a subtle critique of creation stories that imagined the land resulting from a violent war between competing and violent divine powers. See Peter L. Trudinger, "Friend or Foe? Earth, Sea and *Chaoskampf* in the Psalms," in *The Earth Story in the Psalms and the Prophets*, ed. Norman C. Habel. The Earth Bible 4 (Sheffield: Sheffield Academic Press, 2001), 29-41.

Creation. Indigenous ways of knowing (epistemology) believe that there is no end to the knowledge and wisdom that can be gained from closely observing the natural world around us. The close observation of creation, including the fauna, flora, minerals, water, and atmosphere, not only advances our understanding of the world around us; it also has something to teach us about how we should live. As Clarence Yarholar (Muscogee/Creek), a minister for the Oklahoma Indian Missionary Conference, has said, "Nature speaks so loudly and so quietly"—if only we will listen and pay attention. As First Nations Christians, such attentiveness to nature provides a rich way to gain wisdom and to hear from Creator.

For instance, in the summer of 2022, Chris had the honor to visit an esteemed Lakota elder, visionary, and medicine man, Basil Brave Heart, during his visit to Pine Ridge reservation in South Dakota. Basil shared that one day, when he was young and out picking plums with his grandmother and others, Basil's grandmother announced to the group: "When you were going up, somebody stepped on flowers—not on purpose. On the way back, follow your footsteps, see if you can find that flower. Then stoop down and smell it. Because you stepped on the flower, is it going to withhold its fragrance? No, it must still share it. That's nature's way of forgiveness. Even though you stepped on it."[24] Basil treasured his grandmother's lesson about the flower's forgiveness, which has helped him process his own bitterness toward the harm others have caused him.

Other examples of hearing Creator's wisdom abound in Indigenous worshiping communities, such as one that Chris and Danny have both had the pleasure of virtually attending and speaking at: Good Medicine Way.[25] At each service before worship around the ceremonial drum, members have an opportunity to share any creation insights they received during the week. Kimberlee Medicine Horn Jackson (Lakota), a teacher in the community, once shared about her experience watching a poor frog leap to and fro across her yard to avoid the pursuit of a curious blue jay. Observing this scene, she reflected on how, in her own life, she often wants a straight path. And yet, like the frog jumping back and forth, sometimes the good path is not the straightforward path we plan or desire. What she observed was a living parable playing out in front of her, with the Holy

---

[24]Basil Brave Heart also shared this story for publication in Pope Francis and Friends, *Sharing the Wisdom of Time* (Chicago: Loyola University Press, 2018), 84, from which this quote derives.
[25]The Good Medicine Way streams every Monday night out of Albuquerque, New Mexico, and is led by Dr. Casey Church (Potawatomi) along with Brian Grover and Leah Grover.

Spirit guiding her heart to an insight she needed in the moment. Creator has set before us a created order filled with living parables, waiting to be discovered and appreciated for those with eyes to see and hearts attuned to the Spirit to receive. Although this way of looking at the world may not be obvious to Western perspectives—and may even be questionable to many—for countless Indigenous people, this is an obvious way of looking at the world.

Turtle Island hermeneutics poses the question, What if we could learn from creation as we do from Scripture? What if Christians take more seriously in practice Augustine's statement that nature is like a second book written by God?[26] Proverbs invites us to closely observe and learn from nature, pointing out the ant as an example of judicious labor (Prov 6:6-11). Job 12:7-10 invites us to ask nature questions to gain wisdom:

> But ask Behemoth, and he will teach you;
>   the birds in the sky, and they will tell you;
>   or talk to earth, and it will teach you;
>   the fish of the sea will recount it for you.
> Among all these, who hasn't known
>   that the LORD's hand did this?
> In whose grasp is the life of every thing,
>   the breath of every person?

This statement, in the heart of the Bible's Wisdom literature, makes a profound statement about valid sources of divine wisdom. Wisdom and fear of God extend beyond the written words of Scripture (and even the human community of believers) to the wider community of creation. As the scholars of the Earth Bible project express in one of their key guiding principles: "Earth is a living entity capable of raising its voice in celebration and against injustice."[27] If the stars can induce the psalmist to reflect on the smallness and humbleness of humanity

---

[26] "Some people, in order to discover God, read books. But there is a great book: the very appearance of created things. Look above you! Look below you! Note it, Read it. God, whom you want to discover, never wrote that book with ink. Instead, he set before your eyes the things that He had made. Can you ask for a louder voice than that?" Augustine, *Sermon* 126.6, in *Miscellanea Agostiniana* 1:355-68, ed. G. Moran (Rome, 1930), cited in Vernon Bourke, trans. *The Essential Augustine* (Indianapolis: Hackett, 1974), 123.

[27] The Earth Bible is a project by a number of scholars from south Australia. In addition to a series of essay collections, they are also working on a commentary series. The principles are printed in each of the Earth Bible volumes. See "Earth Bible: EcoJustice Principles," Earth Bible, accessed March 3, 2025, www.webofcreation.org/Earthbible/ebprinciples.html. Details on the Earth Bible project can be found at Earth Bible homepage, www.webofcreation.org/Earthbible/earthbible.html.

before the works of God (Ps 8:3) and can be called on to worship the Creator (Ps 148:3), might the psalmist think they can teach us something too? To go even further, if we accept that Jesus of Nazareth "matured in wisdom and years," as the Gospel of Luke puts it (Lk 2:52), what wisdom did Jesus learn from closely observing creation? And what might this mean for Indigenous followers of Christ?

Let's consider a few examples that illustrate how Jesus learned from creation. In particular, recall Jesus' experience in the wilderness as narrated in Mark 1:12-13: "At once the Spirit forced Jesus out into the wilderness. He was in the wilderness for forty days, tempted by Satan. He was among the wild animals, and the angels took care of him." What do we imagine Jesus doing for forty days and nights in the wilderness? Most likely, whatever we imagine, it will be informed by our own experiences of fasting or of the wilderness or some campy Jesus film. Our mind always imagines *something* to fill in the gaps. For some Indigenous people familiar with the ceremonies of First Nations of the Plains, this sounds an awful lot like a vision quest.[28] For the Lakota, a vision quest consists of numerous days of fasting alone in the wilderness in order to demonstrate one's pitifulness before Creator. Out of one's deep humility and vulnerability, a person petitions Creator to receive a vision that sheds light on their authentic self, their calling, and the gifts they have to offer the community—such transformative visions are good medicine or divine blessings. Vision quests also provide opportunities for individuals to reflect on, observe, and listen to the lessons of creation, which surrounds them as they think about their own roles and responsibilities to the community.

Can we imagine Jesus too reflecting on, observing, and listening to creation as he prepares himself for his sacred journey of preaching and healing? Did he notice the flight and beautiful feathers of the hoopoe, Israel's native bird? Or did he observe the resilient grazing habits of the Arabian Oryx? Did he acknowledge and respect the space of the Levant viper slithering by? Did his time abstaining from food and society lead Jesus to be more receptive to the very lessons that would encapsulate what the kingdom of God is like—and did some of these lessons come to him from observing his animal and botanical kin? We suggest that after John the Baptizer mentored and baptized Jesus, creation also mentored him before his ministry commenced.

---

[28]Steven Charleston, *The Four Vision Quests of Jesus* (New York: Morehouse, 2015), 10-22, 51.

Now consider the extent to which Jesus' parables pull from agrarian practices and observations about plants and animals. For example, Luke 12:24-30 reads:

> Consider the ravens: they neither plant nor harvest, they have no silo or barn, yet God feeds them. You are worth so much more than birds! Who among you by worrying can add a single moment to your life? If you can't do such a small thing, why worry about the rest? Notice how the lilies grow. They don't wear themselves out with work, and they don't spin cloth. But I say to you that even Solomon in all his splendor wasn't dressed like one of these. If God dresses grass in the field so beautifully, even though it's alive today and tomorrow it's thrown into the furnace, how much more will God do for you, you people of weak faith! Don't chase after what you will eat and what you will drink. Stop worrying. All the nations of the world long for these things. Your Father knows that you need them.

What if Jesus' parables and teachings that involve creation arose from what Jesus learned from observing and contemplating nature rather than merely an attempt to speak "baby talk" to us infantile humans? Instead, we should see Jesus, the perfect human, as an example for us today, as one who lived out the instructions given in Job 12:7-8. Jesus' attention to the provisions provided to the ravens and hoopoe in the sky, and the beauty of the red anemone and other wildflowers of the fields, inspired some of the teaching he would share with his disciples. Certainly, this example can be multiplied to include the cursed fig tree that doesn't produce fruit (Mt 21:19-21) and a number of Jesus' parables: about the weeds in the wheat (Mt 13:24-30), the tree and its fruit (Mt 7:15-20), the weather signs (Mt 16:2-3), the mustard seed (Mk 4:30-32), and the sower and the seeds (Lk 8:4-8). It's a small turn, but we believe this has significant consequences for how we imagine the possible ways in which the Holy Spirit might speak to us through creation and simultaneously affirm ancient Indigenous ways of knowing.

We admit that this doesn't come naturally to either of us. It must be practiced and experimented with, just like anything else. Indeed, nature is no clearer than Scripture as a source of teaching and wisdom, and it too is full of ambiguity and complexity. And yet, like Scripture, we believe that nature is a vehicle for Creator's message and love for us when we come to it with the proper intentionality and appreciation it deserves. We need to open ourselves to Creator's Spirit to *meet us* in these moments and tell us what our hearts need to hear, and we need to attune our ears to the more-than-human members of the community of creation. Turtle Island hermeneutics leans into the divine lessons that saturate the created world around us and believes that the Holy Spirit meets us among the trees and teaches lessons from the trees, just as the Spirit does in the pages of Scripture produced from the pulp of these very same trees. The teachings from the land enter into the dance through the medicine wheel, interacting with and informing our encounters with Scripture.

Our hearts and minds. Understanding Indigenous concepts of identity enables us to discuss this final domain within the medicine wheel of Turtle Island hermeneutics. Human reason and experience have been recognized as foundational for illuminating Christian faith and interpretation in some theological systems, such as the Wesleyan quadrilateral.[29] Modern Western methods of arriving at knowledge (i.e., epistemology) typically ground reason and experience in the *individual*. However, modern notions of the individual differ from the expansive way in which traditional Indigenous thought conceptualizes the individual within a web of relationships.

Indigenous followers of Christ have a communitarian sense of identity, in which the goal of the individual is not only to achieve self-actualization, but also to contribute to the community's actualization and subsequent cultural perpetuity.[30] For the Indigenous person, one's heart and one's mind are connected to, shaped by, and are themselves shaping the collective heart and mind of one's community. An example of the interplay between the individual and the communal can be seen in an example from what Cree theologian Ray Aldred calls an "ethic of non-interference," which is born out of deep respect for the individual. "The individual is significant because of her ability to respect the other, to realize her significance lies in relationship to the other. It is this ability to find one's significance in the larger group that is vital for a

---

[29]See Donald A. D. Thorsen, *The Wesleyan Quadrilateral: Scripture, Tradition, Reason and Experience as a Model of Evangelical Theology* (Grand Rapids, MI: Zondervan, 1990). Other theologians have been critical of reason and experience as part of theological method. See appendix F of Donald G. Bloesch, *A Theology of Word and Spirit: Authority and Method in Theology* (Downers Grove, IL: InterVarsity Press, 2005).

[30]On this see the discussion and critique of Maslow's hierarchy of needs in Cindy Blackstock, "The Emergence of the Breath of Life Theory," *Journal of Social Work Values and Ethics* 8 (2011): 1-16; Cindy Blackstock, "Revisiting the Breath of Life Theory," *The British Journal of Social Work* 49 (2019): 854-59. A helpful summary, including a useful graphic from one of Blackstock's public presentations, is available at Teju Ravilochan, "The Blackfoot Wisdom That Inspired Maslow's Hierarchy," Resilience, June 18, 2021, www.resilience.org/stories/2021-06-18/the-blackfoot-wisdom-that-inspired-maslows-hierarchy.

theology that considers the communal nature of identity."[31] Consider also the words of Indigenous philosopher Brian Yazzie Burkhart, who states:

> The real Cartesian bias is the idea that knowledge can only be acquired and manifested individually, in or by the individual. The *cogito, ergo sum* tells us, "I think, therefore I am." But Native philosophy tells us, "We are, therefore I am." A Native philosophical understanding must include all experience, not simply my own. If I am to gain a right understanding I must account for all that I see, but also all that you see and all that has been seen by others.[32]

Similarly, Fijian theologian Ilaitia Tuwere describes Fiji identity as "first and foremost a communal phenomenon. It is related to the community and is relational through and through. The dictum, 'I am because we are, and because we are, therefore I am' holds in many ways our understanding of identity, of who we are and what we may become."[33] To add to this conception of identity, Aldred describes how Indigenous identity is inclusive of land.[34] The communitarian nature of Indigenous identity also encompasses our ancestors.[35]

In our interviews with Indigenous believers, the emphasis on the heart as a deep place of knowing was a common theme. Larry Wilson (Cree) spoke about reading Scripture with the heart. He explained that the mind can often hold something as true, but our hearts—that deep seat of emotion, passion, resolve, and action—may not actually follow through with change in our lives and actions. But if our hearts lead, then our minds will follow. Martin Brokenleg (Sicangu Lakota/Rosebud Sioux) states, "Our minds seek information and explanations but our hearts look for experiences and deep inner movement."[36] Seeking the collective experiences and inner movements of a people happens only in community.

Indigenous communities often seek the wisdom of their elders as those who have walked life's journey the longest. Elders have no need to prove

---

[31] Ray Aldred, "An Alternative Starting Place for an Indigenous Theology," (PhD Diss., Toronto School of Theology, 2020), 82-83.
[32] Brian Yazzie Burkhart, "What Coyote and Thales Can Teach Us: An Outline of American Indian Epistemology," in *American Indian Thought: Philosophical Essays*, ed. Anne Waters (Malden, MA: Wiley-Blackwell, 2004), 25-26.
[33] Ilaitia S. Tuwere, "Christian Identity: A View from Fiji," *Pacific Journal of Theology* 56 (2016): 30-31.
[34] Ray Aldred, "The Land, Treaty, and Spirituality: Communal Identity Inclusive of Land," *Journal of NAIITS* 18 (2019): 1-17.
[35] See chap. 4 for more discussion on ancestors.
[36] Martin Brokenleg, Holy Thursday sermon, Vancouver, BC, 2019.

themselves, and the self-interested desires of youth have faded. They practice and pass down the art of heart-based understanding. Indigenous communities recognize that a gathered community that allows everyone to speak is an open space for everyone to contribute. It flattens any hierarchy, allowing anyone to reflect deeply, not just those who can speak with academic and esoteric complexity. It is these voices of heart conviction that guide individual and communal hearts and minds. In some Indigenous nations, this is why it is the grandmothers that choose leaders—grandmothers lead and speak from their hearts.

Both of us authors have had the privilege of being taught by Casey Church in multiple venues and also being led by him many times in a pipe ceremony. There are numerous aspects to the pipe ceremony, but one component beautifully draws attention to our hearts and minds as sites for theological interpretation. In the ceremony, the pipe and the smoke that arises out of it are pointed in the seven directions (north, south, east, west, up, down, internal). In Church's practice of this, the smoke, which represents the prayers of the group, is sent in all of these directions because Creator is everywhere present (Ps 139:7-10). In the last move of the pipe, the smoke is turned to face the heart of the person performing the ceremony: "I point to myself as a seventh direction, because Creator-Jesus is also in me."[37] The performer of this ceremony, in a priestly role, represents the people. As followers of Jesus, we believe that God's Spirit has taken up residence in his people (1 Cor 6:19). To this we can add the biblical teaching on humanity as made in the image of God.[38] The beauty, dignity, and worth of every human being, coupled with the indwelling presence of God's Spirit, make our individual and collective hearts and minds a domain from which we directly encounter the teaching and guidance of Creator's Spirit, the third member of the triune mystery. The integrity and worth of our hearts and the heart's way of knowing are primary reasons Indigenous peoples appreciate encountering the Scripture in their original language. Numerous interviewees, both native and nonnative speakers, expressed the

---

[37]Read Church's description of the pipe ceremony and other contextually adapted Indigenous ceremonies in Casey Church, *Holy Smoke: The Contextual Use of Native American Ritual and Ceremony* (Cleveland, TN: Cherohala Press, 2017), 63.
[38]On the image of God, see J. Richard Middleton, *The Liberating Image: The Imago Dei in Genesis 1* (Grand Rapids, MI: Brazos, 2005).

profound sense of connecting with Scripture as they encounter it in their heart language.[39]

The theological underpinning for our hermeneutical approach (discussed below) does not place a Christian at war with herself. We truly believe that God has created humanity in God's image, which means that when we are at our best, we display the goodness of God. After all, the Holy Spirit resides in the heart of the believer, in both the individual and the collective (1 Cor 3:16; 1 Jn 3:24; 4:13). The message of much of Western Christianity, in its deficit orientation, has by default taught people not to see the best in themselves. Rather, this message overemphasizes without pastoral grace that our hearts are devious (Jer 17:9) and that "there is no righteous person, not even one" (Rom 3:10). We are, of course, in danger when we read single verses outside their wider context. Jeremiah's statement is not an ontological judgment about all humanity but about the state of Israel, who had exceeded the patience of God and would be exiled. And Romans 3:10-18 is a collection of six Old Testament passages to bolster Paul's main point—that both Jews and Greeks are under the (supernatural) power/entity of sin (Rom 3:9). As our friend Matt LeBlanc (Mi'kmaq) astutely states, "How can I love my neighbor as myself when my theology has taught me to hate myself?"

GROUNDING OURSELVES IN GOODNESS: AN ASSET-BASED APPROACH

Turtle Island hermeneutics holds to a certain theological underpinning, namely, an *asset-based theology*. This approach has been operative in much of the writings of Indigenous theologians, but the label and description was pioneered and developed by our dear friend, elder, and founding member of NAIITS, Terry LeBlanc (Mi'kmaq). As we introduce this concept, we want to be respectful and recognize that its proper introduction and explanation belongs to LeBlanc, who is in the process of putting it to print. In briefly sharing it here, we intend to honor Uncle Terry's influence in our lives and the impact it has had on our hermeneutical approach.

---

[39]This has been rendered exceedingly difficult given the cultural genocide that Indigenous peoples have undergone since colonization. Languages were banned, with children in residential schools punished severely for speaking their native language. Language revitalization is a crucial part of the overall goal of cultural revitalization for Indigenous communities.

Asset-based approaches to community development and to ministry have been around in one form or another for some time, but it has been LeBlanc's genius to frame these concepts within an Indigenous Christian theology. Asset-based community development focuses on sustainable development of communities that attends to the strengths and potentials of the community. It avoids focusing on problems and deficits but chooses rather to identify assets already available in a community and leverage them for positive change. This approach empowers people and communities by building on existing strengths, relationships, and networks. Indigenous communities since colonization have been thought of from a deficit-based approach—as problems to be solved. But as Richard Twiss (Sicangu Lakota/Rosebud Reservation) notes, "an asset-based approach to describe life at its best" is more helpful.[40] Terry LeBlanc has helped Indigenous communities globally using an asset-based community development approach, and these experiences have generated new theological insights that formed much of the DNA in the curricular approach of NAIITS.[41]

Deficit-based thinking and beliefs have undergirded so much prior missionary and community work among Indigenous communities. Indigenous communities have always been "problems" for the colonizers:

- They are savages; we need to civilize them.
- This is their land; we need to get it from them.
- They have treaty rights; we need to find ways to extinguish them.
- They are an identifiable people; we need to assimilate or unregister them.
- They are pagans; we need to convert them.

This colonial gaze has always been paternal and judgmental, and often fearful. Western deficit-based theology has made the fall of humankind in the garden (Gen 3) the foundational story, inspiring a continual emphasis on the wickedness of humankind (think John Calvin's "total depravity of man"). This type of theology perpetuates a culture of judgment and

---

[40]Richard Twiss, "Native-Led Contextualization Efforts in North America 1989–2009" (PhD diss., Asbury Theological Seminary, 2011), 65.
[41]See Wendy L. Peterson, "A Gifting of Sweetgrass: The Reclamation of Culture Movement and NAIITS: An Indigenous Learning Community" (PhD diss., Asbury Theological Seminary, 2018), 195-96; Julene Pommert and Terry LeBlanc, "Indigenous Pathways and a Community Spirituality of Wellness," *Journal of NAIITS* 18 (2020): 37-62.

suspicion within Christian communities, labeling and dismissing anything suspicious or unknown. Deficit-based theology inevitably creates bounded-set communities rather than centered-set communities. Bounded-set communities are defined by clear boundaries, in which membership depends on adherence to specific beliefs or behaviors, emphasizing conformity, purity, and a distinct separation between insiders and outsiders. In contrast, centered-set communities are oriented around a central focus (i.e., Christ), with membership determined by the direction of one's movement relative to the center. In bounded-set communities, policing the boundaries becomes a "noble" and ongoing duty required to maintain community cohesion, while centered-set communities emphasize relationship, transformation, and inclusion across varying stages of faith, as members are encouraged to move toward the center.[42]

Deficit-based theology had and continues to have great difficulty in integrating new knowledge into its theological system. Willie Jennings, in his masterful work *The Christian Imagination*, traces this back to supersessionism, the theology that sees the church as the replacement of Israel rather than imagining a new work of God in which Gentiles are grafted into an existing story.[43] As Jennings discusses, this same lack of imagination prevented colonizers from being able to expand their theology to include the vast wonders of Turtle Island and the stories of many First Nations that existed

---

[42] The important work of missiologist Paul Hiebert in this regard continues to be relevant. See Paul G. Hiebert, *Anthropological Reflections on Missiological Issues* (Grand Rapids, MI: Baker Books, 1994), 110-35. This sacred duty of policing the boundary is akin to Willie James Jennings' discussion on the pedagogy of the plantation, in which the self-sufficient man was formed according to the values of possession, mastery, and control. "They imagined they could see the peoples of the world better than the peoples of the world could see themselves, and that their insight was key to forming institutionalizing processes that were crucial to global well-being. They were as indispensable as God. Western education and modern theological education were formed in this condition without entering into lament over its harmful effects; indeed, we became the means through which untold generations were shaped to think inside these troubled forms of gathering and the facilitating obsession of whiteness with its relentless need to perform its indispensability." Willie James Jennings, *After Whiteness: An Education In Belonging* (Grand Rapids, MI: Eerdmans, 2020), 137. This observation by Jennings is certainly alive and well among Christian intellectuals who so often engage other people and their ideas with the goal to find the weakness rather than seeking to understand and appreciate.

[43] Jennings states, "Christian theologians have yet to capture the depth of the supersessionist problematic as it expressed itself in the New World of colonialism." See Willie James Jennings, *The Christian Imagination: Theology and the Origins of Race* (New Haven, CT: Yale University Press, 2010), 251.

with the land. Turtle Island, with the bolstering of the Doctrine of Discovery, was seen as an *un*storied place.

What then of asset-based theology and its implications for Turtle Island hermeneutics? Asset-based theology chooses to root itself in Genesis 1 rather than Genesis 3. In Genesis 1, we see the beauty and goodness of the creation, of which we are a part. This should be our starting place. Grounding ourselves here chooses to focus on the good, and in the human realm chooses to intentionally highlight the reality that humanity is made in the image of God (Gen 1:27). This is not to ignore the realities of sin and its effects, but sin is placed into the context of the goodness of creation, recognizing, for instance, that being considered the image of God does not disappear after the rebellion in the garden but is reiterated later in the story (Gen 9:6). "Instead of starting with the problem and trying to imagine what it would look like corrected, we start instead with the intent of our Creator."[44]

Like asset-based community development, asset-based theology looks to the riches not only of the Western Christian tradition but of Indigenous nations' pre- and post-Christian experiences as well. Rather than seeing Indigenous culture and heritage as deficits to condemn and root out, they are seen as places to find wisdom to walk in a good way as Jesus-followers. Because of our asset-based theological foundation, the medicine wheel of Turtle Island hermeneutics welcomes dialogue with our culture and traditions, with creation, and with our own hearts and minds, because within these spaces we find assets—wisdom for the journey. There is more that could be said about this fundamental reframing of theology, but this will suffice for helping the reader understand the theological presuppositions that undergird Turtle Island hermeneutics and hopefully will whet your appetite for Terry LeBlanc's future work.

CONCLUSION: AN INVITATION TO THE DANCE

Our hope for this book is that it would empower Indigenous followers of Christ to read and interpret Scripture in such a way that speaks to and dignifies their Indigenous heritage and daily concerns. Our hope is that they would see how their Indigenous identity and their identity as believers can

---

[44] Pommert and LeBlanc, "Indigenous Pathways and a Community Spirituality," 45.

come together in beautiful and life-giving ways in their interpretation of Scripture. We have often been taught to read the Scriptures as condemning our lifeways, that our cultural traditions have nothing to offer the church, nor can they help us understand the Scriptures better. But we are persuaded that thoughtful interpretations of Scripture can actually bring dignity and affirmation to our ancestral ceremonies, lifeways, and stories. In the pages that follow, we will demonstrate how the interpretation of biblical texts in their ancient contexts shows how ancient Hebrews, Judeans, and Christ-followers believed and lived in ways surprisingly similar to Indigenous peoples. As we will discuss, there are assets within Indigenous cultures that can help us all be better, even more historically grounded readers of Scripture. We are also persuaded that there are assets in every person's traditional worldview and culture that can illuminate the Scriptures, and so this is also a book for non-Indigenous readers as well. We hope they would find as much nourishment, fresh ideas, and even lessons in history as our Indigenous audiences and further invite them to investigate the assets and theological resources of their own ancestral heritages.

We recognize that for many Indigenous Christ-followers, there is no discernibly different approach to the scriptural text from the wider/whiter Western, Euroamerican church, and there is often a tendency toward a more conservative reading. This trend is due in large part to the theology and legacy of the missionaries and the theological institutions who trained Indigenous ministers.[45] We hope that such Indigenous Christians would read this book with an open mind and gracious spirit. We would invite them into this dance but also want to encourage them in their own steps to the extent that they encounter God in a life-giving way. While Indigenous interpreters seek to reassert the dignity and wisdom of their ancestral stories and customs, Indigenous people disagree with each other on how to reconcile differences between Indigenous and biblical conceptions of creation, divinity, sacrifice, sin, and salvation. If Creator has been present among both Native North Americans and Israelites, then which revelation "corrects" or supersedes the

---

[45]For example, see Mark Clatterbuck, *Crow Jesus: Personal Stories of Native Religious Belonging* (Norman: University of Oklahoma Press, 2017), which contains interviews with numerous Indigenous Christians in Crow Nation, Montana, that illustrate the spectrum of Indigenous Christian attitudes toward holding together Indigenous traditional beliefs and ceremonies and Christian identity.

other? Should we imagine the Great Spirit/Mystery as essentially personal or as an impersonal power, as is the case with some Lakota understandings of *Wakan Tanka*? Can we interpret the story of Corn Mother, which we will discuss in chapter three, and its message of the interconnectedness of creation as inspired by Christ/Logos? Could the Corn Mother story even serve as a helpful corrective to interpretations of Genesis 1:28, a verse that has been used to endorse the domination of creation—an ideology complicit with our deforestation and scarring of the earth in order to extract its resources at unsustainable rates? There may be no simple or universally satisfying answer to these questions.

We are often asked, "How can you be Christian and Indigenous?" This sometimes sincere and sometimes accusatory question recognizes that Christians and policies enacted by Christian institutions have been responsible for the genocide of Indigenous lives and culture. We will address this history of trauma more in later chapters, but it is worth noting here the essential work of Tink Tinker (wazhazhe/Osage) on this topic. In "jesus, the gospel and Genocide," Tinker discusses the genocidal impact that missionaries had in converting Indigenous peoples away not only from their ancestral traditional practices but from their Indigenous worldviews.[46] Tinker has argued that it is impossible to homogenize Christianity with Indigeneity without doing damage to the latter and participating in the cultural genocide of Indigenous culture and worldviews.[47] While Chris considers Tinker a friend, and we both deeply respect his work, Tinker would certainly consider this project complicit in the soft genocide of our people.[48] And we would respectfully disagree.

One surprising answer we can give to the question of how we hold together our Christian and Indigenous identities is that for many Indigenous people, it is now traditional to be Indigenous and Christian. Many of us come from generations of Indigenous ministers and followers of Christ. And so, to

---

[46]Tink Tinker, "jesus, the gospel, and Genocide," in *The Colonial Compromise: The Threat of the Gospel to the Indigenous Worldview*, ed. Miguel De La Torre (Lanham, MD: Lexington Books/Fortress Academic, 2020), 133-60. See also Tinker, "Weaponized christianity: missiology, jesus, the gospel, and Indigenous Genocide," in *T&T Clark Handbook on Intercultural Theology and Missiology*, ed. John Flett and Dorottya Nagy (London: T&T Clark, forthcoming).
[47]See esp. Tinker, "Weaponized christianity."
[48]See also our appendix, where Tinker's weighty arguments are given more attention.

abandon following Christ would also feel like abandoning the teachings of our grandfathers and grandmothers. No culture is pure or static, and this is true for Indigenous culture as it is for all global, historical cultures and peoples. Granted, it has been useful to talk about the role and impact of "Christianity" broadly when discussing and critiquing how European, Christian settlers inflicted cultural genocide on Indigenous peoples. However, to essentialize Christianity with the worst evils of Western settler colonialism would be its own form of cultural erasure and denial of the dignity of both historical and global followers of Christ who neither descend from Europeans nor participate in a settler-colonizing ideology. We also reject the notion that our Indigenous ceremonies, traditional lifeways, histories, and experiences can't inform, critique, and reshape Christianity generally in Spirit-inspired, Christ-honoring ways. Within the medicine wheel of cultural traditions, creation, and even minds/hearts, Turtle Island hermeneutics celebrates a resurgence of communitarianism, an emphasis on spatiality and land for understanding our sense of self, and an egalitarianism that does not reduce other created beings to things or land to private property.[49] Ultimately, we believe that Indigenous communities are at their best when they create enough space and freedom for Indigenous people to determine what flourishing and revitalization looks like for themselves in relation to their web of relations within the community of creation.

To return to our analogy that interpretation is like dance, let us share one final story about Indigenous dancing that illustrates the paradox and tensions of being Indigenous and Christian. In 1883, US Congress issued a general ban on all Indigenous dancing and ceremonies, with the intention of especially targeting the Sun and Ghost Dances popular among Plains Indians. Christian missionaries who worked among the Choctaw, Chris's tribe, were long suspicious of the pagan ceremonial practices and beliefs associated with Choctaw round dances. In 1937, whatever Choctaw dancing was tolerated was forced underground in response to negative pressure from American educators and missionaries. In the 1970s, Rev. Eugene Wilson, a Choctaw Presbyterian minister, consulted with the Mississippian band of the Choctaws to revitalize social dancing. In 1974, Rev. Wilson organized a dance troupe to

---

[49]See Tinker, "Weaponized christianity."

publicly perform traditional Choctaw social dances at Owa Chito Festival at Beavers Bend State Park.[50] At the Choctaw Cultural Center in Durant, Oklahoma, the clothes of Rev. Wilson are prominently displayed, honoring his work to revitalize Choctaw culture and his work as a minister. This story illustrates the paradox of how Christians were responsible for both the suppression and the revitalization of our culture. We name it, and we hold this paradox in tension.

Turtle Island hermeneutics is a proud expression of Indigenous people, allegiant to Christ, who are seeking to revitalize their Indigenous practices and identities. In doing this, we are following Jesus in the way Creator has made us. The drumming has begun. Will you join us in the dance?

Let the reader know: Danny can actually cut a rug with the best of them but didn't want Chris to feel bad about himself. Danny thought Chris's opening was cute, so he went along with the "bad dancer" thing.

---

[50] "Traditional Dance," Choctaw Nation of Oklahoma, accessed December 20, 2024, www.choctawnation.com/about/culture/traditions/dance/.

2

IT'S ALL RELATIVE

The Scriptures, Creational Kinship, and "All Our Relations"

A COMMON CEREMONIAL PHRASE used in a number of Indigenous nations encapsulates a vital part of Indigenous worldviews. For the Mi'kmaq of the East Coast it is *Msit no'kmaq*, and for the Lakota it is *Mitakuye Oyasin*. For some communities, the phrase is used in ceremony. For some, "all my relations" are the final words as people part from one another; for others, it is how a prayer ends. Even if the phrase is not commonly used by a particular First Nation, the philosophy it represents is there. It is the belief in the interconnectedness, interrelatedness, and interdependence of all things. Thomas King states:

> "All my relations" is at first a reminder of who we are and of our relationship with both our family and our relatives. It also reminds us of the extended relationship we share with all human beings. But the relationships that Native people see go further, the web of kinship to animals, to the birds, to the fish, to the plants, to all the animate and inanimate forms that can be seen or imagined. More than that, "all my relations" is an encouragement for us to accept the responsibilities we have within the universal family by living our lives in a harmonious and moral manner (a common admonishment is to say of someone that they act as if they had no relations).[1]

As King notes, these interrelationships extend beyond the human family and into the more-than-human family. "All my relations" recognizes responsibility and reciprocity: "Connectedness positions individuals in sets of

---

[1] Thomas King, *All My Relations: An Anthology of Contemporary Canadian Native Fiction* (Toronto: McClelland & Stewart, 1990), ix.

relationships with other people and with the environment. Many Indigenous creation stories link people through genealogy to the land, to the stars, and other places in the universe, to birds and fish, animals, insects and plants."[2] It recognizes that we have gifts we give to one another. It acknowledges that if we walk in a bad way, those we are interrelated with will suffer. "All my relations" also acknowledges measures of agency in all created things, and to recognize the power and life in all created things is an important aspect of the ongoing recognition of our interrelationships. Some Indigenous peoples will speak about the spirit of a created thing, whether a bird, a tree, or a rock. This is recognition of creatureliness, of our interrelatedness, and of animacy. As Randy Woodley (descendant of the United Keetoowah Band of Cherokee) notes, the closer we look at anything, even a rock, at the atomic and subatomic level, these things are moving—they are animate.[3] And more than that, the subatomic reality of quarks even shows Creator's fingerprint of unity in diversity.[4] When you mention rocks in front of Elona Street-Stewart (Delaware Nanticoke), the first Indigenous woman to be elected co-moderator of the Presbyterian Church (USA), in 2020, her eyes light up. "I love rocks. I always look for them wherever I go. They speak to me." When she was Chris's guest at the 2023 NAIITS Annual Symposium in Winnipeg, Manitoba, she was noticeably excited to see her kin in the formation of turtles both at the meeting of the Assiniboine and Red Rivers and outside the National Center for Truth and Reconciliation at the University of Manitoba. In an Indigenous worldview, rocks are our oldest and most stable relations, mountains are our most majestic of relations, trees are the tall protectors of so many, and the plants are our endlessly generous relations.

An exercise that a friend has done in some churches and community groups helps to illustrate this difference in worldview and is something you can also do as you read this.[5] Take the following and place them in hierarchical order:

---

[2]Linda Tuhiwai Smith, *Decolonizing Methodologies: Research and Indigenous Peoples*, 2nd ed. (London: Zed Books, 2013), 149.
[3]Randy S. Woodley, *Indigenous Theology and the Western Worldview: A Decolonized Approach to Christian Doctrine*, Acadia Studies in Bible and Theology (Grand Rapids, MI: Baker Academic, 2022), 77.
[4]Woodley, *Indigenous Theology*, 49-50.
[5]Our thanks to NAIITS alumnus Marc Levasseur for sharing this exercise in an unpublished paper titled "The Evil That Is the Cure: Perceptions of Land in Western Christian and Native Worldviews."

earth, plants, God, animals, humans. Mentally rearrange these in your mind. Depending on your worldview, you will arrange this list of five items a particular way. Most Western-educated people, and certainly most Christians, will arrange the list in the following way:

1. God
2. Humans
3. Animals
4. Earth
5. Plants

Depending on the person, the final three may have some variation, but the first two were likely written down immediately and without hesitation. But what of a person with a traditional Indigenous worldview? The first thing to note is that an Indigenous person may actually resist listing these in hierarchical order. There is likely to be an inclination to place these things in a circle of relationship (with Creator at the center of the circle or outside the circle altogether) to resist the notion of one thing being better or of more worth than the other. But if pressed, a traditional person may render a hierarchical list this way:

1. Creator
2. Earth
3. Plants
4. Animals
5. Humans

A common theme among Indigenous stories from across Turtle Island is just how needy human beings are in comparison to the rest of creation. In many of these stories, two of which we will share below, it is humans who rely on the help and mercy of animals and plants to survive. Such stories stress the importance of humans treating animals and plants with respect, appreciation, and reciprocity.

In Spokane, Washington, Chris and his wife, Stephanie, had the honor of sitting down for coffee at a comfy fifties diner to listen to some of the stories and wisdom of Lakota elder Lenore Three Stars. Lenore shared with them a story she is fond of sharing about the great race between the animals and humans. One version of the story goes that, a long time ago, when the bison were a plentiful and powerful nation that roamed the plains, there arose a controversy between the bison and the two-legged humans about who should have the right to eat whom.[6] The two nations decided to settle the matter with a race; the winner would be first among the others and have the right to eat the other. Well, apparently humans looked pretty delicious, not only to the buffalo but to a number of four-legged animals who painted themselves (for previously they had no color) and also entered the race for the right to be chief among the animals. Only four birds—the eagle, the hawk, the crow, and the magpie (the smallest and slowest but greatest of heart of the four)—sided with the humans. The race would take place around the Black Hills, which remain sacred to the Lakota to this day. Running Slim Buffalo Woman, the fastest among the bison, would represent the bison, and represent she did. When the race began, she took an early lead among all the animals and kept that lead throughout the race, with the two-legged human trailing behind. One by one, the other four-legged animals began to fall back; even the eagle and the hawk couldn't keep up in this race of stamina and heart. Only the human could keep up with the buffalo, but even he was falling behind. As Slim Buffalo Woman neared the finish line and all hope seemed lost for the humans, the animals cheering the buffalo near the finish line noticed a small black speck on top of the buffalo's head. It was the magpie, hanging on for dear life! And as Slim Buffalo Woman neared the finish line, the magpie launched itself from the buffalo's head forward to the finish line to win the race on behalf of the humans. And so to this day, because of the magpie's help, humans have earned the right to eat the buffalo and other animals—a right that could be easily abused, with fatal consequences.

A Nêhiyawak (Cree) creation story that has been passed along orally speaks about the Creator being upset by the greed of his human children in their excess killing of the animals. Creator decides to take the animals, birds, fish, and bugs to his spiritual home so that the humans can learn the error of their ways. "The animals, knowing that the humans could not survive without them, begged the Creator to take pity on their human brothers and

---

[6]This version follows the retelling preserved by the Akttá Lakota Museum & Cultural Center, which Chris visited during his time with St. Joseph Indian School in Chamberlain, South Dakota. See "The Great Race," Akttá Lakota Museum & Cultural Center, accessed December 20, 2024, https://aktalakota.stjo.org/lakota-legends/the-great-race/.

sisters."[7] Because the animals are good, Creator grants the request. But Creator removes the animals' ability to converse with humans and makes them afraid of humans so that they will hide and aim to preserve themselves.

Many Christian readers may now be ready to pounce—Protestants be protestin', after all. Aren't we only a little "lower than angels" (Heb 2:7), and aren't we the ones made in the image and likeness of God (Gen 1:27)? While not dismissing these theological convictions (which we also hold), it is also worthwhile to consider that the second list above follows more closely the order of creation in Genesis 1. It also, broadly speaking, follows the evolutionary record. We are the youngest among the created order in the world. Think too of how reliant we are as humans on the rest of the list. We are the most needy. The earth, plants, and animals could all survive without us—but we could not survive without them. In the community of creation, we are the needy ones. We are the ones most cared for by the others, given constant gifts for our sustenance. Furthermore, this notion embodies the Christian ethic of putting others before ourselves. The story of the great race shared above and the creation story shared in chapter one showcase humanity's reliance on animals. Our interrelatedness with creation is also frequently recognized by Indigenous peoples in the sacramental understanding of eating. To quote at length Clara Sue Kidwell (Choctaw, White Earth Ojibwe), Homer Noley (Choctaw), and Tink Tinker (wazhazhe/Osage):

> Corn and all food stuffs are our relatives, just as much as those who live in adjacent lodges. . . . Thus, eating is sacramental, to use a euro-theological word, because we are eating our relatives. Not only are we related to corn, beans, and squash . . . but even those other relatives like Buffalo, Deer, Squirrel and Fish ultimately gain their strength and growth because they too eat of the plenty provided by the Mother—eating grasses, leaves, nuts, and algae that also grow out of the Mother's bosom. When we eat, we understand that we are benefiting from the lives that have gone before us, that all our human ancestors have also returned to the earth and have become part of what nourishes us today. Thus, one can never eat without remembering the gift of the Mother, of all our relatives in this world, and of all those who have gone before us.[8]

---

[7]Muskeke Iskew, "Grandmother's Creation Story," IndigenousPeople.net, last updated January 6, 2014, www.indigenouspeople.net/whitwolf.htm.

[8]Clara Sue Kidwell, Homer Noley, and George E. "Tink" Tinker, *A Native American Theology* (Maryknoll, NY: Orbis Books, 2001), 81. While the language and approach is different, the ultimate

The philosophy of "all my relations" compels us to live in right-relatedness within this community of partnerships, a life of reciprocity and appreciation that lives in a constant response to the grace and gifts received. As Norman Wirzba states, "The places and times of your life are made possible by forms of hospitality, sharing, and symbiogenesis that boggle the mind."[9] The individualism of the Western worldview so often blinds us to this reality, and Western Christian theology has reinforced this individualism. But, as Lenore Three Stars eloquently asserts, "If my theology doesn't help me be a better relative, then I need a better theology."[10] In the reality of the Anthropocene, the rapid loss of species diversity, the disappearing ice shelves and coral reefs, and the great Pacific garbage patch, it should go without saying—we have acted as if we have no relations. Instead, we have commodified and enslaved our more-than-human kin: "This enslavement and impoverishment of nature is no more tolerable or sensible than enslavement and impoverishment of other human beings."[11]

This opening section is only a small sampling of an Indigenized worldview as it pertains to creation. This can be deeply unsettling to the Western worldview and especially for the Christian worldview. In the remainder of this chapter, we want to show you that these aspects of the Indigenous worldview are far more at home in the biblical text than we may have realized. In the Scriptures, we encounter a creation that is alive with wonder, beauty, agency, and spirit. We also see a challenge to humanity's hubris and a call to see ourselves within the reality of the interrelations we are a part of.

THE FAMILY TREE OF THE HEAVENS AND THE EARTH

The creation narratives of Genesis speak to the interrelations within creation in several ways. Richard Bauckham states, "The *fundamental* relationship between humans and other creatures is their common creatureliness. . . . We, like them, are creatures of God. To lift us out of creation and so out of our

---

importance and sacramental nature of eating is also argued in Norman Wirzba, *Food and Faith: A Theology of Eating* (Cambridge: Cambridge University Press, 2011), particularly chap. 4.
[9]Wirzba, *Food and Faith*, 13.
[10]Lenore Three Stars, "Mitakuyapi (My Relatives), What Is Your Worldview?," Evangelical Covenant Church, October 31, 2022, https://covchurch.org/2022/10/31/mitakuyapi-my-relatives-what-is-your-worldview/.
[11]Winona LaDuke, *All Our Relations: Native Struggles For Land And Life*, 2nd ed. (Chicago: Haymarket Books, 2015), 6.

God-given embeddedness in creation has been the great ecological error of modernity."[12] The relatedness of humanity with the land is emphasized in the Hebrew word ʼādām for the first human, and ʼădāmâ for the ground—or, as Robert Alter translates, "humans" were made from "humus."[13] It is this kinship connection that is assumed in the later story of Cain and Abel, as the land reacts to the actions against its own kin; in Genesis 4:10 the land "cries out for its murdered child."[14] A further emphasis is placed on the earthiness of the first human by the specific usage of ʽāpār, "topsoil" (Gen 2:7), from which the first human is formed.[15] This word specifies the fertile topsoil, with all its wiggling worms, decayed matter, and fungal filaments. The living soil, which has always been vital for producing fruitful plants, is the soil from which humanity is also formed. This reinforces the common creatureliness and kinship with the rest of creation, and reminds the reader once again of the essential connection between humanity and the land.

Common creatureliness also exists with other land creatures, described as "living creatures of earth" in Genesis 1:24 (author translation). Humans, animals, birds, and bugs all mutually depend on the plants for sustenance (Gen 1:30). Our common creatureliness is also indicated in our shared possession of the breath of life, which animates land animals (Gen 1:24), sea creatures (Gen 1:20-21), and humanity (Gen 1:30; 2:7). Humanity also shares common creatureliness with the fish and birds in that they are also commanded to be fruitful and multiply (Gen 1:22), and the interrelatedness of the whole creation is highlighted on the Sabbath day in Genesis 2:1, with the heavens and the earth being the common home to all.[16]

Our interrelatedness with all creation is very clearly stated, though often missed, in the transition verse between the first creation story and the second creation story: "These are the family tree of the heavens and the earth when

---

[12]Richard Bauckham, *Living with Other Creatures: Green Exegesis and Theology* (Waco, TX: Baylor University Press, 2011), 4, italics original.

[13]Robert Alter, *The Five Books of Moses: A Translation with Commentary* (New York: Norton, 2004), 21.

[14]Mark G. Brett, *Decolonizing God: The Bible in the Tides of Empire*, Bible in the Modern World 16 (Sheffield: Sheffield Phoenix Press, 2008), 35.

[15]M. Stoeber, "עָפָר," in *Theological Lexicon of the Old Testament*, by Ernst Jenni and Claus Westermann (Peabody, MA: Hendrickson, 1997), 939.

[16]Howard N. Wallace, "Rest for the Earth? Another Look at Genesis 2.1-3," in *Earth Story in Genesis*, ed. Norman C. Habel and Shirley Wurst, The Earth Bible 2 (Sheffield: Sheffield Academic, 2000), 52.

they were created" (Gen 2:4, our translation). On Genesis 2, Mark Brett states, "The human belongs to the same kinship group as the animals in the sense that they all descend from the land. In the genealogical terms suggested by the introductory formula in Gen. 2.4a . . . the land is the parent."[17] In Genesis 2:4, the Hebrew word *tôlēdôt* ("generations") invokes strong kinship language. The word is clearly a relational concept, making "family tree" a dynamic and accurate translation.[18] Hebrew, as a verb-based language (like many Indigenous languages), builds this word off the root form *yld* ("to beget"). This Hebrew word *tôlēdôt* appears thirty-nine times in the Hebrew Bible, almost always at the beginning or end of a genealogical record. This is a word that connects people with their ancestors, and in Genesis 2:4 Scripture indicates that our relatives are the entirety of the heavens and the earth. As such, we can never raise ourselves above or even out of these essential relationships, nor can we separate this from our understandings of theology and faith. In Walter Brueggemann's words, land is a "primary category of faith." He states:

> Place is space that has historical meanings, where some things have happened that are now remembered and that provide continuity and identity across generations. Place is space in which important words have been spoken that have established identity, defined vocation, and envisioned destiny. Place is space in which vows have been exchanged, promises have been made, and demands have been issued. . . . Rootedness, in community and in a geographical land, is a conscious choice to be bound to the story of a place, be shaped and molded by it, and to be active in its upkeep. To delight in its beauty and suffer along with it, in sickness and in health. It is a covenant.[19]

---

[17]Mark G. Brett, "Earthing the Human in Genesis 1–3," in Habel and Wurst, *Earth Story in Genesis*, 82.

[18]The LEB translation suggests in a footnote, "These are the family records of the heavens and the earth." This footnoted option, in an English translation currently only available in digital format within Logos Bible software as well as through biblegateway.com, strikes closest to the meaning and full relational implication of the verse. In a similar vein, *The Hebrew and Aramaic Lexicon of the Old Testament* includes the suggestion of "this is the family tree of the heaven and the earth as they were created." See "תּוֹלְדוֹת," in *The Hebrew and Aramaic Lexicon of the Old Testament*, by Ludwig Koehler, Walter Baumgartner, and Johann J. Stamm, trans. and ed. Mervyn E. J. Richardson (Leiden: Brill, 1994–1999), 1700. While this lexicon ultimately does not endorse Gunkel's suggestion, his suggestion is faithful to the use of the word elsewhere.

[19]Walter Brueggemann, *The Land: Place as Gift, Promise, and Challenge in Biblical Faith*, 2nd ed., Overtures to Biblical Theology (Minneapolis: Fortress, 2002), 4.

Indigenous folks well understand the primal connection with one's ancestral lands. This is not simply a matter of loving the outdoors but rather of belonging to a place such that your identity is inclusive of the land.[20] A communal identity that is inclusive of the land is often hard for settlers and colonial peoples to understand, due in part to the brevity of their time, historically speaking, within particular lands. But for Indigenous peoples, including Jesus, the land of one's people holds memories. It is not simply a place in which we theologize but a relationship from within which we theologize.

HUMANITY'S ROLE IN THE COMMUNITY OF CREATION

Humanity is the constant recipient of gifts from Creator and the rest of the community of creation. Gifts initiate a relationship of reciprocity.[21] The second creation story describes how humanity ought to live into a life of reciprocity with the rest of our creational kin. Humanity is placed in the garden, but to do what? Well, that depends on the English translation one reads. Modern translations of Genesis 2:15 have objectivized the land, resulting in a nonrelational translation such as the ESV's "to work (or till) it and keep it."[22] Yet the first Hebrew verb in the verse is *'bd*, often translated as "to serve" elsewhere.[23] The second Hebrew verb in Genesis 2:15 is *šmr*. While "keep" is the most frequent choice of modern translators, "keep" in modern English no longer conveys the same sense it once did. This word is used specifically in the context of covenant discussions in the Mosaic law, suggesting a different nuance.[24] In many examples, almost always in a covenantal context,

---

[20]See Ray Aldred, "The Land, Treaty, and Spirituality: Communal Identity Inclusive of Land," *Journal of NAIITS* 18 (2019): 1-17.

[21]The role of gifts as initiators of relationships of reciprocity in the ancient world has become increasingly clear in biblical scholarship thanks to the helpful work of John Barclay, *Paul and the Gift* (Grand Rapids, MI: Eerdmans, 2015), especially chap. 1.

[22]The modern translation that comes closest to the relational framing in the text is the NET, "to care for it and to maintain it."

[23]See the note in *Hebrew and Aramaic Lexicon of the Old Testament* that the verb with *lə* means "to work for someone, serve" ("עבד," *Hebrew and Aramaic Lexicon of the Old Testament*, 1:773). Note also Gen 4:12 and the disharmony within the established reciprocity because of Cain's sin. The choice of "serve" is further strengthened by the recognition that Eden is sacred space. See John H. Walton, *The Lost World of Genesis One: Ancient Cosmology and the Origins Debate* (Downers Grove, IL: InterVarsity Press, 2009), 70.

[24]Some examples: in Gen 17:9, God tells Abraham that he must "keep my covenant"; throughout Exodus in the law, the Israelites are told to "keep" the feasts (Ex 12:17), to "keep" customs (Ex 12:25), to "keep" commands and statutes (Ex 13:10; 16:28), to "keep" the Sabbath (Ex 31:13-16).

"to keep" something is to conform one's life and actions to it. In the Mosaic law, the call is not just to know the commandments, not simply to conserve them, but to order one's life around them. Regardless of the English words used, the Hebrew words intimate a more relational understanding, framed within Creator's establishment of ongoing reciprocal relationships. Our translation of this verse is, "The LORD God took the human and placed him in the garden of Eden to serve her and conform to her."[25] The land takes care of us; the Creator has deemed it to be so. And because of these gifts we receive from the land, and our utter reliance on these gifts, humanity is to do its best to reciprocate in service and conformity. We adapt to the land and its rhythms, and honor it for its generosity. We treat it like a mother that is always self-giving and nourishing us.

Humanity is the more dependent within the circle of relationship, yet the creation narrative also makes clear that there is a measure of dependence on humanity for creation to flourish as Creator intends. Before God declared that it was not good for the human to be alone (Gen 2:18), it was first not good for the land to be alone in Genesis 2:5-8. Humanity's service to the land displays interdependency within the community of creation.[26] We are called to take our responsibilities to our creational kin seriously and to hold the reality of our power lightly. As the image of God, we have incredible and beautiful creative potential, in imitation of Creator. But we also wield the most destructive power. The present reality that humanity is the greatest threat to the environment and to other members of the community of creation stands in stark contrast to Creator's intent.

CREATION, WITHOUT US

Once we rid ourselves of an anthropocentric worldview, it becomes easier to appreciate the biblical portrait of God's relationship with creation. We are not the mediators of this world; Creator delights and has a relationship with our

---

[25]This translation is presented more fully in Mark Brett and H. Daniel Zacharias, "To Serve Her and Conform to Her: An Intercultural Reading of Gen 2:15," in *The Critic in the World: Essays in Honor of Fernando F. Segovia*, ed. Amy Lindeman Allen, Francisco Lozada Jr., and Yak-hwee Tan (Atlanta: SBL Press, 2024), 221-40.

[26]Norman Habel also points out this conditional parallel, as the earth is also on its own (*tōhû wābōhû*) and without interdependent relationships at the beginning of the seven day creation story. See Habel, "Geophany: The Earth Story in Genesis 1," in Habel and Wurst, *Earth Story in Genesis*, 38.

creational kin that has nothing to do with us. The seven-day creation story in Genesis 1 portrays a clear relationship between Creator and more-than-human creation. In Genesis 1:22 aquatic life and bird life are commanded to be fruitful and multiply just as humanity is. The language is clearly reciprocal: God commands that they do something (be fruitful and multiply); this is their response to his gracious gift of life—but the very command is at the same time called a blessing. In the act of procreation, all life simultaneously delights in the gift of God and reciprocates the gift with ongoing obedience and cocreative activities.

Perhaps the most theologically dense expression of the continued relationship between Creator and more-than-human creation is Psalm 104.[27] After the psalmist describes the act of creation in Psalm 104:5-9, the text moves in Psalm 104:10-13 to offer "a portrayal of God's continuing creativity and lavish care of the earth that he has made."[28] In Psalm 104:14-23 the Creator's gift is described as being lavishly excessive—the earth has more water than it needs, creatures have more than enough food, and wine provides not just satiation but gladness for humanity: "The bounty of God, the outpouring of his goodness and plenty, go beyond what is essential to maintain life."[29] The psalm goes on to talk about mountains, trees, and a variety of animals, all of which are described as valuable in and of themselves. So too do the created sun, moon, day, and night serve other parts of the community of creation. The night is in service to the animals that hunt at night, and the day serves humans to hunt by the sun's light (Ps 104:19-23).

The psalm moves to speak of great sea creatures in Psalm 104:25-26, including the formidable Leviathan, who in Canaanite/Ugaritic creation stories was a primeval sea monster defeated by the Canaanite god Baal.[30]

---

[27]See also Jerry Hwang, *Contextualization and the Old Testament: Between Asian and Western Perspectives*, Logia Series 1 (Carlisle, UK: Langham Global Library, 2022), 170-74. Hwang brings to our attention both that Ps 104 illustrates how "God's electric presence" permeates all creation and how this psalm likely adapts a fourteenth-century BCE Egyptian hymn, The Great Hymn to the Aten. The former point connects to our discussion of theological (mis)constructions of animism below and exemplifies how the scribes of Scriptures found the songs of other cultures useful to *think with theologically*, as discussed in chapter one.

[28]Walter J. Harrelson, "On God's Care for the Earth: Psalm 104," *Currents in Theology and Mission* 2 (1975): 20.

[29]Harrelson, "On God's Care for the Earth," 20.

[30]Ps 104:26 may be better translated "Leviathan that you formed to play with." This would further indicate the relationship and pleasure God takes in his creation.

Here, Leviathan, whom God "formed to play with" (Ps 104:26, our translation), has become domesticated and is indicative of the Creator's relationship and pleasure in his creation.[31] Such a reading aligns with Job 41:1-34, where God praises various aspects of Leviathan's body and its dangerous strength in a poetic manner comparable to how the lover in Song of Songs describes his beloved (e.g., Song 4). Old Testament scholars Brian Kolia (Samoan Islander) and Emily Colgan suggest that the book of Job seems to have rebranded the image of the Leviathan from a cosmological monster to a wild friend of God—however ferocious the Leviathan may remain for humans.[32] As Psalm 104 nears its end, it focuses once again on the gracious gift of Creator:

> All your creations wait for you
>   to give them their food on time.
> When you give it to them, they gather it up;
>   when you open your hand, they are filled completely full!
> But when you hide your face, they are terrified;
>   when you take away their breath, they die and return to dust.
> When you let loose your breath, they are created,
>   and you make the surface of the ground brand new again. (Ps 104:27-30)

Another significant passage that speaks to the ongoing relationship between Creator and more-than-human creation is God's response to Job in Job 38–41. God's response provides a creational collage: "YHWH's answer to Job presents a cosmic panorama, focusing specifically on what is considered alien to human perception."[33] Through the variety of descriptions of the ordered world and fellow creatures, Job and the reader are shown that the world and its wild inhabitants are not dependent on humanity. God's long response to Job makes it clear that he continues to have a relationship with more-than-human creation that humanity has no part in. The eco-theology of Psalm 104 and Job helps us reframe and limit what it means to be God's image-bearer,

---

[31] William P. Brown, *The Seven Pillars of Creation: The Bible, Science, and the Ecology of Wonder* (Oxford: Oxford University Press, 2014), 149-50.

[32] Brian Kolia and Emily Colgan, "Whose Trauma Is It Anyway? A Tausua Reading of God and the Leviathan in Job 41" (paper presented at the Annual Meeting of the Society of Biblical Literature, San Diego, CA, November 24, 2024).

[33] William P. Brown, *Wisdom's Wonder: Character, Creation, and Crisis in the Bible's Wisdom Literature* (Grand Rapids, MI: Eerdmans, 2014), 16.

who is called to rule and subdue creation (Gen 1:28).[34] It ought to also cause us to find more inclusive ways of doing theology such that all creation is encompassed.[35] Indeed, in Job readers are encouraged to seek wisdom from more-than-human creation (Job 12:7-10). Old Testament scholar Terence Fretheim even suggests that due to human sin, God's relationship with more-than-human creation might be closer and more intense.[36] Our elder kin have lived with Creator for much longer than we have, and as the youngest and most needy of creation, we have required the most effort on Creator's part. Just as more-than-human creation dies for us daily in order to sustain us, so too Creator died for the youngest of his creational family.

Creator's relationship with creation is not simply one of care over an object, nor is it simply delight over something made, like a painter enjoying art on a canvas. The care is relational. This can be stated confidently because the Scriptures also indicate God's displeasure at times with more-than-human creation and God's delivering consequences on more-than-human creation. Two examples in Scripture show this to be the case. The first is the covenant God creates in Genesis 9:5 after the flood. The Common English Bible rightly subtitles this "God's Covenant with All Life," while many modern English translations provide a more anthropocentric subtitle such as "God's Covenant with Noah" (NIV) or "The Covenant with Noah" (NRSV).[37] Not only is the covenant with all the living creatures, but God also makes it clear that animals are held accountable for impermissible shedding of blood.[38] This is why Chris thinks outdoor cats, who often murder their prey for *fun*, are among Creator's least favorite animals.[39] God's reciprocal relationship with more-than-human

---

[34]It should be noted that the repeated command for humanity to multiply changes through the narrative, with the command to "subdue" from Gen 1:28 not being repeated later (Gen 9:1). See the discussion in Brett, *Decolonizing God*, 32-34.

[35]Vicky Balabanski, "Critiquing Anthropocentric Cosmology: Retrieving a Stoic 'Permeation Cosmology' in Colossians 1:15-20," in *Exploring Ecological Hermeneutics*, ed. Peter L. Trudinger and Norman C. Habel, Society of Biblical Literature Symposium Series (Atlanta: Society of Biblical Literature, 2008), 152.

[36]Terence E. Fretheim, *God and World in the Old Testament: A Relational Theology of Creation* (Nashville: Abingdon, 2010), 278.

[37]The NKJV also properly subtitles the section of Genesis 8:20–9:17 "God's covenant with Creation," with some NKJV Bibles beginning a new subtitle "God's Promise to Noah" for Gen 9:1-17.

[38]See also Teresa Morgan's discussion on how animals and creation commit wrong, experience suffering, and stand in need of reestablishing a relationship of trust with Creator, in *Trust in Atonement: God, Creation, and Reconciliation* (Grand Rapids, MI: Eerdmans, 2024), 169-76.

[39]While we mean this as a joke, it's interesting to point out that the indiscriminate predatory habits of our fluffy feline friends have been linked to 26 percent of bird, mammal, and reptile extinctions

creation is ongoing, and Creator has expectations of the ecological community. Exodus 21:28 continues to hold up this law from Genesis 9, with an ox that kills a person being put to death for its action.

Another example of more-than-human creation being held accountable for improper action is Ezekiel 6. In this chapter God condemns both the people and the mountains for allowing the pollution of idolatry: "For Ezekiel, the mountains are . . . harborers of other gods that are in league with the people who commit crimes against Yahweh, implying that they have a moral condition and that they are guilty by their association with the Israelites."[40] Ezekiel views the people and the land as intimately connected, both deserving of punishment.[41] Yet, in this condemnation, God is said to be "crushed" or "broken" in Ezekiel 6:9, a striking metaphorical picture that indicates brokenness of spirit.[42] "God is so entwined with the relational web of the world that everything that happens in creation has an effect on the divine realm."[43]

AGENCY IN CREATION

In the creation story of Genesis 1, the days of creation follow the pattern of creating the place or habitat (the sky, the water, the land) and then filling that place with occupants (the celestial bodies, aquatic creatures, land creatures—which includes humanity).[44] Through the days of creation, there is a basic pattern of God issuing forth a command for something to be created or to come forth, followed by God either creating the thing commanded, and/or naming the created thing, and/or placing the created thing into its functional position. In all cases, the work is theocentric, with God issuing the command and then God also completing the command, either implicitly or explicitly.

---

across the globe—it's almost as if they think they're people! See Christopher A. Lepczyk, Jean E. Fantle-Lepczyk, Kylee D. Dunham, Elsa Bonnaud, Jocelyn Lindner, Tim S. Doherty, and John C. Z. Woinarski, "A Global Synthesis and Assessment of Free-Ranging Domestic Cat Diet," *Nature Communications* 14 (2023), https://doi.org/10.1038/s41467-023-42766-6.

[40]William Briggs, "Idols and Land Grabs, Ancient and Modern: Creation and Ecotheology in Ezekiel 6; 35:1–36:15," *Horizons in Biblical Theology* 40 (2018): 48.

[41]Briggs, "Idols and Land Grabs," 49.

[42]"שׁבר," in *Hebrew and Aramaic Lexicon of the Old Testament*, 1403-4.

[43]Briggs, "Idols and Land Grabs," 49.

[44]John H. Walton, *Genesis*, New International Version Application Commentary (Grand Rapids, MI: Zondervan, 2001), 65.

Table 2.1. Command and response in the creation narrative

COMMAND	RESPONSE
"Let there be light" (Gen 1:3)	**God** separates light from dark (Gen 1:4) **God** names light day and darkness night (Gen 1:5)
"Let there be a dome in the middle of the waters" (Gen 1:6)	**God** made the dome (Gen 1:7) **God** names the dome "sky" (Gen 1:8)
"Let the waters under the sky come together into one place so that the dry land can appear." (Gen 1:9)	**God** named the dry land "earth," and the waters "seas" (Gen 1:10)
"Let the earth grow plant life" (Gen 1:11)	**The earth** produced plant life (Gen 1:12)
"Let there be lights in the dome of the sky to separate the day from the night" (Gen 1:14)	**God** makes the stars, sun, and moon (Gen 1:16) **God** places them in the sky to rule the day and night (Gen 1:17-18)
"Let the waters swarm with living things, and let birds fly above the earth up in the dome of the sky" (Gen 1:20)	**God** creates the sea creatures and birds (Gen 1:21)
"Let the earth produce every kind of living thing" (Gen 1:24)	**God** makes every kind of creature (Gen 1:25)
"Let us make humanity" (Gen 1:26)	**God** creates humanity (Gen 1:27)

All translations CEB.

The table above shows the issuing of the commands and their subsequent fulfillment. We see, for example, the created thing given a job: the celestial bodies are to rule over the day and night (Gen 1:18), and the marine creatures are commanded to be fertile and fill the seas, and the birds to fill the sky (Gen 1:22). A clear pattern is in the text: the gift of being created by God includes a sphere in which the created thing occupies and fulfills its responsibility, with the sphere itself being incomplete until it fulfills its function for the inhabitants. This gift establishes a reciprocity, with the celestial bodies performing their proper function and marine and sky creatures being fertile. For all created things, to fulfill their responsibility is to obey the command of their Creator as a continual act of reciprocity.

Given this pattern, it is important not to miss one extremely important break from the established pattern, something that speaks to the agency within the community of creation. Day three completes the creation of the inhabitable spaces and is also the first day that has a second act of creation. On day three, as expected, God issues forth a command beginning in Genesis 1:11:

> God said, "Let the earth grow plant life: plants yielding seeds and fruit trees bearing fruit with seeds inside it, each according to its kind throughout the

earth." And that's what happened. *The earth produced* plant life: plants yielding seeds, each according to its kind, and trees bearing fruit with seeds inside it, each according to its kind. God saw how good it was. (Gen 1:11-13)

Whereas in all other instances God gives the command and then explicitly or implicitly is the one who fulfills the command, in this verse it is mother earth herself that actively obeys the command by producing plant life.[45] The land here is described as a participant, or cocreator, in the creation of vegetation.[46] Like the other created things, which have reciprocated the gift of being created with fulfilling their function, the land also does so. The language of cocreator is appropriate and should cause no concern, as other created things are also invited into the cocreation process through the function of reproduction (Gen 1:22, 28). And while the cocreation language is most explicit in this instance, the cocreative connection on the sixth day with the creation of wild animals is certainly implied, with the same verb being used, and the wild animals created are living creatures brought forth from the land in Genesis 1:24.[47] The cocreation of vegetation in Genesis 1:12 is very important to recognize, as the vegetation from the third day is spoken of again on the sixth day. God gives this cocreated vegetation as food for everything that breathes: humanity, wildlife, bug life, and bird life (Gen 1:29-30). The land takes care of us like a mother, and our response ought also to be borne of relational affection.

In its own agency, the more-than-human creation is also active in honoring Creator. Psalm 104, discussed earlier, ends the way many psalms end, with praise and thanksgiving. In the face of such great gifts and care, God is offered back due honor. The psalmist hopes that the Lord will find joy in what he has made (Ps 104:31), as his creatures fulfill their roles and duties that have been described through the psalm. Other psalms say that the heavens tell the glory of God (Ps 19:2), the heavens declare his righteousness (Ps 50:6; 97:6),

---

[45]The Hebrew nouns used to refer to the land are all feminine (*yabbāšâ*, *'ereṣ*, *'ădāmâ*), as are the Greek equivalents in the LXX (*gē*, *chōra*). More than that, though, is my attempt to heighten the relational language with which we talk about the land.
[46]Habel states, "Earth and Elohim are both characters with major roles to play" ("Geophany," 34).
[47]Noted also by Habel, "Geophany," 43. Pasifika scholar Jione Havea also notes the cocreative description that the waters have in Gen 1. See Jione Havea, "A Moana Reading of Genesis 1," in *Kōrero Mai: Earth, Our Parish*, ed. Te Aroha Rountree and George Zachariah (Auckland, NZ: Trinity Methodist Theological College, 2024), 35-42.

the heavens praise his wonderful deeds, and the entire psalter concludes with the call, "Let every living thing praise the LORD" (Ps 150:6). In Revelation 16:4-7, water itself, represented by or personified as an "angel [or messenger] of the waters," affirms Creator's righteous judgment against Roman imperial forces who shed the blood of the saints.[48] Creation also mourns in the Scriptures. Particularly in the prophets, the community of creation mourns along with the people of Israel (Is 24:1-20; 32:15-20; 33:7-9; Jer 4:23-28; 12:1-4, 7-13; 23:9-12; Hos 4:1-3; Joel 1:5-20; Amos 1:2). As Mari Joerstad notes, "Aridity, the loss of animal life, and famine are all signs of the earth's grief."[49]

One final story from the Gospel of Matthew tells of the agency in more-than-human creation and shows how creation aligns itself with the marginalized. At the close of Matthew 17, Jesus and his disciples return to their home base in Capernaum, where Peter is asked whether they pay the temple tax. A short but important exchange then takes place between Peter and Jesus on the shores of the Sea of Galilee.[50] Jesus' exchange with Peter indicates that in the Roman imperial economy (inclusive of the temple economy), taxes are levied against the subjects and not against the ruling oppressive class. This certainly is an oppression, but Jesus will change it to an act of defiance. If the oppressive ruling class is exempt from taxes, then to not pay the tax is to seek to belong to that group. If not paying taxes is a social marker of the imperial oppressive class, Jesus will have none of it. He and his disciples will pay the tax and thus align with the oppressed masses in an act of solidarity and defiance.

As the story goes on, we see that creation too will stand in solidarity with those who are oppressed by the Roman colonizers and the local leadership who align themselves with the colonial powers. In order to pay the current tax, Jesus instructs Peter to go catch a fish, in whose mouth is a coin covering the tax for both of them. As with Matthew 17:25, Jesus here shows the gift of foresight. All fishermen know that fish go after shiny and colorful items; it is the basis of the fishing lure industry. Jesus knows that the first fish Peter will

---

[48]Barbara Rossing, "Waters Cry Out: Water Protectors, Watershed Justice, and the Voices of the Waters," in *Decolonizing Ecotheology: Indigenous and Subaltern Challenges*, ed. S. Lily Mendoza and George Zechariah (Eugene, OR: Pickwick, 2022), 39-57.

[49]Mari Joerstad, *The Hebrew Bible and Environmental Ethics: Humans, Nonhumans, and the Living Landscape* (Cambridge: Cambridge University Press, 2019), 140.

[50]See Warren Carter, *Matthew and Empire: Initial Explorations* (Harrisburg, PA: Trinity Press International, 2001), 133-43.

catch will have a coin in its mouth, one that had been dropped by someone in the past and grabbed by the fish. It is now the fish that provides what is needed for this subversive act of solidarity and defiance. The fish, the more-than-human community of creation, is also on the side of the marginalized and oppressed and willing to serve Jesus. The lake and its fish inhabitants will partner with these acts of defiance—the community of creation also aligns itself against the oppressive powers. Even the fish will participate in the paying of taxes if it means demarcating themselves from the ruling class, who aim at oppression and oppressive resource extraction.[51]

This creaturely act of solidarity ought to spurn Christ-followers, attuned to the lands that sustain them, to reciprocal deeds of solidarity and partnership to the wider community of creation of which we are a part. Like in the primordial story of Cain and Abel, "the earth itself is in solidarity with the victim of violence," in this case the taxation practices of a Jewish establishment that is aligned with Rome.[52] This exchange was a reminder for Peter, and a reminder for the reader today, of the gifts provided by Creator and creation. Peter and his community had relied for their whole lives on the fish of the lake, and now in addition to the continuous self-giving comes another gift from the fish. Gifts invoke relationships of reciprocity and remind humanity once more of our reliance on creation and accompanying responsibilities—and "when we rely deeply on other lives, there is urgency to protect them."[53] As we can see from these verses, agency within creation extends well beyond the story of Balaam talking with his donkey (Num 22:22-35).[54]

THE CREATION SONG

With all that has been laid out so far in the chapter, it should now come as no surprise that all of creation, of which we are a part, is in relationship with

---

[51] The restriction of hunting grounds, suppression of treaty hunting rights, and continual battles over fishing rights continue to the present in many countries. See, for example, the documentary on the Burnt Church conflict of 2000: Alanis Obomsawin, dir., "Is the Crown at War with Us?," 2002, www.nfb.ca/film/is_the_crown_at_war_with_us/.

[52] Ched Myers and Elaine Enns, *Ambassadors of Reconciliation*, vol. 1, *New Testament Reflections on Restorative Justice and Peacemaking* (Maryknoll, NY: Orbis Books, 2009), 63.

[53] Robin Wall Kimmerer, *Braiding Sweetgrass: Indigenous Wisdom, Scientific Knowledge and the Teachings of Plants* (Minneapolis: Milkweed Editions, 2013), 177.

[54] See also Arthur W. Walker Jones and Suzanna Miller, *Ask the Animals: Developing an Animal Hermeneutic* (Atlanta: SBL Press, 2024).

Creator. And part of the relationship between a covenanted community with its God is the act of worship. The book of Revelation provides us with the most extensive portrait of a worship service in the entirety of the Bible.

> At once I was in a Spirit-inspired trance and I saw a throne in heaven, and someone was seated on the throne. The one seated there looked like jasper and carnelian, and surrounding the throne was a rainbow that looked like an emerald. Twenty-four thrones, with twenty-four elders seated upon them, surrounded the throne. The elders were dressed in white clothing and had gold crowns on their heads. From the throne came lightening, voices, and thunder. In front of the throne were seven flaming torches, which are the seven spirits of God. Something like a glass sea, like crystal, was in front of the throne.
>
> In the center, by the throne, were four living creatures encircling the throne. These creatures were covered with eyes on the front and on the back. The first living creature was like a lion. The second living creature was like an ox. The third living creature had a face like a human being. And the fourth living creature was like an eagle in flight. Each of the four living creatures had six wings, and each was covered all around and on the inside with eyes. They never rest day or night, but keep on saying,
>
> > "Holy, holy, holy is the Lord God Almighty,
> > who was and is and is coming."
>
> Whenever the living creatures give glory, honor, and thanks to the one seated on the throne, who lives forever and always, the twenty-four elders fall before the one seated on the throne. They worship the one who lives forever and always. They throw down their crowns before the throne and say,
>
> > "You are worthy, our Lord and God,
> > to receive glory and honor and power,
> > because you created all things.
> > It is by your will that they existed and were created." (Rev 4:2-11)

In this heavenly throne vision, Creator sits at the center on a throne and is described using precious stones, jasper and carnelian (Rev 4:3). The beauty and power of the skies also symbolizes Creator's presence, with a rainbow surrounding Creator, and lightning and thunder signifying his presence and power (Rev 4:3-4). The twenty-four elders on twenty-four thrones encircle Creator's throne, and four living creatures stand even closer around the throne and encircle the central throne on each side, possibly symbolic of the four directions (Rev 4:6-8). The four creatures each have a different face, one as a lion, the other an ox, the third a human, and the fourth an eagle. They are described in such a way so as to be understood as superior to any other heavenly or earthly creature. They have six wings, unlike earthly birds or other angels described in the Scriptures (e.g., Ezek 1:23-25). And unlike most creatures, which are restricted to a set of two eyes, they are constantly wakeful and attentive to the entirety of creation and are full of eyes.[55]

There is much that could be said about this central vision of Revelation, but the relevant component for the current discussion is the four living creatures.[56] These beings encircle closest to Creator around the throne. The clue to what the living creatures represent is in the description of their faces: lion, ox, human, and eagle (Rev 4:7). In the same way that the eagle is revered by many First Nations because it soars the highest and sees the farthest, these faces represent the greatest of creatures in their corresponding domains. The lion is the greatest of the wild animals, the ox is the greatest of the domesticated animals, and the eagle is the greatest of the birds. Bauckham states: "They embody pre-eminently all that is most magnificent in the whole creation. . . . They are representatives of the world of earthly creatures in the sense that they worship on behalf of the latter. They act as the priests of creation, offering continuous praise to God in the heavenly sanctuary on behalf of all creatures."[57]

The symbolic power of the four living creatures is striking. Together, not only do they represent the world of creatures, but they do so in a nonhierarchical way. The human-faced one, representing humanity, does not stand apart or above the rest. The living creatures, full of eyes that represent their wakefulness and attunement to all creatures, show the intimacy that Creator has with the totality of creation—they stand closest to the throne as a united and equal group. And it is the living creatures together that lead in the worship of Creator. As the vision continues, the twenty-four elders, the symbolic representation of the people of God, follow the lead of the four living creatures.

---

[55]Bauckham, *Living with Other Creatures*, 173.
[56]For a fuller discussion, see H. Daniel Zacharias, "The Throne and the Round Dance: An Ethnomusicological and Intercultural Look at Revelation 4–5," *Journal of NAIITS* 21 (2023): 146-57.
[57]Bauckham, *Living with Other Creatures*, 176-77.

When the gathered people of God today honor Creator, we simply join in the creation song that is continually offered by all of creation. We are not doing something new; we are not initiating worship, nor are we leading worship. We are, rather, joining the community of creation in the honor that is continually being offered to God. Just as the living creatures stand between the throne and the twenty-four elders, it is the community of creation that mediates and facilitates our relationship with Creator as followers of Jesus. As the living creatures offer their praise (Rev 4:9), the twenty-four elders join in the song (Rev 4:10), something that will happen again later in the vision in Revelation 5:8-14, when the innumerable number join in the song, followed by every living creature. This beautiful vision helps us to see ourselves as creatures, interreliant and interdependent, with the rest of creation and its honor of Creator and the Lamb. This final worship service is led by creation. It is intimate. It is extravagant. It is communal. It is multiethnic. Any worship Christians participate and organize today should be building toward and in anticipation of this vision. We suggest that Indigenous followers of Jesus can help the wider church fall back into line as creation leads us in the creation song.

ENCOUNTERING CREATOR IN AND THROUGH CREATION

At various times in the Scriptures, humans are permitted to enter or glimpse into the spirit world. Prophets catch glimpses of the future; apocalyptic visionaries such as Daniel, Ezekiel, and John see the concomitant spiritual dramas that align with and affect the dramas that happen in the physical realm. And sometimes unique people such as Enoch and Elijah surpass death and move directly into the unseen realm. But the majority of the story in the Scriptures takes place on earth, just as it should. This is our home, the dwelling that God has designed for all of his children, and it is the place he continues to hold together (Col 1:17). The place for encounter with God is on the land. God's design from the outset was to walk with his people in the beauty of the land (Gen 3:8). God's desire to be fully present with us on earth is the picture of our future in the final chapters of Scripture as well (Rev 21–22). In the interim period, the Israelites encountered God on the land in limited ways, either through an intermediary such as Moses, who spoke with God on Mount Sinai, or as the priests encountered him in the tabernacle and temple. There is no sense in the Scriptures that the ideal encounter with Creator takes place in a noncorporeal way. The ideal encounter with God is profoundly earthy. The interaction God desires is not in the mystical or psychical encounters so often sought after but in the everyday embodied experiences of flesh and blood, rocks and roots.

Yet, creation is not simply a place *in* which we encounter God. God is also encountered *through* creation. The most obvious, yet most profound and mysterious, way is in the incarnation of Christ. In Jesus we encounter the Creator-made-flesh (Col 1:15). As the Gospel of John speaks of the incarnation, it is significant that he does not say, "the word became a man" or "the word became a human." It is, rather, that the word became "flesh" (Jn 1:14). *Flesh*, of course, indicates being human. But it also speaks more generally to the reality of Creator truly moving through the Creator-creation divide. Catholic theologian Elizabeth A. Johnson would invite us to imagine a "deep incarnation" that understands the mystery as not only wedding "Jesus Christ to other human beings in the human species" but also reaching "beyond us to join the incarnate one to the whole evolving biological world of living creatures and the cosmic dust of which they are composed."[58] When the Word incarnated into Jesus, did this not include the water, the carbon, the oxygen, the minerals, and the community of bacteria that live within all human flesh? Not only are humans composed of flesh (Gen 2:21-24), but so too are our animal kin (Gen 6:17). And as we situate ourselves into the Hebrew creation story, we remember that this flesh was fashioned from the topsoil of mother earth. We are not above creation; we are part of creation. And when God the Son became flesh, he entered into the community of creation too. The Gospels indicate that creation recognized its Creator. The wind and waves obey the command of Jesus; because creation has agency, it is able to respond.[59] We also see Jesus in a dangerous situation in the wilderness, yet he is able to be with the wild animals (Mk 1:14).[60] The

---

[58]Elizabeth A. Johnson, *Creation and the Cross: The Mercy of God for a Planet in Peril* (Maryknoll, NY: Orbis Books, 2019), 186.

[59]"A classic Greek (Western) world view would say that any Native who believes a tree could talk would be involved in animism, spiritism, and/or pantheism, though Jesus spoke directly to the winds and the waves and they 'heard' Him and actually obeyed." Richard Twiss, Terry LeBlanc, and Adrian Jacobs, "Culture, Christian Faith and Error," *Journal of NAIITS* 1 (2003): 13.

[60]On this, see Bauckham, *Living with Other Creatures*, chap. 5.

incarnation of Christ shows us that we encounter Creator through creation. But what of more-than-human creation?

It is noteworthy that the first physical manifestation of the Great Spirit is as wind (Gen 1:2). Both the Hebrew word (*rûaḥ*) and the Greek word (*pneuma*) can be translated "spirit," "breath," or "wind." Indeed, we must remember that these three options are due to the limitations of our language. The precision of English in this case overshadows the expansive meaning of this word. When ancient readers encountered either of these two words, it was conceived of as a single thing rather than three different things. While most English translations choose "Spirit of God," two modern translations choose "wind" (NRSV, CEB). In light of the description of Genesis 1, with the *rûaḥ* hovering over the waters, "wind" is a more potent translation. The wind of God, or God-as-wind, hovered over the waters, preparing to do the work of creation. God is also encountered in another element, in a fire that does not consume a bush at Horeb (Ex 3:1). This burning bush is more than just a miraculous event to get Moses' attention. As the verse indicates, it is out of the bush that God calls Moses (Ex 3:4), and the command for Moses to remove his sandals because he is on holy ground (Ex 3:5) indicates that God is manifest there and is fully present.

Finally, all four Gospels are witness to an extraordinary though often unrecognized manifestation of God in more-than-human creation. Whereas God the Son is enfleshed, there is a period of time in which God the Spirit is enfeathered. After Jesus' baptism, the heavens open, God speaks from the heavens, and the Spirit descends on Jesus in the form of a dove. This triune presence at the baptism scene will later correspond to the commission to go out and baptize in the name of the Father, Son, and Spirit (Mt 28:19). Significant too is the nature of the Holy Spirit, a physical, if temporary, manifestation in dove form.[61] Creation is not simply a location of divine encounter, but divine encounter occurs *in*, *through*, and *as* creation.[62] Jesus experienced the companionship of the Holy Spirit as Dove. Matthew notes the immediacy

---

[61]Although the physical nature of the Holy Spirit in dove form is clear in Matthew, Luke makes it the most explicit (Lk 3:22).

[62]See Mark I. Wallace, *Finding God in the Singing River: Christianity, Spirit, Nature* (Minneapolis: Fortress, 2005); Wallace, *When God Was a Bird: Christianity, Animism, and the Re-enchantment of the World*, Groundworks: Ecological Issues in Philosophy and Theology (New York: Fordham University Press, 2018).

of moving from the baptism to the temptation in the wilderness, but the common separation of these two scenes in modern Bibles (almost always broken with a subtitle) causes readers to miss the continuity of the narrative and the implication that Jesus followed the enfeathered Holy Spirit into the wilderness. In other words, we should not read this story as an internal Holy Spirit prompting that Jesus received to go to the wilderness but as a manifest leading, with Jesus following Dove into the wilderness.

Many traditional Indigenous peoples have a worldview characterized by animacy, holding to creation as sacred and infused with divine presence and its own power. That Gospel authors portray the Holy Spirit enfleshed/enfeathered in other-than-human form ought to at least soften Western Christian perspective on differing worldviews that are often labeled animist or panentheist.[63] In the same way that God the Son, the second member of the triune mystery, transgressed the Creator-creation divide, so too has God the Holy Spirit. It is no surprise that many people would say they have felt closest to God when out in nature. Nature is alive and brimming with the breath and presence of Creator. Just as Jesus looked on Dove and felt the real and manifest presence of the Great Spirit, so too do many Indigenous people today look on the eagle and feel the real and manifest presence of Creator.

CONCLUSION

This foray into the Scriptures with an Indigenous worldview hopefully helps us see "all our relations" with fresh eyes, spurring us to relational responsibility to the inherent partnerships in the community of creation. Creation is loved by God, is engaged directly by God, and holds its own agency and spirit. As we recite the most well-known verse in all of the Bible, we hopefully recognize that God truly so loved the *whole* world that he gave his one and only son (Jn 3:16). Jesus seeks the restoration not just of humanity but of the

---

[63]While animism as a label and concept has a long and troubled history, some modern scholars seek to refine and renew its usage. See, for example, Mari Joerstad, *The Hebrew Bible and Environmental Ethics: Humans, Nonhumans, and the Living Landscape* (Cambridge: Cambridge University Press, 2019), chap. 2. In short, to *relate* to the earth and luminaries as persons with dignity and ability to effect change does not necessarily imply making such beings into gods. Panentheism, as the word's Greek roots imply (all-in-God), holds that all that exists is contained within and by God's ultimate power but that God is simultaneously separate from and greater than all that exists. For more on panentheism, see John W. Cooper, *Panentheism, the Other God of the Philosophers: From Plato to the Present* (Grand Rapids, MI: Baker Academic, 2006).

entirety of his community of creation—to make all things new (Rev 21:5). The apostle John indicates that when Christ came, he came to "what was his own [i.e., all of creation], and his own *people* didn't welcome him" (Jn 1:11, modified, emphasis ours). Creator-made-flesh was welcomed by more-than-human creation, while it continues to be the youngest and most immature of creation that has trouble accepting his transformative gifts and our requisite responsibilities. Yet Creator's heart is ever toward us, as he is "pleased to reconcile to himself all things, whether on earth or in heaven, by making peace through the blood of his cross" (Col 1:20). Until such time as we grow up to stand in our call to be the sons and daughters of God, creation itself awaits to be free from the bondage we have placed on it (Rom 8:21).[64] Our interrelationships with the community of creation mean that we are bound together, that we have interrelated destinies. And so mother earth continues to groan in labor pains even to the present (Rom 8:22), calling us forth to step into our role and responsibility as image bearers of God and be good kin, because it's all relative.

---

[64] See T. Christopher Hoklotubbe, "Restoring Harmony with Creation: Reading Romans 8:18-23 with Indigenous Stories," in *Preaching Romans from Here: Diverse Voices Engage Paul's Most Famous Letter*, ed. Lisa M. Bowens, Scot McKnight, and Joseph B. Modica (Eugene, OR: Cascade Books, 2023), 91-95. See also Laura Donaldson, "Theological Composting in Romans 8: An Indigenous Meditation on Paul's Rhetoric of Decay," in *Buffalo Shout, Salmon Cry: Conversations on Creation, Land Justice, and Life Together*, ed. Steve Heinrichs (Waterloo, ON: Herald, 2013), 142-48.

3

READING ALONG THE BRIGHT PATH

How Jesus' Jubilee Teachings Can Lead Us Back into Shalom/Harmony with All Our Relations

AFTER A DAY OF SETTING UP tipis and tending the surrounding grounds at Eloheh Indigenous Center for Earth Justice outside Portland, Oregon, Randy Woodley (descendant of the United Keetoowah Band of Cherokee) and Edith Woodley (Eastern Shoshone) gathered Chris and a visiting Princeton Seminary intern to talk on their porch. The conversation soon turned to the importance of plants, and to that end Randy shared a Cherokee story he has also shared most recently in *Indigenous Theology and the Western Worldview*.[1]

Long ago, maybe not so long after the two-legged people won their race against the four-legged ones around the Black Hills, across the continent humans were overhunting the animals. This was of grave concern to the forest animals, who held council to determine how to get back at the humans. In this council, led by the bears, all manner of ideas were suggested, including acquiring humans' bows and arrows and shooting them back. However, with few among the animals with opposable thumbs, this effort comically failed. Eventually, the council turned to the earthworm, who suggested that they "put disease upon the Cherokee" to get revenge. This diabolical idea gained traction and was met with approval. So the animals sent plague and sickness on the Cherokees. And it worked. It worked too well, in fact. Disease ravaged the Cherokee to such an extent that they faced extinction. And in these dark days,

---

[1] Randy S. Woodley, *Indigenous Theology and the Western Worldview: A Decolonized Approach to Christian Doctrine*, Acadia Studies in Bible and Theology (Grand Rapids, MI: Baker Academic, 2022), 54-56.

the plants began to pity the suffering two-legged ones and held council themselves. The plants agreed with one another to help the humans and began to appear to two-legged ones deemed worthy in dreams, teaching them how to make use of plants to bring medicine and healing. And so the Cherokee dreamed and received instruction from the plants about which plants provided healing properties and how to make use of them during the present epidemic. The Cherokee survived by the mercy of the plants and learned why it is important to respect both their animal and plant kin. To this day, the Cherokee, among other Indigenous peoples, show their appreciation to the plants from which they harvest by burying or sprinkling small pinches of tobacco beside the base of the plants.[2]

This Cherokee story illustrates the serious consequences of living in disharmony with the community of creation and invites audiences to walk well in the world. This idea of "the Harmony Way," what the Choctaw call the "Bright Path," is a common metaphor shared among North American Indigenous peoples for conceptualizing what it means to live in a good way. In *Shalom and the Community of Creation*, Woodley shares how for his dissertation he surveyed one hundred Native Americans from forty-five different tribes and spoke in depth with eight elders who were familiar with their own tribal traditions about how they each conceptualized what it looks like to live in a good way.[3] While some details differed among those interviewed, Woodley observed thematic patterns that supported his hunch that tribal traditions across North America generally share common principles and ways of living that comprise a harmonious life, often understood as aspects of the Original Instructions given by Creator to the people. These core values and principles that comprise what Woodley calls the Harmony Way include:

- a respect and gratitude for creation; recognizing the interconnected nature of all life and our duties to seek out balance, harmony, and reciprocity with our kin

---

[2]Tobacco is one of the four sacred medicines in several First Nations traditions (along with sage, cedar, and sweetgrass). Tobacco used in ceremony is often harvested separately (i.e. not purchased at the cigarette counter). Among other things, ceremonial tobacco is used especially to give thanks.
[3]See Randy S. Woodley, *Shalom and the Community of Creation: An Indigenous Vision*, Prophetic Christianity (Grand Rapids, MI: Eerdmans, 2012), which incorporates his dissertation, "The Harmony Way: Integrating Indigenous Values Within Native North American Theology and Mission" (PhD diss., Asbury Theological Seminary, 2010).

- respecting the sacred roles that everyone in the community has, from our children to our elders
- appreciating humor and play
- making decisions through consensus building and respecting diversity
- respecting the power of both words and silence
- being present in the present
- working as needed in meaningful ways and not simply for acquiring more material possessions
- giving and hosting generously[4]

If these principles flesh out what life at its best looks like according to Indigenous values and ancestral traditions that bear Creator's fingerprint, in what ways might these core values be present in the ancestral traditions of Jesus, and how might they be incarnated in his life and ministry? Moreover, how might reading Scripture along the Bright Path help us to appreciate nuances of Scripture and the ministry of Jesus that have been underappreciated or unnoticed by Western readings? Woodley identifies the concept of shalom ("peace") in Scripture as illustrating what life looks like at its best according to Creator's vision in the Hebrew Scriptures.[5] This vision is established in the Hebrew creation stories of Genesis 1–2, particularly the story of the Garden of Eden. Shalom is envisioned in the Sabbath system and the practice of Jubilee, which we will discuss below. Shalom is the peaceful resolution of conflict and coexistence among the nations and among creation as envisioned by the prophet Isaiah (Is 2:3-4; 11:6-9). Shalom is the manifestation of the kin(g)dom of God as taught and incarnated by Jesus and advanced by Paul:

> Therefore, as God's choice, holy and loved, put on compassion, kindness, humility, gentleness, and patience. Be tolerant with each other and, if someone has a complaint against anyone, forgive each other. As the Lord forgave you, so also forgive each other. And over all these things put on love, which is the perfect bond of unity. The peace of Christ must control your hearts—a peace into which you were called in one body. And be thankful people. (Col 3:12-15)

---

[4]Woodley, "Harmony Way," 155-57. See also Richard Twiss, *One Church, Many Tribes: Following Jesus the Way God Made You* (Bloomington, MN: Chosen Books, 2000), 90-110.
[5]Woodley, *Shalom and the Community*, 1-24.

Woodley further describes shalom as communal, holistic, tangible, dynamic, a constant journey, transformative, and worked out in our everyday relationships and activities with one another.[6] What Old Testament scholar Walter Brueggemann identifies as God's dream of one community "living in harmony and security toward the joy and well-being of every other creature" is consistent with the Harmony Way/Bright Path.[7]

We believe that this understanding of the Bright Path as shalom makes a significant contribution toward Indigenous Christian interpretations of Scripture, as it centers shalom in Creator's vision for all of creation. To read Scripture along the Bright Path invites Indigenous readers to understand such scriptural notions as sin and salvation in dialogue with their ancestral traditions, ceremonies, and experiences, which include their experiences with Western Christians. During Chris's visit to a rural Muscogee/Creek church in Oklahoma, Rev. Clarence Yarholar (Muscogee/Creek), who ministers within the Oklahoma Indian Missionary Conference of the United Methodist Church, shared about translating Christian concepts so that they might be more relatable to Indigenous people:

> It is all about balance. . . . If I have balance when it's peaceful, maybe that's what salvation might be. And some spiritual entity may be helping me do that. When some natives hear the word salvation, they feel offended. They feel like they are being told that something is wrong with you. Yeah, we are not perfect; but the word saved, I reinterpret that as coming back into balance, peacefulness, and harmony.[8]

Casey Church (Potawatomi) shared with Chris that in a Native context, one way of describing sin is "falling short of your culture's highest ideals."[9] Uncle Casey explained that natives have an allergic reaction to the word *sin*—not so much because natives do not have a concept of unholy living or morality but because of the legacy of Western Christians labeling Indigenous lifeways and ceremonies as categorically demonic and sinful. The discussion of sin in the modern church, shaped as it is by Western individualism and notions of

---

[6]Woodley, *Shalom and the Community*, 21-22.
[7]Walter Brueggemann, *Peace: Living Toward a Vision* (St. Louis: Chalice, 2001), 13-14, quoted in Woodley, *Shalom and the Community*, 19.
[8]Clarence Yarholar, interview, February 22, 2022.
[9]Casey Church, interview, June 9, 2021.

moral and cultural superiority, sees sin solely at the individual level and rarely extends the discussion to the collective.[10]

There is a lot of baggage and hurt associated with the concept of sin, and Indigenous peoples have their own ways of describing similar negative behavior and attitudes in other productive ways. For example, within Diné (Navajo) culture, Donnie Begay (Diné) explained to Chris that there isn't a straightforward concept that encapsulates pure evil or sin, since their worldview is structured around notions of coexistence, duality, and balance. A common term used to describe harmony and balance is *hòzhǫ́*, and the word is used in many prayers and songs. Yet, there can be no *hòzhǫ́* without *hóchxǫ́*, which can be considered the counterpart or duality of *hòzhǫ́*. The term *hóchxǫ́* perhaps gets closest at capturing a concept of moral deficiency and can be thought of as ways of living that seek to extend one's own life at the expense of others. *Hòzhǫ́*, on the other hand, is seeking balance and harmony for self, others, and creation. Certainly many Western social, political, and economic practices of the modern world illustrate this Diné concept of *hóchxǫ́*. Life at its best within Diné culture is *Są́ah naagháii bekʼeh hòzhǫ́*, which is difficult to translate but conveys ways of life that promote longevity, harmony, balance, and beauty.[11] Steven Charleston explains that origin stories and Original Instructions given to Indigenous peoples generally affirm human pitifulness and the human tendency to exhaust their resources or disrespect their human and nonhuman kin when ceremonies and protocols are forgotten. Such stories lack a concept of original sin as a central, primordial problem, but they certainly speak to living out of balance among our relations.[12] Interpreting Scripture within the framework of the Bright Path emphasizes how human sin disrupts our relationship with Creator, defiles or pollutes our spirit, and creates an imbalance in our web of relationships that leads to disharmony and harm.

In this chapter we will explore how reading Scripture along the Bright Path can help us better appreciate how biblical stories and values align with

---

[10]See further discussion on the concept of sin from Indigenous perspective in Lisa A. Dellinger, "Sin—Ambiguity and Complexity and the Sin of Not Conforming," in *Coming Full Circle: Constructing Native Christian Theology*, ed. Steven Charleston and Elaine A. Robinson (Minneapolis: Fortress, 2015), 119-32.
[11]Donnie Begay, interview, January 21, 2022.
[12]Steven Charleston, *The Four Vision Quests of Jesus* (New York: Morehouse, 2015), 93-94.

Indigenous stories and concepts of what life looks like at its best, as our elder Terry LeBlanc would say, which entails harmonious relationships with all our relations. Moreover, this chapter will explore how Indigenous stories, ceremonies, and values can contribute to our interpretation of how Scripture describes the work and role of Christ in restoring our shalom and our relationships with Creator, with humans, and our more-than-human relatives. Turtle Island hermeneutics asserts that our ancestral stories, ceremonies, and lifeways have something to contribute to envisioning Creator's dream of shalom in our world today and how we can participate in that dream.

HOW JESUS RESTORES OUR SHALOM WITH CREATOR

Since the resurrection of Jesus, followers of Jesus have told different stories and relied on metaphors and symbols recognizable to their own cultures to explain how Jesus restores humanity's relationship with Creator. As we will discuss below, even Paul of Tarsus relied on many different stories and symbols to express the great mystery of how Christ establishes shalom or peace between Creator and humanity. This observation might surprise many Christian readers who have been taught that the salvation story is simple and clear. In a sense, the broad strokes are simple and clear: "If you confess with your mouth 'Jesus is Lord' and in your heart you have faith [or trust] that God raised him from the dead, you will be saved" (Rom 10:9). But *how* precisely does Jesus save, and what does salvation look like? The responses to this have historically come in symbols and stories arising from believers' experiences of the Spirit of Christ in their own cultures. And if each of these contextualized stories and symbols helped followers of Christ to grasp the mystery of their salvation in creative and illuminating ways, how might Indigenous stories and symbols enrich how we understand and experience the mystery of Christ's peace and salvation? If there have always been a multitude of stories and symbols on hand to explain how Christ saves, there is certainly room for more. The problem with some modern theologies of salvation is that they flatten the diverse scriptural witness and prioritize a handful of stories and symbols to the exclusion of others that are both based on and resonate with the witness of ancient Christian experience and stories.

For nearly the past millennium, Western Christians have explained how Jesus restores humanity's relationship with Creator with reference to some version of Anselm's atonement theory. Anselm, an eleventh-century Benedictine monk and archbishop of Canterbury, creatively referenced feudal concerns for honor that were familiar to his medieval European context to explain why God needed to become human and die to save humanity. According to Anselm, the Creator's honor had been so offended by the rebellious and sinful offenses of humanity that only the sacrificial death of God's son, being of infinite value himself, was sufficient to atone for the infinitely grave offense of dishonoring God.

Anselm's story of atonement, deriving from his cultural location, seems particularly attuned to address the perpetually pressing question about *why* Jesus' death was necessary in the story of restoring our relationship with Creator. This story is adept at instilling attitudes of humility, loyalty, and reverence within Christians who reflect on the terrible cost that their sinful and disobedient behavior merited. And yet, the excesses of Anselm's story raise the question of whether God's ego and honor are so fragile that God *needs* the sacrifice of his son's blood to forgive. "From the Native experience of God and life," Episcopalian Bishop Steven Charleston (Choctaw) explains, Anselm's atonement theory, "seems irrational, perhaps even barbaric."[13] Anselm's atonement theory also seems to have nothing to say to the rest of creation. Indigenous thinkers have often turned to their ancestral traditions in order to understand what role Christ's death plays in the story of God and of bringing the whole of creation back into harmonious relationship, balance, and shalom.

In summer 2023, Chris was honored to be a guest at a Lakota Sun Dance ceremony outside the Rosebud Indian Reservation in South Dakota. So as not to betray the trust of his hosts, we won't reveal anything about this sacred ceremony that has not already been discussed in print or is public knowledge. Generally speaking, Sun Dances, which are common among a number of northern Plains tribes across Turtle Island, take place over a period of days during the summer months, during which dancers pledge to dance each day around a tree and to abstain from food and water for long periods of time.[14] Throughout each of these days, the Sun Dancers will endure either their chest

---

[13]Charleston, *Four Vision Quests*, 97.
[14]For an appreciative account of the Sun Dance and comparison with the Easter tradition, see William Stolzman, *The Pipe and Christ: A Christian-Sioux Dialogue*, 7th ed. (Chamberlain, SD: St. Joseph's Indian School, 2007), 157-65.

or back being pierced and a small piece of wood inserted into the holes. These small pieces of wood are tethered by a long rope to a cottonwood tree at the center. These dancers will then dance until the wood tears the flesh from their bodies. Such experiences of deprivation, discomfort, and pain are sacrificial gifts to creation and/or Creator. They express their deep appreciation for all that Creator gives and the generative force of creation that sustains human life and well-being, to invite divine pity in their display of reverent humility, and to reinforce their prayers and requests for healing to Creator on behalf of the community.

In the afternoon of the third day of the Sun Dance, a healing round is conducted in which members of the community gather around the dancers and present themselves to be prayed over and blessed by power accrued and harnessed by the Sun Dancers. Stephen Charleston explains that the Sun Dancers believe that "the sacrifice of their own bodies, of their own blood, will offer to God a small part of the life that God bestows on humanity.... Ultimately, it is also a request, an appeal on behalf of humanity that God will continue to bless the people, and all of creation, with a bounty of health and well-being."[15] On the car ride back to their motel from the ceremony, Chris's host, Doug Anderson, who has been a welcomed guest to this particular Sun Dance for years, reflected, "What can you give to the Creator and to nature that it does not already have? Everything done inside the sacred circle of the dance is for the healing and well-being of those outside."

Lakota visionary and Catholic catechist Nicholas Black Elk understood Jesus as the ideal Sun Dancer, whose gift of flesh restores and maintains a harmonious relationship with God and all of our relations.[16] For Charleston, to identify Jesus as a Sun Dancer provides him a vantage point to reflect on the meaning of Jesus' suffering apart from a Western story that emphasizes sin as the central framework for interpreting the cross.[17] Jesus' sacrifice, like the sacrifice of a Sun Dancer, channels divine power that translates into

---

[15]Charleston, *Four Vision Quests*, 135. It should be noted that some Indigenous followers of Jesus have differing perspectives on the Sun Dance. Some Indigenous believers choose not to participate at all (though they are cultural practitioners), and others would choose not to participate in only certain aspects of the ceremony.

[16]Damian Costello, *Black Elk: Colonialism and Lakota Catholicism* (Maryknoll, NY: Orbis Books, 2005), 119-22; Clara Sue Kidwell, Homer Noley, and George E. "Tink" Tinker, *A Native American Theology* (Maryknoll, NY: Orbis Books, 2001), 62. See also, Charleston, *Four Vision Quests*, 92.

[17]Charleston, *Four Vision Quests*, 92-93.

divine healing and empowerment for the community. Both Black Elk and Lakota medicine man Frank Fools Crow likened the cottonwood tree at the center of the sacred hoop of the Sun Dance ceremony to Jesus on the cross.[18] As Frank Fools Crow explains:

> So the tree . . . becomes a living thing for us. It becomes human, and it dies for us like Jesus on the cross for everyone. The Sioux received the Sun Dance from *Wakan-Tanka*, and we honor him by doing it as he told us to. Since the white man has come to us and explained how God sent his own son to be sacrificed, we realize that our sacrifice is similar to Jesus' own. As to how the white man feels about what we do, there was a far more terrible thing done by Jesus Christ. He endured more suffering and more pain. He was even stabbed on his side, and he died. . . . The Indian tribes must speak for themselves, but the Sioux feel a special closeness to God in the dance and in the piercing and flesh offerings. We even duplicate Christ's crown of thorns in the sage head wreath the pledgers wear.[19]

While many Christians might have concerns about Frank Fools Crow's equivocation of Christ's suffering with the Lakota's suffering, such an idea resonates with Paul's framing of his own suffering: "I'm completing what is missing from Christ's sufferings with my own body. I'm doing this for the sake of his body, which is the church" (Col 1:24). Moreover, ancient Christian martyr theology poetically and theologically framed Christian suffering as participating somehow in Christ's suffering for the world.[20]

The sacred story of the life-giving death of Christ finds further resonance with the story of Corn Mother, versions of which have been told across Turtle Island. While Corn Mother stories vary, each tale portrays a divine woman who willingly accepts her death so that her people might live. In one Penobscot retelling, the First Mother, compelled by the cries of her starving children, instructs her husband to kill her and to drag her body across the fields so that her flesh, blood, and bones might mix with the soil. Months later, corn begins to grow. In a word reminiscent of the Christian Eucharist, the

---

[18]Damien Costello, "Black Elk Speaks," *Journal of NAIITS* 4 (2006): 46-50.
[19]Costello, "Black Elks Speaks," 46, quoting Thomas E. Mails, *Fools Crow* (Lincoln: University of Nebraska Press, 1990) 133, 136.
[20]See Judith Perkins, *The Suffering Self: Pain and Narrative Representation in the Early Christian Era* (London: Routledge, 1995); Candida Moss, *The Other Christs: Imitating Jesus in Ancient Christian Ideologies of Martyrdom* (Oxford: Oxford University Press, 2010).

First Man tells his people: "Remember and take good care of First Mother's flesh, because it is goodness become substance. . . . She has given her life so that you might live."[21] Similar to Jesus' sacrifice, Corn Mother's sacrifice invites people to gather around the table, recognize our shared kinship—which here includes plants and the earth—and offer gratitude for the gifts of the Corn Mother. George "Tink" Tinker (wazhazhe/Osage) adamantly argues that Indigenous peoples should not give up stories such as Corn Mother, which encompass "God's unique self-disclosure to us."[22] Christ, as God's eternal and pervasive *logos*, or communication, of "creativity and healing or salvation to human beings," inspired this story among the First Nations across Turtle Island.[23] Reading the sacrifice of Corn Mother together with Christ's sacrifice can lead us to ponder how the religious symbolism of death and blood can metaphorically point to new life and, similar to Anselm's story, still instill attitudes of humility, loyalty, and reverence apart from some of the perceived excesses of his story's characterization of Creator's *need* for blood. There is imaginative space within the Christian tradition for Indigenous metaphors, stories, and ceremonies to think about the work of Christ.

The apostle Paul weaves together a diversity of theological stories and metaphors to articulate his mystical experience of the risen Christ and the significance of Christ's faithful life and death for restoring shalom.[24]

---

[21]Richard Erdoes and Alfonso Ortiz, *American Indian Myths and Legends*, Pantheon Fairy Tale & Folklore Library (New York: Pantheon Books, 1984), 13. William Baldridge (Cherokee) shares a Cherokee version where the mother produces corn by rubbing her body and is murdered by her own children, who mistake her for a witch upon discovering how their mom was providing food for them. In this story too, the mother's buried body produces corn forevermore, the source of life-nourishing bread for the Cherokee. See Baldridge, "Reclaiming Our Histories," in *Native and Christian: Indigenous Voices on Religious Identity in the United States and Canada*, ed. James Treat (New York: Routledge, 1996), 87.

[22]Kidwell, Noley, and Tinker, *Native American Theology*, 76-83.

[23]Kidwell, Noley, and Tinker, *Native American Theology*, 79.

[24]Elizabeth Johnson helpfully summarizes these stories in *Creation and the Cross: The Mercy of God for a Planet in Peril* (Maryknoll, NY: Orbis Books, 2019), 113-57. Other recent works on the spectrum of stories and metaphors of atonement, including their strengths and weaknesses, include Ben C. Blackwell, "Paul and Salvation," in *The State of Pauline Studies: A Survey of Recent Research*, ed. Nijay Gupta, Erin M. Heim, and Scot McKnight (Grand Rapids, MI: Baker Academics, 2024), 42-60; Teresa Morran, *Trust in Atonement: God, Creation, and Reconciliation* (Grand Rapids, MI: Eerdmans, 2024); Brian Zahnd, *The Wood Between the Worlds: A Poetic Theology of the Cross* (Downers Grove, IL: InterVarsity Press, 2024); Oliver D. Crisp, *Approaches to the Atonement: The Reconciling Work of Christ* (Downers Grove, IL: InterVarsity Press, 2020); Eleonore Stump, *Atonement* (Oxford: Oxford University Press, 2018); Fleming Rutledge, *The Crucifixion: Understanding the Death of Christ* (Grand Rapids, MI: Eerdmans, 2017).

In 1 Corinthians 15:53-57, Paul references a military story of Christ giving us victory over death. Christ is also a diplomat, reconciling us to God, even though we were his enemies (Rom 5:10-11). Paul also tells a financial story of God purchasing humanity for a price as if they were slaves (1 Cor 6:20), so Christ-followers should remember which master they serve (Rom 7:23). This financial story seems to be at its rhetorical best when it instills a profound sense of gratefulness within us at the price that was paid on our behalf. From gratefulness springs loyalty and obedience to the Bright Path of Christ. Paul's metaphors of justification and redemption (e.g., Rom 3:23-24) evoke the image of a courtroom wherein humanity has been acquitted of all charges of not living up to God's covenantal expectations, with Christ as our defense attorney (Rom 8:34). This merciful acquittal doesn't come cheap, though, although it is not clear whether it is Jesus' blood (Rom 5:9) or his resurrection (Rom 4:25) that brings about our justification. Paul also evokes the Passover story in describing Jesus as our paschal Lamb that has been sacrificed, around whom we gather to celebrate as a community (1 Cor 5:7), a metaphor that John is equally keen on (Jn 19:14, 36).

In the first Passover story, the blood of the Passover lamb does not atone for sins but distinguishes the Hebrew people from the Egyptians, so that the angel of death might pass over their households. Paul's ceremonial words over the Eucharist cup, "This cup is the new covenant in my blood" (1 Cor 11:25), likely call back to the blood that Moses dashed on the basins, against the altar, and on the people to signal the "blood of the covenant that Yahweh now makes with you [the Israelites]" (Ex 24:4-8 modified). Paul also likens Jesus' death to the sin offering of blood that would cleanse a person of their sins (Rom 3:25). "God did not need sacrifice in order to forgive sin," Elizabeth Johnson clarifies, as if this transaction comprised a "quid pro quo." "When a person approached with a sincere heart to repent," Johnson continues, "then an animal's life poured out in blood could function to seal the giver's recommitment."[25] While God remains steadfast in his mercy and grace, ever ready to restore relationships, the ceremony of confessing sins and purifying ourselves with blood is to change us. Such stories that liken Jesus to the sacrificial cult around the Jewish temple carry forward in the anonymous

---

[25]Johnson, *Creation and the Cross*, 138.

letter to the Hebrews. In Hebrews 9:14 the blood of Christ functions like the blood of goats and bulls that sanctifies and purifies what has been defiled and made impure. Here again, the blood of Jesus purifies and does not placate the wrath of an angry God.

Less familiar to many Western Christians is the focus on theosis ("being made divine") and union with God in the Eastern Christian tradition. In Romans 8:9-11 Paul variously speaks of the "Spirit of God," the "Spirit of Christ," "Christ," the "Spirit of him who raised Jesus," and the "Spirit" as dwelling within the believer (Rom 8:9-11; see also 1 Cor 3:16). It is Christ's resurrection that occasions a pouring out of God's Spirit (Acts 2:17-18) and empowers Christians to imitate Christ and to "become participants of the divine nature" (2 Pet 1:4). This is a gift imparted by God to humanity, with the Holy Spirit working within us to ever live into what it means to be "in Christ."[26] This story of empowerment resonates with Indigenous teaching that connects the Sun Dance with Christ and emphasizes how Christ is a conduit of divine power that enables harmonious living and healing.

One last metaphor that holds a special place among two Indigenous ministers Chris spoke with is that of adoption. In Paul's letter to the Galatians, he declares, "God sent the Spirit of his Son into our hearts, crying, 'Abba, Father!' Therefore, you are no longer a slave but a son or daughter, and if you are his child, then you are also an heir through God" (Gal 4:6-7). In this filial metaphor, God brings people into his family through adoption. This metaphor becomes even more profound when we consider how Roman adoption worked in Paul's day. Whereas we often think of adoption as happening to young children, Roman adoption was usually of a young adult, who would carry on the name and be the heir of an older male with no male heirs.[27] Paul's use of this metaphor is beautiful in that he treats all believers, male or female, slave or free, with a metaphor that normally only applied to males. In God's family, male and female are equal inheritors of God. The other

---

[26]James R. Payton Jr., *The Victory of the Cross: Salvation in Eastern Orthodoxy* (Downers Grove, IL: InterVarsity Press, 2019), 115-16. On union with Christ, see the thorough exegetical work in Constantine R. Campbell, *Paul and Union with Christ: An Exegetical and Theological Study* (Grand Rapids, MI: Zondervan, 2012).

[27]On the adoption metaphor in Paul's writings, see Erin M. Heim, *Adoption in Galatians and Romans: Contemporary Metaphor Theories and the Pauline* Huiothesia *Metaphors*, Biblical Interpretation 153 (Boston: Brill, 2017).

interesting component of Roman adoption is that it involved a young adult rather than a child. The adoption of a child in the modern day provides some opportunity for the adoptive family to welcome, pour into, and shape the child in the traditions and ethos of the family. In the case of Roman adoption, the adopted son was full grown, already shaped by the traditions of his family—his identity had largely been established. This identity was brought into the new family as he took on himself a new name, gained a new inheritance, and took on new traditions. The young man's past was not denigrated or erased in the process of adoption.

Metaphors of God's adoption of us into his family can be powerful stories within Indigenous communities that have significant adoption ceremonies, as in Cree, Lakota, and Crow traditions. In fall 2024, Chris and Danny witnessed a Cree adoption ceremony in Winnipeg in which a star blanket was placed over the individual being adopted. In an extremely rare moment of theological brilliance, Danny leaned over to Chris and observed how Jesus is our Star Blanket, whom we put on (Gal 3:27) when we are baptized and adopted into Christ's family. Paul Sneve (Lakota), an Episcopal minister who served the Tiospaye Wakan (Sacred Family) Lakota congregation at Calvary Episcopal Cathedral in Sioux Falls, South Dakota, metaphorically frames the work of Christ and baptism within the Lakota adoption ceremony. "We call God 'Father' in our congregation," Sneve shared with Chris, "because we are adopted in his family."[28] Kenny Pretty on Top Jr. (Crow), who ministers at a Foursquare church in Crow Agency, Montana, just a freeway exit away from where the Battle of the Greasy Grass (or the Battle of Little Bighorn) took place, told Chris how he has referenced the Crow adoption ceremony when illustrating Jesus' parables of God seeking out the lost in Luke 15 and bringing them back into God's family.[29] In one version of this ceremony, an announcement will be made during a large community gathering such as a dance or powwow that a child has gone missing. A dancer from the center stage will dance on into the stands searching for the lost child. Soon the dancer will identify an individual from the crowd and bring them down to the floor, where they will be met by the family intending to adopt the individual. In this beautiful display of communal celebration and support of

---

[28]Personal communication, July 28, 2023.
[29]Personal communication, June 2022.

making relatives, it can be a powerful story to imagine Jesus having incarnated in the form of a Crow dancer and warmly inviting others into the family dance.

It should not be lost on Christians today that the language of adoption in the Bible not only encourages us to call Creator "Father" but also encourages us to think of Jesus as our elder brother (Rom 8:17). This in turn helps us to think of Jesus and Creator as our ancestors. Matthew's and Luke's genealogies of Jesus connect him to his Jewish and non-Jewish ancestors, to the first human, Adam (himself made of the dirt), and ultimately to Creator himself. This is the family story and kinship that we are invited into. And just as Jesus was a good ancestor for us, so we are called to be a good ancestor to others.

While Western Christianity may prefer atonement stories such as that of Anselm, Indigenous people have in Christ the theological invitation to imagine within their cultural traditions and stories the Christ story for themselves. Steven Charleston summarizes his own atonement story this way:

> [Jesus] had to live in a new way in order to heal the whole circle of humanity. He had to become the "we" to the farthest limit of that definition. In order to call back every person from exile, he had to go where they are, on the very margins of society, cut off and alone, rejected and abused. The death of Jesus, therefore, was not required by God to stave off divine retribution against a fatally flawed humanity that deserves eternal punishment, but an act of self-sacrifice and love so profound that it brought enough Good Medicine in the world to heal the broken hoop of the nation for every person on earth. . . . [It restored] the most essential aspect of creation: kinship. . . . He came that we might have his vision.[30]

For some Native North Americans, Jesus' suffering at the cross is not about what God *needs* in order to forgive but the ultimate display of Creator's love for us and the tragic culmination of humanity being out of balance and out of line with the Original Instructions of Creator. As Jace Weaver (Cherokee) puts it: when Jesus was murdered, God wept but then laughed at the folly of humanity (Ps 2), and resurrected Jesus in vindication of his life and teachings.[31]

To be fair to Anselm, and to every story or metaphor that attempts to explain the mystery of Christian salvation, there are inherent gaps, plot holes,

---

[30]Charleston, *Four Vision Quests*, 106-7.
[31]Jace Weaver, *That the People Might Live: Native American Literatures and Native American Community* (New York: Oxford University Press, 1997), 182n172.

excesses, and questions that lie beyond the scope of the plot and intended effect of the story and metaphor. And yet, all these stories come together to form a beautiful photomosaic, their individual hues and contours form an awe-inspiring picture of Christ reconciling all creation to himself that can be appreciated when you step back and take in all the stories together.[32] As we sing around the big drum, "Jesus is good medicine, the good medicine way," we assert that there is room enough in the sacred photomosaic of the mystery of salvation to hold together the diversity of scriptural stories and other encultured stories inspired by Christ, in all their resonances and tensions. What would it look like if we spent a little more time being curious about the kinds of work that our diverse and encultured stories do to cultivate attitudes of courage, devotion, generosity, gratefulness, healing, humility, and faithfulness that encompass shalom? As the gospel continues to be shared into new cultures and peoples across time, the photomosaic of salvation will become all the more textured and extravagant.

JESUS AS JUBILEE

Just as Jesus restores our shalom with Creator, Jesus works to restore our shalom with both our human and other-than-human kin, and he calls us into this ongoing work. Out of the foundational Hebrew construct of shalom came a unique and unparalleled instruction in the ancient world: the Jubilee year (Lev 25:8-55). While other ancient societies sometimes had royal announcements of a Jubilee nature (debts forgiven and/or land returned), Leviticus enshrined this practice into the calendar of Israel.[33] This year drew on the shalom construct as exemplified in the laws of Sabbath in order to enact a great national work for socioeconomic justice every fifty years. In the Jubilee year, lands that were sold returned to the original family's stewardship, slaves were released, all debts were canceled, and the land laid fallow, with the people permitted to reap whatever was produced but not allowed to sow and work the fields. This last aspect of Jubilee meant that the Jubilee year was also a Sabbath year for the land, meaning that what the land chose to produce

---

[32]We give our thanks to our friend and Old Testament scholar Michael J. Rhodes for this metaphor for how images and stories in the Bible are juxtaposed together, in all their continuities and tensions, and yet can contribute to a greater, more complex picture and story.

[33]See Michael J. Rhodes, *Just Discipleship: Biblical Justice in an Unjust World* (Downers Grove, IL: IVP Academic, 2023), 161-63.

during its time of rest was for the owners, the foreigners, the poor, and the animals to make use of, as the land cared for all (Lev 25:3-6). The Jubilee, then, was also for the poor, the hungry, the foreigner, the widow, the orphan, the livestock, and for the wild animals. This was the great leveling effect. Greed was halted, as the Jubilee was expressly "to prevent the accumulation of ownership in the hands of a wealthy few."[34] Poverty was halted. Everyone started over again so no one person or family or generation lived forever in their present marginalized state. Extreme poverty and extreme greed were silenced. The Jubilee "unequivocally advocates wealth redistribution as a matter of justice for the poor."[35]

In the Jubilee, our circle of care and relations is reset, reminding us of the web of relations we are part of—the humans, the more-than-humans, and the land. The Jubilee, as a major societal overhaul, shows that Creator is concerned about individuals who are suffering and so expects other people to create systems and structures to provide a safety net for those who are disenfranchised. The Jubilee also indicates that socioeconomic justice extended beyond the individual and into the socioeconomic health of the entire community intergenerationally, as those who may have sold their land out of necessity would often not have been alive to see the restoration of the land to their family at the fifty-year mark. And for those at the top, who had accumulated wealth and land, the Jubilee was for their healing too, as they were challenged each generation to covenant faithfulness and community health over their own ambitions.

The Jubilee instructions show that shalom was not simply a spiritual, disembodied reality but was expected to be incarnated in actions. Jubilee was eventually incarnated ultimately in Jesus of Nazareth and his teachings, the themes of which are evoked in his first sermon according to Luke 4.[36] When Jesus came home to Nazareth, he proclaimed that he was the fulfillment of this shalom way of living—Jesus was the Jubilee bringer. This sermon is unique to Luke's Gospel and becomes a lens through which Luke wants his

---

[34] Christopher J. H. Wright, *The Mission of God: Unlocking the Bible's Grand Narrative* (Downers Grove, IL: InterVarsity Press, 2006), 296.

[35] Michael Barram, *Missional Economics: Biblical Justice and Christian Formation* (Grand Rapids, MI: Eerdmans, 2018), 116.

[36] See especially Randy Woodley, *Mission and the Cultural Other: A Closer Look* (Eugene, OR: Cascade Books, 2022), 126-29; see also Rhodes, *Just Discipleship*, 192-94.

readers to encounter the life and teachings of Jesus and their continuance into the early church, as narrated in Acts.

As Jesus finishes reading from Isaiah 61 and its proclamation of Jubilee, his words are initially met with favor as he declares, "Today, this scripture has been fulfilled just as you heard it" (Lk 4:21). The warm fuzzies are short lived as the people begin to dismiss Jesus in skepticism or envy. Jesus, in response, begins to "story" them, disrupting their thoughts and pushing them to think far more inclusively than they have been. He first speaks of the widow from Zarephath, a Gentile, who had no food for her family. As the story goes, Creator sent the great prophet Elijah to her, and Elijah performed a miracle, and it gave her food. But Jesus adds that Creator did not send Elijah to the hungry widows in Israel at that time (1 Kings 17:8-24). He then tells them the story of the Gentile soldier Naaman of Syria, who was part of an army that invaded Israel. In fact, Naaman was a captain in the occupying army. The people of Israel hated this army and the man, but Creator wanted this man to be healed from the dreaded disease of leprosy. So, Creator sent another great prophet named Elisha to cure this man, and he was healed. Then Jesus adds that Creator did not send Elisha at the time to people in Israel with leprosy (2 Kings 5:1-14). The people in Jesus' hometown become livid and want to throw Jesus off a cliff and kill him. But somehow Jesus gets away from them (Lk 4:28-30).

What can we learn from Jesus' stories and Luke's broader story of Jesus' Jubilee sermon? And where might we see reverberations of these Jubilee stories through the rest of Luke's Gospel?

Jesus wanted the people in his hometown of Nazareth to know that they were not the only people loved by Creator. The people of Nazareth had succumbed to the thought that they were special, above everyone else in the world, but Jesus was telling them that everyone made by Creator was special, loved, and sometimes even preferred over those who claimed to know Creator the most. The people of Nazareth had forgotten just how great Creator's love and concern for all people was. It would take many years for that first Jesus community to understand Creator's plan for a global and multiethnic faith family, and Luke most fully tells this story in Acts.

Perhaps Jesus had in mind not just Isaiah 61 but other Scripture passages that demonstrate a God who has dealings with all people, such as

Deuteronomy 2 or Amos 9:7: "'Are you Israelites more important to me than the Ethiopians?' asks the Lord. 'I brought Israel out of Egypt, but I also brought the Philistines from Crete and led the Arameans out of Kir'" (NLT). Perhaps the Abrahamic covenant was also in his mind, with the call for Abraham and his people to be a light to the nations (Gen 18:18). Being a man shaped by his genealogy, Jesus recognized that his family tree extended outside the people of Israel (Mt 1:3-6), and indeed he knew from the Hebrew creation story that the entire heavens and earth was a giant family tree (Gen 2:4).[37] Additionally, knowing that the land was also a teacher for Jesus through his life, and most intensely during his time of vision quest in the wilderness, Jesus knew the truth that Creator and creation do not hold to any notions of ethnic superiority, with the gifts of creation given to everyone (Mt 5:45) and mother earth taking care of us all—the four-leggeds, the two-leggeds, the bird life, and the bug life.[38]

This Jubilee vision is not confined to this first sermon of Jesus but reverberates throughout the rest of Luke's writings. This inclusivity is already signaled in the early chapters of Luke. The great leveling of Jubilee narrated in Luke begins prior to Jesus, with a simple peasant girl being spoken of in exalted terms and the announcement that she will bear the Messiah (Lk 1:28-30). The song of Mary in Luke 1 becomes a template for her son as she praises God for his mercy, that he has "scattered those with arrogant thoughts and proud inclinations . . . pulled the powerful down from their thrones . . . lifted up the lowly . . . filled the hungry . . . sent the rich away empty-handed" (Lk 1:51-53). We might say that the Jubilee was first decreed by his Father, then sung by his mother, before being preached by Jesus in the Nazareth synagogue. Jesus was in the family business.

As this first sermon highlighted those considered outsiders during the times of Elijah and Elisha, it is important to notice that outsiders have already been featured prominently prior to the start of Jesus' ministry. The shepherds who received the announcement from the spirit world were an economically marginalized group, working for those who owned the land and sheep and gained all the profit and benefits. Widows are also highlighted in Luke (Lk 2:36-38; 7:11-12; 21:1-4), as are debtors and tenant workers (Lk 7:41-42;

---

[37]See chapter two above.
[38]See discussion in chapter one above; Charleston, *Four Vision Quests*, 65-77.

8:18; 12:58-59), and the shunned lepers (Lk 17:11-19). Luke and Acts, taken together, highlight (and condemn) more than any other Gospel the social stratification of the world.[39]

As the ministry of Jesus begins, he is characterized as one who surrounds himself with the marginalized (Lk 5:30; 7:34; 15:1-2), and his closest followers come from the working poor of Galilee (Lk 6:12-16). In a world where it was wealthy landowning males who sat at the top of the hierarchy and were the patrons of a society full of clients, in Jesus' ministry it was a group of women who functioned as the patrons for Jesus and his ministry (Lk 8:2-3).[40] It was these same women who provided the sacred balance of man and woman at the crucifixion, as all of Jesus' male followers fled but they remained (Lk 23:27, 49, 55-56).[41] It was this same group of women who became the first preachers of the resurrection (Lk 24:6-10).

Finally, encounters between Jesus and other characters enact Jubilee justice, encounters that are labeled as salvation. For instance, in the story of the woman with incurable blood flow, salvation (*sōzō*) is her being made whole and her bleeding stopped (Lk 8:48). Another example is the story of Zacchaeus, where salvation (*sōtēria*) looks like financial reparations for those who have been wronged (Lk 19:8-9). We will return to the Zacchaeus story in chapter five in connection with the story of Jesus' encounter with the rich young man (Mk 10:17-31; Mt 19:16-30; Lk 18:18-30).

It is an unfortunate reality that there are no recorded examples of the Jubilee year ever being practiced in Israelite history.[42] However, there are at least some glimpses of Jubilee-like principles being put into practice in the Hebrew Bible. Jeremiah describes an attempt at Jubilee-like practice in Jeremiah 34:8-20, where King Zedekiah proclaims liberty for Judean slaves,

---

[39]On this, see Douglas E. Oakman, "The Countryside in Luke–Acts," in *The Social World of Luke–Acts: Models for Interpretation*, ed. Jerome H. Neyrey (Peabody, MA: Hendrickson, 1991), 151-80.

[40]On the patron-client system, especially as it relates to Luke's writings, see Halvor Moxnes, "Patron-Client Relations and the New Community in Luke–Acts," in Neyrey, *Social World of Luke–Acts*, 241-68.

[41]Charleston, *Four Vision Quests*, 152-56.

[42]See Niels P. Lemche, "Manumission of Slaves—the Fallow Year—the Sabbatical Year—the Jubilee Year," *Vetus Testamentum* 26 (1976): 38-59. See also Rhodes, *Just Discipleship*, 178-96, who makes the case that it may in fact have been practiced in light of other surrounding societies engaging in similar debt-relief and land-return practices. Moreover, he shows how a "jubilary imagination" or paradigm developed and informed the politics and practices of Jeremiah, Ezekiel, Nehemiah, Jesus, and Luke.

declaring that all should release slaves. The elite initially comply with the decree, but very soon after the release, they are brought back into slavery. Another example of a Jubilee-like event occurs in Nehemiah 5:1-13. The people are complaining that the excessive taxes mean they have to borrow money and that their children are being forced into powerless lives of enslavement. Nehemiah brings the outcry to the elite and calls them to enact Jubilee justice. He implores them to stop charging interest and to restore to the people their lands that very day. Under oath, the elites promise to do this, and Nehemiah 5:13 indicates that they did as was promised. Finally, we see a climactic example of Creator enacting Jubilee/Sabbath rest for the land in 2 Chronicles 36:15-21. As the Chronicler narrates the slow demise of the Northern and Southern Kingdoms, the fall of Jerusalem by the king of the Chaldeans is described, with the temple destroyed and the vessels of the temple taken to Babylon. The remaining people who were not killed in the battle are exiled in servitude to Babylon. The Chronicler states:

> Finally, he exiled to Babylon anyone who survived the killing so that they could be his slaves and the slaves of his children until Persia came to power. This is how the LORD's word spoken by Jeremiah was carried out. *The land finally enjoyed its sabbath rest. For as long as it lay empty, it rested, until seventy years were completed.* (2 Chron 36:20-21, emphasis added)

These verses should disabuse us of any notions of human superiority over the rest of the community of creation. These verses tell us that the land's need for its Jubilee rest is a prime reason for the exile to Babylon. God himself enacted the Jubilee for the sake of the land.

JESUS AS JUBILEE FOR OUR MORE-THAN-HUMAN KIN

If we continue to follow the Bright Path in looking for how salvation encompasses a restoration of relationships and balance with our more-than-human kin, then we can begin to see how shalom with the more-than-human creation is already present in the Jesus Way. The most famous verse in the Bible declares God's love for the whole world (Jn 3:16), and it is a peculiar symptom of diseased Western theology that has conditioned us to read this verse as only about humans. The Christ hymn of Colossians 1:15-20 also declares strongly that *all created things* are within the purview of the cosmic Christ's reconciling work, a work we are also called into. Christian conservationists and theologians who advocate for creation care are often, in our opinion, missing a crucial detail within their theological framing. Our work in and for creation is not simply caring for "God's things" because he asked us to, as if we were house-sitters for a friend. This perspective still holds creation at a distance and objectivizes it. But as we argued in an earlier chapter, we are part of creation and are involved in many layers of relationships within creation. Creation itself has its own agency, and our relationship to creation is largely one of reliance. Before we can talk about creation care, we must first acknowledge creation's care for us.[43]

Looking to the story of Jesus in the Gospels, we see that the work toward restoring shalom for the more-than-human community of creation is evident in the life and ministry of Christ. Prior to Jesus' ministry, the wilderness, which was so often spoken of as a wasteland, becomes the place where God's prophet John spends his days (Lk 1:80), and it is in the wilderness and in the waters of the Jordan that John prepares the way for all flesh to see God's salvation (Lk 3:2-6). *Flesh* is certainly a reference to humankind, but both the Greek word and the Hebrew word from Isaiah 40:5 encompass both human and animal. In Luke, the open fields become the place for the angelic announcement of the Messiah (Lk 2:8). As Jesus undergoes his vision quest in the wilderness, Mark notes that Jesus was with the wild beasts and that angels waited on him (Mk 1:13). As Bauckham observes, the peace teachings of Jesus are evident here in his "peaceable and friendly companionship with the animals."[44] This shows that the time in the wilderness was also a time of communion with the more-than-human creation around him, including the spirit world. Consider also how Jesus speaks words of healing and peace, not just to people but also to the wind and the waves (Mk 8:22-25), signaling his relationship with creation and creation's own agency. Creation itself laments Christ's death as darkness covers the land and the sun ceases sending its light (Lk 23:44-45).

Many Indigenous traditions, stories, and ceremonies emphasize the importance of maintaining or restoring shalom with our creation kin.

---

[43]See the thought experiment provided in H. Daniel Zacharias, "The Land Takes Care of Us: Recovering Creator's Relational Design," in *The Land: Majority World and Minoritized Theologies of Land*, ed. K. K. Yeo and Gene L. Green (Eugene, OR: Cascade, 2020), 69-70.

[44]Richard Bauckham, *Living with Other Creatures: Green Exegesis and Theology* (Waco, TX: Baylor University Press, 2011), 131. See also Job 5:22-23; Is 11:6-9.

Vine Deloria Jr. (Hunkpapa Lakota/Standing Rock Sioux) says, "Stories explaining how the people came to hunt the buffalo, how the salmon came to be the major food supply, how bird feathers were incorporated into ceremonial costumes and medicine bundles, all derive from early interspecies communications in which other forms of life agreed to allow themselves to be used in ceremonial and economic ways."[45] Relationship, reciprocity, and sacrificial giving sit at the heart of these stories. Bernie Gobin Kia-Kia (Tulalip) shares a story about the origin of the Salmon Ceremony of the Tulalip Tribes.[46] Like many other Pacific Northwest tribes, many of the lifeways and ceremonies center on the salmon, their central food staple. In this story, humans and animals could become one another and understand one another.

The human people and the salmon people have an agreement—a covenant—that the humans have begun to disregard. They are to clean the rivers each year and to return to the rivers the bones of the salmon that have been eaten. As the humans begin to neglect their responsibilities, the salmon come less and less and are becoming sicker. One day, a young man comes to the shore, asking why the salmon numbers are fewer. A salmon person suddenly emerges from the water and brings the young man to the salmon village to meet the king of the salmon, who himself is suffering terribly. Many of the other salmon are sickly and missing limbs. The king of the salmon has a fishhook in his head that is invisible to all but the young man. After the young man removes the hook, the king reminds him of what has been forgotten, the agreement between the salmon people and the human people. The salmon king then renegotiates the terms of their agreement. Humans are still expected to keep the river clean. But in recognition that the humans are having trouble keeping all of the bones of the salmon season by season, the salmon king teaches the young man songs to sing for a salmon ceremony, where only the bones of a scout salmon need to be returned to the river. This scout will check to make sure the humans hold up their end

---

[45] Vine Deloria Jr., *Spirit and Reason: The Vine Deloria, Jr., Reader* (Golden, CO: Fulcrum, 1999), 51-52.
[46] Bernie Gobin Kia-Kia, "The Story of the Salmon Ceremony," Hibulb Cultural Center and Natural History Preserve, accessed November 5, 2023, www.hibulbculturalcenter.org/Storytelling/The StoryOfTheSalmonCeremony. The Tulalip tribes are Coast Salish tribes, consisting of the Snohomish, Snoqualmie, Skykomish, and other allied tribes and bands that are signatories to the Treaty of Point Elliott.

of the agreement to keep the river clean, and this scout's bones are to be returned to the river in a ceremony accompanied by songs that the salmon king teaches the young man. And now, year by year, as the human people see the salmon fighting to go upstream, leaping at great heights to move upriver, they are reminded how diligently the salmon people work to uphold their end of the agreement.

Like the Tulalip tribes, many Galilean followers of Jesus had centered their lives on the life-giving relationship with the Sea of Galilee and its fish. One surprising story where we might interpret Jesus as reconstituting peace between the Galilean peoples and their more-than-human kin is Luke's account of Jesus' calling his first disciples (Lk 5:1-11). The story goes that Jesus politely commandeers Simon's boat and asks him to set off from shore so that he might make good use of the lake's acoustics while also giving himself a little breathing room. When Jesus finishes teaching, he tells Simon that they should go fishing. Simon, clearly annoyed, replies that he had fished all evening and hadn't caught anything. But Simon decides to humor Jesus. He rows to deeper water, casts his net, and takes in more fish than he had ever caught before. What happened? Luke's telling of the story doesn't address how this miracle precisely occurred. And so readers are invited to supply their own explanations about how the fish came to fill the nets.

Reading along the Bright Path leads us to picture Jesus as healing the Sea of Galilee and its fish inhabitants, reconciling Galileans to the lake and fish. Otherwise, what do we imagine happening? Did Jesus magnetically pool the fish together to be captured? We invite you to imagine that Jesus restored balance to the lake such that the fish knew that they could freely present themselves as food and that there would still be an abundance. Perhaps the reason the fish refused to present themselves to the fishermen earlier was that the fishermen had been overfishing the lake, succumbing to the extractive economy of empire.[47] The fish present themselves to the Jubilee bringer, and the response of the fishermen is to drop their nets. Might we even interpret the fishermen leaving behind their nets as also a symbolic gesture of recognizing the lake needs its Sabbath too? We can only presume that as these fishermen followed Jesus that their fishing was minimal. And thus the Sea of

---

[47]On the realities of the Galilean fishing economy at the time of Jesus, see Kenneth C. Hanson, "The Galilean Fishing Economy and the Jesus Tradition," *Biblical Theology Bulletin* 27 (1997): 99-111.

Galilee, which had become a place of oppressive economics, once again teems with life and abundance. Jubilee for fish and sea.

While believers may be persuaded that Christ's atoning work is indeed for all of creation, we may at the same time be at a loss to understand how disciples today can and ought to participate in this work toward new creation today.[48] The story of the first salmon ceremony not only can encourage imaginative readings of Scripture but also provides a model for thinking about our own ongoing relationship with "all our relations" and responsibilities placed on us. These relationships of reciprocity and respect are reinforced habitually and ceremonially by the community. Appreciating that these stories and ceremonies are location based, readers are invited to call to mind the *specific rivers* that they are to watch over and keep clean in their own watershed. Finally, audiences should recognize that there is nothing utopian about what is envisioned in the relationships represented in these stories. The salmon work hard to make it upstream. The humans find it an imposition to keep the salmon bones and return them to the river but will continue to do so as a tangible act of respect for the agreement. Keeping the river clean is ongoing toil. Maintaining relationships with our created kin is challenging work for all involved—but worth it to realize the kin(g)dom of Creator in our midst. Like our first parents in the Garden of Eden, who were to "serve and conform to the land" (Gen 2:15), our work striving for shalom balance with creation is an ongoing work because relationships continually require something from us.[49]

CONCLUSION: HAND IN HAND ALONG THE BRIGHT PATH

We need to embrace the partnerships and reciprocity within the community of creation, and we believe that Jesus shows us the way. However, it seems that Western Christians generally struggle with embracing such a place-based spirituality because most have shallow roots at best or are simply

---

[48] For articulations of Christ's atoning work as for all creation, see Teresa Morgan, *Trust in Atonement: God, Creation, and Reconciliation* (Grand Rapids, MI: Eerdmans, 2024), 159-95; Johnson, *Creation and the Cross*, 158-226.

[49] I (Danny) and Mark Brett argue for this translation of Gen 2:15 in "To Serve Her and Conform to Her: An Intercultural Reading of Gen 2:15," in *The Critic in the World: Essays in Honor of Fernando F. Segovia*, ed. Amy Lindeman Allen, Francisco Lozada Jr., and Yak-hwee Tan (Atlanta: SBL Press, 2024), 221-40. See chapter two under "Humanity's Role in the Community of Creation."

rootless. In the Western world, a very limited number of people can trace their ancestors back six or more generations to the same place that they inhabit today. This lack of ancestral connection means that our identity is not rooted to a place. In contrast, Indigenous people's sense of identity is bound to the land.[50] It takes extra, concerted effort for modern people to root themselves to their place.

At times, our (mis)understanding of theology has compounded this lack of connection to place. Our belief that we are citizens of heaven (Phil 3:20) has uncritically warranted a lack of concern with the lands we are part of. But being a citizen of the kin(g)dom of God is not a replacement of other citizenships and partnerships but rather an additional circle of relationships we are brought into. When Jesus spoke of the kingdom of God, he not only spoke of an alternative place in the future but said, "God's kingdom is already among you" (Lk 17:21). Being a citizen of the kingdom of God is not only a future orientation but also a present reality. It also does not replace other partnerships we are a part of. We suggest, rather, that by virtue of our heavenly citizenship, all other relationships of responsibility take on additional significance as we now strive to bring a new-creation kin(g)dom-of God-ethic into these relationships.

We ask the question, "What does it look like for our relationship with 'all our relations' to be at its best in Creator's eyes?" Following Jesus' example, the answer to this will always mean being servants, emptying ourselves of any power we may hold, lifting up those in the relationship that are marginalized, and always working toward shalom. As our friend Randy Woodley eloquently puts it: "Jesus showed humanity how to use power, not to gain advantage over the vulnerable and marginalized, but rather to empower those who are disenfranchised, even to the point of viewing them as our teachers."[51]

The work of shalom with creation begins with recognizing the relationships and framing them in some sense as a covenant. Vine Deloria Jr. says:

> A covenant places responsibilities on both parties and provides a means of healing any breach in the relationship. . . . [For instance,] although Indians hunted and fished wild game, they made it a rule that unless they were starving

---

[50]For more on this, see Ray Aldred, "The Land, Treaty, and Spirituality: Communal Identity Inclusive of Land," *Journal of NAIITS* 18 (2019): 1-17.
[51]Woodley, *Mission and the Cultural Other*, 44.

and needed food for survival, they would not take the animals and birds until these creatures had enjoyed a full family life and reproduced their kind.[52]

No matter where you live today, there is a body of water that is sustaining you and those you love—what is your responsibility to that water source? Depending on where you live, you are either shaped by the grandeur of the mountains, by the roar and salt of the ocean, or by the open expanse of flat landscapes and their winding rivers and creeks. What is your responsibility to see these places continue to flourish and to heal from the mistreatment they have suffered due to human greed?

Recognition must be followed by habits, rituals, and practices that reinforce what we believe. What customs, habits, and ceremonies in Christian life today recognize the importance of place and work for shalom with more-than-human creation? We would dare say this is almost entirely absent from most Christian spirituality and almost entirely absent from the communal Sunday morning gathering of the average church.[53] Believers today, in the individual and the collective, need to be radically re-placed and then re-membered into the community of creation in which they find themselves. If we do not do this hard work of rooting ourselves to place and seeing ourselves and our well-being as being intimately bound to our community of creation, our dis-membered status will leave us impotent to the work of shalom with our more-than-human kin and create a vacuous existence that is instead filled with excessive materialism and media consumption.

In the end, human beings are created for relationship with Creator and the entire community of creation. As we have seen, this story is told in many different ways in the creation stories of Indigenous peoples, including the Hebrew creation stories. These stories speak to ways in which relationships are broken and the work needed to restore balance and respect. We suggest that the Bright Path emphasizes Jesus as Jubilee bringer and provides disciples of Jesus today with a framework to identify and enact what it means to live in a good way. The Bright Path helps us to measure how we are working out our salvation (Phil 3:12) as we join Creator in his work of justice and healing

---

[52]Deloria, *Spirit and Reason*, 51-52.
[53]This lack in the modern church has given rise to alternative worshiping Christian communities. See, for example, the Wild Church Network, www.wildchurchnetwork.com, and Victoria Loorz, *Church of the Wild: How Nature Invites Us into the Sacred* (Minneapolis: Broadleaf Books, 2021).

in this world. The teachings of Jesus and the teachings of our Indigenous traditions from Turtle Island teach us this good way as we strive for shalom with Creator, our human kin, our more-than-human kin, and mother earth, who is always caring for us. Creator's dream of shalom is more expansive than we can begin to conceptualize; it is a work to restore all things. Indigenous voices and teaching are gifts and can contribute to the life of God's people as we work together to walk the Bright Path of the Jesus Way.

4

CRYING FOR A VISION OF WHO WE ARE

Seeing Our Ancestors and Ourselves in Scripture

IN FALL 2022, Chris was invited by Bishop David Wilson (Choctaw), who was ordained the next year as the first Indigenous bishop of the United Methodist Church, to join the Oklahoma Indian Missionary Conference at a weekend retreat. The purpose of the retreat was to bring together Indigenous Methodist ministers and traditional ceremonial leaders to build bridges and possibly dispel misconceptions about one another's traditions. The conversations were heartfelt and powerful, and it became clear from the stories shared by the traditionalists that they harbored great pain from being shunned by Christian Indians for practicing traditional medicines and ceremonies. These traditionalists were made to feel like they were backwards, superstitious, uncivilized. It was a pain that was familiar to these Indigenous pastors. There were tears shed by all that afternoon.

During our coffee break, the conversation turned to our collective love for the hit television series *Reservation Dogs*. If you have not seen it yet, it is a television series created by Sterlin Harjo (member of the Seminole Nation with Muscogee heritage) and Taika Waititi (Māori, New Zealand) that centers on the exploits of four Native teenagers in rural Oklahoma, navigating their relationships with their families and with each other as they process their grief over the death of their friend Daniel. One scene in particular that had recently aired had everyone at the gathering talking.[1] This scene, which Bishop Wilson referenced in his sermon the previous week, was a poignant depiction

---

[1] The *second* scene on everyone's mind was the brief cameo that Rev. David "Hollywood" Wilson made while tabling for the "Rock the Native Vote" movement.

of prayer in season two, episode nine. Willie Jack (played by Paulina Alexis), one of the four teenagers, is visiting with her auntie Hotki (played by Lily Gladstone) in prison to learn how to pray in such a way that might cast away the darkness that Willie Jack thinks is causing her friends to drift apart. Hotki is processing her own bitterness and grief for her son Daniel and reluctantly agrees to teach her niece to pray. Hotki instructs Willie Jack to open up her hands, close her eyes, take long slow breaths, and remember the stories she had told her about the people she comes from, "generations of medicine people, caretakers." Hotki begins: "These are the ones who held us together as we arrived from our homelands. The healers who carried us and buried us as we marched. Men and women whose songs led us through the dark. They're watching you, my girl. You don't need me. You have them. This is the power we carry. When you really pray, they are all around you. All the time."[2]

As Hotki speaks, the camera focuses on Willie Jack praying. A low voice begins to intone a solemn ceremonial song. Suddenly, generations of her ancestors begin to appear behind Willie Jack in prayer. While Willie Jack's eyes are closed, the audience is privileged to see this vision that only Hotki can see. One of the ancestors even puts her hand on Willie Jack's shoulder, which elicits an irreverent response that is characteristic of Willie Jack and the show's charm. Tears stream down Willie Jack's face, who is otherwise stoic and harder than nails.[3] The Indigenous pastors agreed that this was one of the most powerful portrayals of what it feels like to pray and to sense that the ancestors are watching over you all the time.

Turtle Island hermeneutics rejects the Euroamerican Christian framing of Indigenous practices, ceremonies, and lifeways as inherently idolatrous, pagan, or sinful. Instead, beginning with the assumption that Creator was and has been present among our ancestors and the wisdom, teachings, and rituals they have passed down to us embody our Original Instructions from Creator, Turtle Island hermeneutics reads the Bible with a spirit of curiosity about how our ancestral lifeways may resonate with those depicted in Scripture. And surprise! Wouldn't you know it, the ancient Hebrews and early Christians, along with ancient Mediterranean peoples in general, often

---

[2]*Reservation Dogs*, episode 9, season 2, "Offerings," directed by Sterlin Harjo, September 21, 2022 on FX/Hulu.
[3]*Reservation Dogs*, "Offerings."

look more like Indigenous peoples in their lifeways and worldviews than modern Euroamericans. In this chapter, we will discuss ways in which Indigenous experiences of relating to the ancestors and of experiencing dreams and visions are evidenced in Scripture in ways underappreciated by many Christian communities.

A CLOUD OF ANCESTORS

Many Indigenous people carry a deep respect for their ancestors. Our ancestors connect us back to Creator, root us to our traditional territories as their remains return to the land, and have shaped us with their lives and teachings. Whereas Western individualism emphasizes the hard work and triumph of the individual to "make something of yourself," communitarian communities emphasize the hard work and journeys of our ancestors that have shaped our journey and that we continue on. "We would not be here," Martin Brokenleg reflects, "if our ancestors had not given us the spiritual tools and the strength that we need to be the people that we are today."[4] Acknowledging our ancestors is a tangible act of gratitude and recognition of the history that has shaped us. Seeking their guidance and wisdom in the present is about looking to our communal heart and mind and meditating on what has been passed down to us.

Having just referenced *Reservation Dogs* above, we would be remiss not to mention one of the most beloved recurring characters of the show, William Knifeman, also known as the Unknown Warrior or Spirit (played by Dallas Goldtooth). Knifeman is a self-proclaimed Lakota warrior who offers sage encouragement in irreverent ways that causes us to laugh out loud. "Being a warrior, it's not always easy," the Lakota spirit admonishes Bear, one of the teenagers, in a vision. "You and your thuggy . . . friends, what are you doing for your people?"[5] The Israelites also looked to the wisdom of their ancestors:

> Listen, my people, to my teaching;
>   tilt your ears toward the words of my mouth.
> I will open my mouth with a proverb.
>   I'll declare riddles from days long gone—

---

[4]Martin Brokenleg, "Circles of Courage," *Journal of NAIITS* 18 (2020): 10.
[5]*Reservation Dogs*, episode 1, season 1, "F*ckin' Rez Dogs," directed by Sterlin Harjo, August 9, 2021 on FX/Hulu.

> ones that we've heard and learned about,
> ones that our ancestors told us.
> We won't hide them from their descendants;
> we'll tell the next generation
> all about the praise due the LORD and his strength—
> the wondrous works God has done. (Ps 78:1-4)

Each time the writers in Scripture looked back on and named the patriarchs and matriarchs or recalled Moses and his teachings, they were recalling their ancestors and the life and teaching they passed on, as well as the hard lessons learned from their mistakes. The honoring *and retelling* of the wisdom and stories of their ancestors is in large measure why we have a Hebrew Bible today. These stories and teachings existed for many years as oral traditions, passed on from one generation to the next before being written down. Without a culture that honored ancestors, we would not have a Hebrew Bible to speak of. Any time the Jewish people, including Jesus and the earliest Jewish followers of Jesus, read or recalled the Hebrew Bible, they were engaging the wisdom of their ancestors. To name one's ancestors was to invoke their stories and remind others of the stories and traditions that shaped an individual and community, something Luke and Matthew do for Jesus in their genealogies.[6]

The ancient Israelites, among other Near Eastern and ancient Mediterranean civilizations, had a deep regard for ritual systems around their ancestors.[7] Tobit 4:17 in the Apocrypha and archaeological evidence of bowls and food platters found among Judean tombs attest to the practice of "feeding" the dead.[8] And yet it certainly is the case that ancient Jewish literature condemns consulting the dead (Lev 19:26-31; Deut 18:9-14; 1 Sam 28–29;

---

[6]Johannes A. Loubser, "Invoking the Ancestors: Some Socio-rhetorical Aspects of the Genealogies in the Gospels of Matthew and Luke," *Neotestamentica* 39 (2005): 127-40; H. Daniel Zacharias, "Gospel of Matthew," in *The New Testament in Color: A Multiethnic Bible Commentary*, ed. Esau McCaulley, Janette H. Ok, Osvaldo Padilla, and Amy L. B. Peeler (Downers Grove, IL: IVP Academic, 2024), 45-48; Wayne Manaaki Rihari Te Kaawa, "Re-visioning Christology Through a Māori lens" (PhD diss., University of Otago, 2020), chap. 5.

[7]See the discussion in chap. 3 of Mark G. Brett, *Decolonizing God: The Bible in the Tides of Empire*, Bible in the Modern World 16 (Sheffield: Sheffield Phoenix Press, 2008).

[8]Markus Cromhout, "The 'Cloud of Witnesses' as Part of the Public Court of Reputation in Hebrews," *HTS Theological Studies* 68, no. 1 (2012): 1-6; Pieter Craffert, *Meeting the Living Among the Dead: Perspectives on Burials, Tombs, and the Afterlife* (Pretoria: Biblia Publishers, 1999); Elizabeth Bloch-Smith, *Judahite Burial Practices and Beliefs About the Dead* (Sheffield: Sheffield Academic Press, 1992), 122-26. See Deut 26:14; Sirach 30:18.

2 Kings 21:6; Job 7:7-10; Is 8:18-20).⁹ Deuteronomy 18:9-14 exhorts the Israelites to remain faithful to the Lord and prohibits them from imitating the "detestable things" of the Canaanites, which include consulting "ghosts or spirits" or seeking oracles from the dead (Deut 18:9, 11). The passage elaborates that it is because of such abhorrent practices that the Lord will dispossess and drive out the Canaanites from their land (Deut 18:13-14). The prophet Isaiah mocks those who say, "consult the ghosts and the spirits that chirp and mutter" as hopeless (Is 8:19).

Nevertheless, the collective ancestors of Israel are honored throughout ancient Jewish literature, their genealogies recounted, their stories remembered so that their virtues could be emulated and their failures learned from. The stories of their ancestors were embedded in the land, as parcels of land stayed within families, marked by boundary stones placed by their ancestors (Prov 22:28). Jewish literature, including the Maccabean literature and the pseudepigraphal Testaments of the Twelve Patriarchs, likely edited together in the second century BCE, strongly emphasizes the connection between authentic Jewish identity and remembering the covenantal oaths and virtues of one's ancestors. It is not a stretch for Indigenous peoples to recognize some commonality with ancient Judeans who were struggling to preserve their ethnic and national identities in the face of Greek pressures to assimilate. Moreover, Indigenous readers can recognize the power of stories celebrating warriors who proudly declare their loyalty to their ancestral traditions (e.g., 1 Macc 2:19): "Remember the deeds of the ancestors," the dying Jewish war leader Mattathias tells his son in 1 Maccabees, "and you will receive great honor and an everlasting name" (1 Macc 2:51, NRSV).

Renee Begay (Zuni Pueblo), who serves as the director of Nations, is one of numerous Indigenous Christians who have wrestled with what it looks like to relate with her ancestors in a good way. Renee grew up in a traditional Zuni home in New Mexico, where she and her family regularly set aside food in honor of their ancestors. Was this idolatrous or an acceptable ritual to honor the dead? How is it any different from Euroamericans placing flowers beside a gravesite for a relative who presumably can't smell them? Crystal Porter (Mi'kmaq), a captain in the Salvation Army Canada, shares that her Mi'kmaq tradition holds that the

---

⁹Choon Sup Bae and P. J. van der Merwe, "Ancestor Worship: Is it Biblical?," *HTS Theological Studies* 64, no. 3 (2008): 1299-1325.

ancestors reside in their shadows, protecting and walking alongside them. When Porter reflects on her ancestors' presence, she becomes simultaneously aware of "the intergenerational shame and pain" her people carry and of "the strength of our people amid forced assimilation" as she reclaims her Indigenous identity.[10] Cheryl Bear (Dakehl, Bear Clan), who has written on Indigenous ministries and is a founding member of NAIITS, has recounted with Danny how the NAIITS leadership also struggled with this question. After mulling over the question, Cheryl recalled Terry LeBlanc reflecting aloud whether the idea of acknowledging one's ancestors was not recognized in the biblical image of the "cloud of witnesses" described in Hebrews 12:1. In Hebrews 11–12:12, the anonymous author sets out to encourage audiences to persevere through hardships by painting a picture of what faithfulness looks like. The author proceeds to detail the faithfulness of their shared ancestors, which include Enoch, Noah, Abraham, Moses, and other Israelite men and women of renown (Heb 11). For Christina Quintanilla (Indigenous Xicana, Cherokee descendant), the author of Hebrews is "in line with Indigenous understanding . . . that perfection and holistic healing is unattainable without a reciprocal relationship between the ancestors and the living."[11] What, then, is to prevent us from understanding this cloud of witnesses from including our ancestors and families too?

To sit with the text of Hebrews a bit longer, the author seems to be addressing an audience that has faced some hardship for being neither civilized nor ceremonial enough. Shortly after seeing "the light," this community seems to have "stood [their] ground while [they] were suffering" at the hands of local authorities and neighbors, which comprised "insults and abuse in public," being imprisoned and seeing their friends imprisoned, and having their possessions stolen (Heb 10:32-34). Chris has written extensively about how early followers of Christ were sometimes mocked by Greeks and Romans for abandoning their ancestral traditions to follow some foreign, uncivilized superstition (Christianity). He won't bore you with the details here.[12] But it goes without saying that experiences of imprisonment and theft are clear

---

[10]Crystal Porter, "A Search to Belong: Cultural Reclamation on the Jesus Way," *Journal of NAIITS* 17 (2019): 121.

[11]Christina Quintanilla, "The Cloud of Good Ancestors: An Examination of Hebrews 11:35–12:3 Through Multiethnic Indigenous Eyes" (unpublished paper, December 2022), 7.

[12]If you want to dig deeper, see T. Christopher Hoklotubbe, *Civilized Piety: The Rhetoric of Pietas in the Pastoral Epistles and the Roman Empire* (Waco, TX: Baylor University Press, 2017).

messages that someone doesn't belong. Regarding the community's ceremonial or "Jewish" identity, it seems that the community is worried that they lack something insofar as they are not fully complying with Jewish ancestral traditions or seem to be following something derivative to the dominant, more authentic stream of tradition. Such a situation might explain the author of Hebrews' sustained interest to show that Christ fulfills Jewish rituals and ceremonies and that followers of Christ have a better mediator (Heb 8:6), who offers better sacrifices (Heb 9:23), a better covenant (Heb 7:22), better hope (Heb 7:19), and better promises (Heb 8:6).[13] It is into this situation of not feeling "enough," whether civilized or ceremonial enough, that the author of Hebrews invites the audience to remember the ancestors. Like Hotki's encouragement to Willie Jack in *Reservation Dogs*, the author of Hebrews exhorts followers of Christ to remember who they come from, "generations of medicine people, caretakers... whose songs led us through the dark."[14] We are enough. And if the world does not recognize us as such, our ancestors do.

Now, we suspect that some of our Protestant audiences may still be protestin' against how many Indigenous people think about their ancestors. But let us suggest one analogy that might address some of their concerns. Most Christians today can and do readily acknowledge the work and presence of angels in both prayer and song. In these prayers and songs the angels are not praised, nor are they petitioned. But they are acknowledged, recognized for the work they do, the roles they play, and the power they have to discharge the will of Creator. In the midst of this type of recognition, those leading prayer or songs do not seem to be overly concerned with "accidentally" worshiping or praying to the angels. Recognition and acknowledgment of angels is not an act of worship, nor is it typically feared as a slippery slope into idolatry. For our Catholic and Orthodox kin, we could also point to both traditions' nuanced approach to the veneration of saints as distinguished from worship directed to the triune God. We suggest that these are close parallels to Indigenous acknowledgment of our ancestors. The unfortunate

---

[13]In constructing this possible backstory to Hebrews, it is important to acknowledge that the logic of the author's argument will be referenced within a dark history of Christians harmfully erasing the dignity and integrity of Jews, claiming to be the true and exclusive inheritors of the religious tradition, and justifying programs and policies that persecute the "lesser" Jews. And so to describe the rhetoric here of Hebrews is not to endorse its legacy or even its theological implications.

[14]*Reservation Dogs*, episode 9, season 2, "Offerings."

reality of Christians using Old Testament prohibitions against consulting the dead to condemn an aspect of Indigenous worldviews and practices is a product of colonialism, ignorance, and fear of the unknown.

And let us not forget that Jesus too benefited from a word of encouragement from his ancestors. In the story of his transfiguration (Mt 17:1-8; Mk 9:2-8; Lk 9:28-36), Jesus ascends up a mountain to pray and takes Peter, James, and John along. While Jesus is praying, he begins to shine in a dazzling glow, and suddenly Moses and Elijah show up and begin speaking with him. None of the Gospel stories narrate their dialogue, but Luke indicates that they "spoke about Jesus' departure, which he would achieve in Jerusalem" (Lk 9:31), and later Jesus shows his determination to head toward Jerusalem (Lk 9:53). Christ received encouragement from his ancestors for the sacred duty he was called to undertake. With Moses in his role as lawgiver and Elijah as wonderworking prophet, Indigenous readers can recognize this scene as Jesus' ancestors encouraging him in these same roles and responsibilities. If Jesus had any internal doubts about whether he was enough for what lay before him, his resolve and courage was greatly strengthened from the support of his ancestors. Even God the Father affirms Jesus before his disciples: "This is my Son, my chosen one. Listen to him!" (Lk 9:35). When the voice had spoken and the cloud had lifted, the Scriptures say, "Jesus was found alone" (Lk 9:36). But Jesus knew he wasn't alone; his ancestors were watching, and his Father was with him.

Finally, for Indigenous communities, our ancestors are part of our collective memory and collective heart and mind, part of the dance of the medicine wheel discussed in chapter one. The acknowledgment of ancestors and the desire to honor the wisdom that they passed on to us reminds us that we in turn need to be good ancestors, a driving ethic in most Indigenous worldviews. Some Indigenous traditions look forward seven generations, stating that our decisions affect the next seven generations.[15] Richard Twiss (Sicangu Lakota/Rosebud Reservation) expresses his understanding of a seven-generation continuum: "We learn from the previous three generations, who then inform our current generation to help us prepare the way for the next

---

[15]Randy S. Woodley, *Shalom and the Community of Creation: An Indigenous Vision*, Prophetic Christianity (Grand Rapids, MI: Eerdmans, 2012), 119.

three generations."¹⁶ In either case, we recognize the impact of the previous generations on us, and we feel the weight of responsibility as we take up a sacred role of being a good ancestor for the next several generations. This sits contrary to individualistic cultures but finds deep resonance in communitarian understandings such as those encountered in Indigenous nations and the Israelite nation. More and more we are facing the consequences of industrial pollution, air pollution, resource extraction, biodiversity loss, and piles of unrecyclable plastics filling the land and ocean. These are the results of generations unconcerned about being good ancestors. The reality of the seemingly unstoppable juggernaut of climate change threatens our future, and youth are increasingly subject to climate-induced mental-health challenges.¹⁷ We are not being good ancestors, but we have the capacity to change course.

DREAMS AND VISIONS

For many of our Indigenous friends, dreams and visions play a vital role in how they interpret Scripture and the Spirit's directions and encouragement in their lives. Kelly Montijo Fink (Apache, Mexican), who has won multiple awards for her Indigenous gospel albums, including a prestigious Native American Music Award, shared with Chris how she regularly contemplates her dreams every morning for what they might signify. She then recited Joel 2:28:

> I will pour out my spirit upon everyone;
> > your sons and your daughters will prophesy,
> > your old men will dream dreams,
> > and your young men will see visions.

On occasion, Kelly has emailed Chris when her dreams may bear some significance for his life. Danny has also received similar messages from Indigenous friends, mostly recently from a Māori colleague who shared that he could see Danny's ancestors circling in support of him while Danny gave a

---

¹⁶Richard Twiss, *Rescuing the Gospel from the Cowboys: A Native American Expression of the Jesus Way* (Downers Grove, IL: InterVarsity Press, 2015), 238.

¹⁷Reem Ramadan, Alicia Randell, Suzie Lavoie, Caroline X. Gao, Paula Cruz Manrique, Rebekah Anderson, Caitlin McDowell, and Isabel Zbukvic, "Empirical Evidence for Climate Concerns, Negative Emotions and Climate-Related Mental Ill-Health in Young People: A Scoping Review," *Early Intervention in Psychiatry* 17 (2023): 537-63; Ashlee Cunsolo and Neville R. Ellis, "Ecological Grief as a Mental Health Response to Climate Change-Related Loss," *Nature Climate Change* 8, no. 4 (2018): 275-81.

short homily and shared a song during a smudging circle in his hometown of Winnipeg.

During the preparation for this book, Indigenous Christians, including Larry Wilson (Cree), Dean Shingoose (Anishinaabe, Cote First Nation), Tony Snow (Nakota, Stoney Nakoda First Nation), and Christina Dawson (Nuu-Chan-nulth), shared with Danny about Spirit-inspired dreams or visions they have had, sometimes confronting them very powerfully or regularly informing both their interpretations of Scripture and their discernment of what God was telling them in their life.[18] While such methods of interpretation and discerning the voice of Creator may make some protestin' Protestants uneasy (our charismatic and Pentecostal friends notwithstanding), they are well documented in Scripture. In our dance through the medicine wheel, we suggest that reading stories of Indigenous visionaries and medicine people side by side with stories of Jesus and Paul can give us a fresh perspective on both. In particular, we suggest that Paul looks much like Indigenous Christians we have spoken with, whose dreams and visions inform how they interpret Scripture and help to guide their lives as followers of Jesus.

INDIGENOUS DREAMS AND VISIONS

Dreams and visions have been core experiences for countless Indigenous peoples, including prophets and medicine people.[19] Speaking about his own tribe, the Hunkpapa Lakota or Standing Rock Sioux, Vine Deloria Jr. writes, "Dreams are critical to understanding cosmology, space and time, family structure, and relations with animals and the non-human world."[20] For the Lakota, David C. Posthumus expands, "a dream might determine which dream society an individual belonged to, which non-human person(s) he was related to, from where he received power/knowledge or medicine, what

---

[18]Larry Wilson, interview with author, October 15, 2022; Dean Shingoose, interview with author, September 9, 2022; Tony Snow, interview with author, October 21, 2022; Christina Dawson, interview with author, September 22, 2022.

[19]While this study primarily engages with Indigenous experiences located on Turtle Island (North America), we want to shout out to our Aboriginal kin in Australia, for whom "dreaming" is an essential component of their spirituality, as discussed by Brooke Prentis (Waka Waka) in her interview on episode 129 of the podcast *The Bible for Normal People*, https://thebiblefornormalpeople.podbean.com/e/episode-129-brooke-prentis-reading-the-bible-through-aboriginal-eyes.

[20]Vine Deloria Jr., *Jung and the Sioux Traditions: Dreams, Visions, Nature, and the Primitive*, ed. Philip J. Deloria and Jerome Bernstein (New Orleans: Spring Journal Books, 2009), 167.

career or role he would pursue in his community, and so on."²¹ Dreams, as documented among the Hopi, may materialize the hopes, fears, desires, and guilt of their dreamers, whether for the revitalization of traditional religious practices, reconciliation with elders, or a new romantic partner.²² Among the Yuman tribes along the Gila River, including the Mojave, success in life, including the gaining of spiritual powers, learning of songs, conceiving children, identification of chiefs, and victory in war, was often attributed to dreams.²³ It is a rare privilege for a dream or vision to be shared publicly, out of a concern that some of its power might be lost or that some divine connection become untethered in the divulging of such intimate details.

The vision of Nicholas Black Elk, as edited by poet John G. Neihardt in *Black Elk Speaks*, is among the most recognizable Indigenous visions available. Black Elk, a Lakota medicine man and a devoted Catholic, experienced a powerful vision in 1872 when he was nine years old, during a seemingly paralyzing, near-fatal bout with illness, and then again when he was eighteen.²⁴ The vision, concisely put, comprises a bay horse who directs Black Elk's attention to four groups of twelve dancing black, white, sorrel, and buckskin horses, each representing the powers of the four directions, west, north, east, and south, respectively. The bay horse then leads Black Elk into a tipi with a rainbow, where six grandfathers await him, each representing one of the six directions (east, south, west, north, sky, and earth) and each with his own admonition and message about Black Elk's path as a medicine man and the troubles that await his nation. In his vision, Black Elk receives a number of powerful objects, including a flowering stick, a sacred pipe, herbs that bring light and understanding, powerful songs, and instructions for leading a sacred Horse Dance. Each gift is integral for healing the Lakota nation's sacred hoop and restoring harmony, healing, and prosperity to his people. In an eschatological vision comparable to Isaiah, Daniel, and John of Patmos,

---

²¹David C. Posthumus, *All My Relatives: Exploring Lakota Ontology, Belief, and Ritual* (Lincoln: University of Nebraska Press, 2018), 139.

²²Dorothy Eggan, "The Significance of Dreams for Anthropological Research," *American Anthropologist* 51 (1949): 177-98.

²³Benjamin Kilborne, "Pattern, Structure, and Style in Anthropological Studies of Dreams," *Ethos* 9 (1981): 175.

²⁴On how Black Elk's recollections of his visions were influenced by his Catholic theology, see Damian Costello, *Black Elk: Colonialism and Lakota Catholicism* (Maryknoll, NY: Orbis Books, 2005).

Black Elk sees that "the sacred hoop of my people was one of many hoops that made one circle, wide as daylight and as starlight, and in the center grew one mighty flowering tree to shelter all the children of one mother and one father. And I saw that it was holy."[25] And like these prophets, Black Elk waited for the day when his vision would be fulfilled and the sacred hoop of his nation restored. Like Black Elk, followers of Christ know something of this waiting, watching for the return of the Messiah and restoration of all creation. Some Indigenous followers of Christ may even continue to remain vigilant, watching for the fulfillment of Black Elk's vision, for the sacred hoop to be restored and the world reconciled into balance and harmony through Christ.

Another notable Indigenous visionary is Wovoka or Jack Wilson, Paiute prophet. Wovoka received a vision on New Year's Day 1889 while in a comatose state brought about by a high fever. In this vision, Wovoka spoke with God, who gave him *booha* (power) over the weather. He also saw a utopian world and received instructions in leading a ceremonial circle dance that would usher this world into existence. In Wovoka's revelation, echoing the apocalyptic notes of Daniel 7 and 1 Thessalonians 4, the Messiah would soon return appearing like a cloud, deceased Indigenous people would be resurrected, and the land restored to its original Indigenous inhabitants.[26] Instructions not to fight and steal, to be peaceful and good to one another, and to work productively with their white neighbors accompanied Wovoka's prophetic vision. Wovoka's Ghost Dance would spread like wildfire across the Plains, culminating in the 1890s Ghost Dance movement—the very dance that Black Elk and his tribe participated in and which precipitated the 1890 Massacre of Wounded Knee. Often participants dancing in the Ghost Dance would induce themselves into a trancelike state where they too would see deceased family members waiting to return to life and manifestations of respected spirits, Crow and Eagle. Some even saw Jesus.[27] Black Elk too experienced a visionary journey while participating in a

---

[25]Black Elk and John G. Neihardt, *Black Elk Speaks: The Complete Edition* (Lincoln: University of Nebraska Press, 2014), 26.
[26]T. Christopher Hoklotubbe, "Reimagining the Thessalonians at the End of the World with Ghost Dancers," in *Scripture, Cultures, and Criticism: Interpretive Steps and Critical Issues Raised by Robert Jewett*, ed. K. K. Yeo (Eugene, OR: Pickwick, 2022), 208-22.
[27]Louis S. Warren, *God's Red Son: The Ghost Dance Religion and the Making of Modern America* (New York: Basic Books, 2017), 250-51.

Ghost Dance, wherein he traveled to a beautiful land, presumably the new earth that awaited the Lakota, where the deceased dwelled, and learned how to design powerful Ghost Dance shirts that would presumably protect his people from bullets.[28]

Indigenous dreams and visions also endowed medicine people with powers and directions to bring healing to those in their community, as exemplified by the life of Bole Molu dreamer, healer, and renowned basket weaver Mabel McKay (1907–1993) of the Long Valley Cache Creek Pomo tribe in Northern California. Mabel McKay "talked" to plants before using them and credited the Spirit for showing her in her dreams basket designs to replicate.[29] These baskets not only won her national recognition but held curative power. Throughout her life, McKay experienced powerful dreams through which the Great Spirit continuously communicated to her, appointing and reaffirming her calling as a medicine woman/doctor, disclosing dreadful threats and auspicious omens, foretelling future events, and endowing her with great power to heal the sick. Visions and dreams empowered other Indigenous prophetic figures and medicine people, among whom we could have also discussed Hiawatha of the Haudenosaunee (Iroquois), Sweet Medicine of the Cheyenne, Handsome Lake of the Seneca, Tenskwatawa of the Shawnee, Kennekuk of the Kickapoo and Potawatomi, Smohalla of the Wanapum, or Frank Fools Crow (son of Black Elk) and Lame Deer of the Lakota, bestowing glimpses into possible climactic futures involving social-political change in ways that resonate with the prophetic visionaries of Israel.[30]

DREAMS AND VISIONS IN THE BIBLICAL LITERATURE

Within the Hebrew Bible, examples of dreams and visions abound as recognized ways in which the Lord communicates to the Israelites, in particular their prophets: "If there is a prophet of the Lord among you, I make myself known to him in visions. I speak to him in dreams" (Num 12:6). While dreams and visions are distinct, they are conceptually linked. Dreams in the Hebrew Bible generally consist of straightforward messages that the

---

[28]Black Elk and Neihardt, *Black Elk Speaks*, 151-52.
[29]Gree Sarris, *Mabel McKay: Weaving the Dream* (Berkeley: University of California Press, 2013), 2-3, 31.
[30]See esp. Clifford E. Trafzer, ed., *American Indian Medicine Ways: Spiritual Power, Prophets, and Healing* (Tucson: University of Arizona Press, 2017).

dreamer hears (e.g., 1 Sam 3:2-15) and/or sees (e.g., Gen 37:5-8), or bizarre messages that must be interpreted (e.g., Gen 41:1-45). Similar to Black Elk, the prophet Zechariah sees four chariots in a dream, each led by different-colored horses, who represent the four winds/directions of the earth (red/east, dappled gray/south, white/west, and black/north; Zech 6:1-8). Visions are distinct from dreams insofar as they occur when the visionary is awake and often entail some kind of physical change (e.g., falling down, seizure, etc.). Memorable visions include Amos's vision of a basket of fruit symbolizing the destruction of the kingdom of Israel (Amos 8:1-2) and the prophetic visions of destruction by Ezekiel (Ezek 9:1-10) and Isaiah (Is 21:1-10).

While visions abound, ancient Jewish texts also caution audiences about the ambiguity of dreams and their potential for abuse. In the Hebrew Bible, the Lord is described as placing a "lying spirit" into the mouths of King Ahab's prophets, who falsely predict military victory for the Israelites (1 Kings 22:19-23; 2 Chron 18:18-22). Ecclesiastes describes dreams as nothing but vanity (Eccles 5:6-7). Jeremiah warns against false prophets who "dream up lies and then proclaim them" (Jer 23:32) and whose visions come from their own minds, not from the mouth of the Lord (Jer 23:16). The abuse of dreams and visions among Indigenous tribes is also acknowledged. Among Chris's own tribe, the Choctaw, historically, when *alikchi* ("medicine people") determined that there was nothing more they could do for a patient, they might sometimes justify their prognosis of the patient's inevitable death on the basis of a received vision or dream and recommend that the family and community members euthanize the patient. In one troubling if slightly comedic story, a patient overhears an *alikchi* offering just such a recommendation to his family and, determined not to die, escapes to a neighboring town occupied by another tribe that owed him some favors. Upon discovering his patient had gone missing, the *alikchi* tells the family that the patient simply died alone in the forest. However, upon recovery, the patient returns to his home, only to be dismissed as a ghost! Slowly, the family comes to terms with the fact that the *alikchi* had lied to them and enacts their retribution on the false diviner by killing him.[31]

---

[31]John R. Swanton, *Source Material for the Social and Ceremonial Life of the Choctaw Indian*, Smithsonian Institution Bureau of American Ethnology Bulletin 103 (Washington, DC: U.S. Printing Office, 1931), 213-14.

Dreams and visions abound in the New Testament as well. Revelation itself is a literary account of John of Patmos's vision. In Matthew, the Lord appears in dreams to Joseph, directing him to remain with Mary and to flee with his family from harm (Mt 1:20-25; 2:13, 19-23); the wise men are warned in a dream not to return to Herod (Mt 2:12); and Pilate's wife seems to experience some nightmare regarding Jesus (Mt 27:19). Moreover, consider the abundance of dreams and visions that are central to Luke's account of the story of Jesus and the early church. Angels visit Zechariah (Lk 1:8-23), Mary (Lk 1:26-38), shepherds (Lk 2:8-14), the apostles in prison (Acts 5:19-21), Philip (Acts 8:26-40), the Roman centurion Cornelius in an afternoon vision (Acts 10:1-6), and Peter in prison (Acts 12:7-10). The apostles witness a vision of Moses and Elijah in the transfiguration of Jesus (Luke 9:28-36), Ananias receives a vision to help Paul (Acts 9:10-19), and Peter receives a vision while falling into a trance (Acts 10:10-20)—not to mention Paul's visions, which we will discuss below. The prevalence of dreams and visions in Luke's Gospel and Acts conveys that God is constantly at work to guide people individually as well as to enact situations that guide an entire community. This underlines that followers of Christ have a complex role in interpreting God's plan as revealed in dreams and visions in conversation with Scripture and community.[32]

THE VISION QUESTS OF JESUS

In *The Four Vision Quests of Jesus*, Stephen Charleston (Choctaw) interprets Jesus as undergoing vision quests at four significant moments in his ministry: during his time in the wilderness where he overcame temptations from the devil (Mt 4:1-11), on the mountain where he saw Moses and Elijah (Mt 17:1-8), in the garden of Gethsemane where he accepted his sacrificial fate (Mt 26:36-46), and on the cross where the depth of his lament and feeling of being exiled from his elders and nation gave way to Jesus embodying all humanity within himself (Mt 27:32-55). Vision quests and their precise protocols vary across Indigenous nations but seem to have been a nearly universal practice among Indigenous nations prior to colonization.[33]

---

[32]See John B. F. Miller, *Convinced That God Has Called Us: Dreams, Visions, and Perception of God's Will in Luke–Acts* (Leiden: Brill, 2007), 241-42.

[33]Vine Deloria Jr., *The World We Used to Live In: Remembering the Powers of the Medicine Men* (Golden, CO: Fulcrum, 2006), xxiv.

A vision quest is often a rite of passage from childhood to manhood but also is practiced by those who are in the midst of life transitions, or for times of spiritual renewal. Vision quests will sometimes have the seeker led by an elder to the place of the quest, which is often a demanding and even hostile environment. Those undertaking such a quest often begin with a period of prayer and purification. Then their endurance and spirit are tested, which invites self-reflection, a spirit of humility, lamentation, and a recognition of their own vulnerability and need for Creator. A person may even receive a powerful vision that reveals something about their identity, their character, or the role they are to serve in their community. These transformative visions are "good medicine" or divine blessings.[34] This description of a vision quest characterizes elements of Jesus' story in ways yet to be appreciated by many Euroamerican audiences.

To flesh out but one example from Charleston's work, let us turn to Jesus' vision in the wilderness. After Jesus completes the purification ceremony of his baptism, he follows the Holy Spirit in dove form like an elder into the wilderness to fast and focus on prayer (Mt 4:2). The Scripture never describes Dove as leaving Jesus once he is in the wilderness, and we might imagine the enfeathered Holy Spirit perched just out of sight, like an elder supervising someone under their care.[35] At the end of his forty days of prayer and fasting, Jesus encounters the tempter, who tries to persuade Jesus to misuse his spiritual power for self-serving ends. The vision quest is seen as a liminal space in which the seeker interacts directly with the spirit world, which includes both helpful and harmful spirits. This melding of the physical and spiritual world began at the baptism with the heavens opening up (Mt 3:16) and continues through into the vision quest. Vine Deloria notes how vision quests are sometimes referred to as dreaming, and often the recounting of one's dreaming/vision quest blurs the lines between visionary experience and physical experience. This is similar to the recounting of Jesus' temptation, with a blurring of the lines between the visionary and the physical. Part of the work of a vision quest is to solidify one's sacred calling in life, expand one's knowledge, and receive power from Creator. Like many Indigenous seekers, Jesus' vision quest propels him forward into his sacred duties.

---

[34]Steven Charleston, *The Four Vision Quests of Jesus* (New York: Morehouse, 2015), 10-22, 51.
[35]For further discussion on this passage, see Zacharias, "Gospel of Matthew," 52-54.

PAUL THE VISIONARY

Now we turn to Paul of Tarsus and the formative roles that dreams and visions played in his own interpretation of Scripture and understanding of what God was doing in the world. Visions abound in the stories that Paul shares about his life and that are shared about Paul. Paul, who probably never met Jesus of Nazareth during his earthly ministry, writes, "[God] was pleased to reveal his Son to me, so that I might preach about him to the Gentiles" (Gal 1:15-16; see also 1 Cor 15:8). Paul proudly declares through his gospel that Gentiles can become children of God "through faith" (Gal 3:26) and not works of the law, through Christ's life, death, and resurrection (e.g., 1 Cor 15:3-5). He also states that his gospel is not of human origin: "I didn't receive it or learn it from a human. It came through a revelation from Jesus Christ" (Gal 1:11-12). Further on in Galatians, Paul references another revelation that spurs him to travel to Jerusalem to give an account of his gospel (Gal 2:2-3). Throughout 1 Corinthians, Paul describes his message as proclaiming the "mystery" of God (1 Cor 2:1, 7; 4:1; see also 1 Cor 14:2; 15:51). In the Dead Sea Scrolls, claims to possess the "mystery" (*rāz* in Hebrew) of God signaled to audiences that the speaker had obtained insight into God's secret plans *through* divine revelation, and Paul is likely doing the same here (see also Eph 1:9; 3:3-4; 6:19; Col 1:26-27; 2:2; 4:3).[36] Like Wovoka, some of the content of this "mystery" concerns the dramatic culmination of history that will come soon, resulting in the return of Christ, justice, and the resurrection of the dead (1 Cor 15:51).

In 2 Corinthians 12:2-7, Paul coyly describes his experience (i.e., "I know a man in Christ") of being caught up to "the third heaven" and "into paradise." Paul may actually be describing two separate heavenly journeys, wherein he heard such magnificent things that it would be impious for him to repeat. Paul's celestial flights are not so dissimilar to other early Jewish literature (e.g., 1–2 Enoch and the Ascension of Isaiah) and those of Black Elk or of Yupik medicine men of Alaska, about whom stories were told of their flights to the moon to retrieve divine knowledge and advice.[37] Paul's reticence to describe

---

[36]For example, see 1QpHab VII, 5; 4Q204 5 II, 26-27; 4Q417 1 I, 3-4, 8-9; Matthew Goff, "Heavenly Mysteries and Otherworldly Journeys: Interpreting 1 and 2 Corinthians in Relation to Jewish Apocalypticism," in *Paul the Jew: Reading the Apostle as a Figure of Second Temple Judaism*, ed. Gabriele Boccaccini and Carlos A. Segovia (Minneapolis: Fortress, 2016), 136.

[37]James W. Henkelman and Kurt H. Vitt, *Harmonious to Dwell: The History of the Alaska Moravian Church 1885–1985* (Bethel, AK: Tundra, 1985), 18.

his visionary experience in detail, while intended to address the foolishness of competing over whose revelatory experience is superior, resonates with an Indigenous hesitancy to reveal such intimate visionary details beyond one's elders. Charleston models this hesitancy in his own partial description of his vision of a crow while standing on a rooftop overlooking Harvard University.[38] After Paul has appealed to the Lord three times that his "thorn in the flesh" be removed from him, which may reflect Paul's struggle against demonic powers preventing him from ascending further through the heavens, the Lord responds to Paul in a vision: "My grace is enough for you, because power is made perfect in weakness" (2 Cor 12:9).[39]

In the Acts of the Apostles, Luke also describes the essential content of Paul's gospel as deriving from visionary experiences (Acts 9:1-9; 22:6-11, 21; 26:12-18). When Paul tells his story before Herod Agrippa II and Bernice (Acts 26:12-18), he explains that Christ appointed him to testify to the Gentiles about his visions, both his revelation along the road to Damascus and those he continued to receive ("those in which I will appear to you," Acts 26:16, NRSV), so that the Gentiles may "receive forgiveness of sins and a place among those who are made holy by faith in [Christ]" (Acts 26:18). Elsewhere in Acts, Paul receives dreams and visions that instruct him regarding his travel and ministry (e.g., Acts 9:11-12; 16:6-10; 18:9-11; 22:17-21; 27:23-24). Like Lakota vision questers who seek the meaning of their dreams among a circle of elders, so too must Paul confer with his colleagues in order to discern God's will for them to travel to Macedonia to preach (Acts 16:6-10). When we read Paul now, Mabel McKay's own description of how she learned the art of basket weaving seems all the more striking for how it resonates with Paul's words just quoted: "It's no such thing as art. It's spirit. My grandmother never taught me nothing about baskets. Only the spirit trained me. . . . I only follow my Dream. That's how I learn."[40]

The importance of visions for Paul's gospel message is all the more striking when we contrast our image of Paul as being akin to an Indigenous visionary against a typical, anachronistic view of Paul hunched over a desk and methodically poring over texts to arrive at his grand theology. Certainly, Paul

---

[38] Charleston, *Four Vision Quests*, 24, 26-28.
[39] Christopher Morray-Jones, "Paradise Revisited (2 Cor 12:1-12): The Jewish Mystical Background of Paul's Apostolate. Part 2: Paul's Heavenly Ascent and Its Significance," *Harvard Theological Review* 86, no. 3 (1993): 268.
[40] Sarris, *Mabel McKay*, 2.

steeped himself in Jewish Scriptures. But a crucial, underappreciated ingredient to the "tea" of Paul's theology—to carry forth the steeping metaphor—are the visions that caffeinated his creative approach to interpretation. Richard B. Hays argues that Paul interprets and cites Scripture in a manner that would often make modern interpreters uneasy. "True interpretation depends neither on historical inquiry nor on erudite literary analysis but on attentiveness to the promptings of the Spirit, who reveals the gospel through Scripture in surprising ways."[41] For example, in 2 Corinthians 3, Paul describes Jewish readers of Scripture as having a "veil" over their minds, preventing them from grasping the "glory" of the true meaning of Moses' laws. Only when readers turn to Christ is the veil removed (2 Cor 3:15-16). For Paul, Scripture's true meaning can only be unveiled through the Spirit; this is sometimes allegorical (i.e., Gal 4:21-31) and ultimately points to Christ. Paul's reliance on his encounters with the Spirit and on his dreams and visions, according to Christopher Rowland and Christopher Morray-Jones, subverts "dominant ways of reading via a conviction that the Spirit enabled a deeper (Christological) understanding of Scripture to come to the fore."[42]

Paul discerns the activity of God and the Holy Spirit in the world, especially with respect to God's inclusion of Gentiles among his elect or chosen people, by placing Scripture in conversation with his experimental ministry among the Gentiles and his visionary experiences. We think that Paul's vision-inspired interpretation of Jesus and Scripture helps us further imagine and perhaps sympathize with the number of Jews and law-observant followers of Christ who zealously argued against Paul's gospel (e.g., Gal 1:6-9; 5:11-12; 6:13; Phil 3:2). For such people, the idea that Gentiles could worship the Lord as *uncircumcised* Gentiles while inheriting the covenantal promises of Abraham was not at all the *obvious* way to interpret Scripture. Imagine what shock Vine Deloria Jr. might feel if another Lakota proclaimed that *Wasichus* ("white people") could inherit the promises and blessings of *Wakan Tanka* without having to adopt Lakota ancestral ceremonies and rituals? Apart from a few biblical scholars, most notably Seyoon Kim and John Ashton, most

---

[41]Richard B. Hays, *Echoes of Scripture in the Letters of Paul* (New Haven, CT: Yale University Press, 1993), 156.

[42]Christopher Rowland and Christopher R. A. Morray-Jones, *The Mystery of God: Early Jewish Mysticism and the New Testament* (Leiden: Brill, 2009), 150.

Euroamerican Christians seem to privilege Paul's eschatological Jewish culture and his interpretation of Scripture as the essential sites that formed Paul's self-understanding and gospel message.[43] However, we invite you to imagine Paul as more akin to an Indigenous visionary or like our friends mentioned earlier. Such envisioning of Paul not only dignifies our Indigenous experiences of dreams and visions but even leads us to be better readers of Paul.

Turtle Island hermeneutics takes seriously the impact and significance that visions held for Paul, not only in introducing him to Jesus and realizing his prophetic calling but also in delivering the essence of much of his gospel—if not in his revelation on the road to Damascus, then perhaps over a series of dreams and visions. It is interesting to note here that, similar to Paul, Black Elk saw Jesus in a powerful vision while leading a Ghost Dance not long before the Massacre of Wounded Knee. In his vision, he is led to a beautiful land, presumably the eschatological restored earth that awaits his nation, where he is led to a holy tree in bloom, before which stands a man unlike any he has seen before:

> Against the tree there was a man standing with arms held wide in front of him. I looked hard at him, and I could not tell what people he came from. He was not a Wasichu [white man] and he was not an Indian. His hair was long and hanging loose, and on the left side of his head he wore an eagle feather. His body was strong and good to see, and it was painted red. I tried to recognize him, but I could not make him out. He was a fine-looking man. While I was staring hard at him, his body began to change and become very beautiful with all colors of light, and around him there was light. He spoke like singing: "My life is such that all earthly beings and growing things belong to me. Your father, the Great Spirit, has said this. You too must say this."[44]

Like Paul, Black Elk not only saw the resurrected Jesus, which affirmed Jesus' place within Black Elk's Lakota cosmology, but also was given *content*, a message—a *gospel*, even—to share with others. Turtle Island hermeneutics, then, appreciates and expresses curiosity and wonder not only about the significance of dreams and visions for advancing the story of Creator and his people in Scripture but also about how such phenomena remain powerful

---

[43]See Seyoon Kim, *The Origins of Paul's Gospel*, 2nd rev. and enl. ed. (Tübingen: Mohr, 1984); John Ashton, *The Religion of Paul the Apostle* (New Haven, CT: Yale University Press, 2000).
[44]Black Elk and Neihardt, *Black Elk Speaks*, 154.

experiences for discerning the Spirit of Creator among Indigenous peoples today in conjunction with interpreting Scripture.

CONCLUSION: HONORING OUR ANCESTORS, RESPECTING OUR VISIONS

Turtle Island hermeneutics invites Indigenous Christians to hold together both our Indigenous and Christian identities when we interpret Scripture and to know that we are enough. More than that, our Indigenous insistence to honor our ancestors and to respect their dreams and visions as well as our own has something to contribute to our broader understanding of the stories and figures detailed in Scripture. In writing these chapters, there were many times in which both Chris and Danny felt the presence of our ancestors and their dreams and visions as we reflected on the Scriptures and the many stories we have shared. Acknowledging our ancestors calls us to live into the story we have been born into. A moving example of Indigenous Christians living into their story as well as seeing themselves in Scripture can be found in a children's book, *The Story of Joseph*, published by the Northern Manitoba Area Mission of the Indigenous Spiritual Ministry of Mishamikoweesh. Not only does the book feature Indigenous-themed artwork by a Cree illustrator, but it is translated and recorded into two dialects of Cree along with Ojibwe and Dene.[45] Joseph's coat, now a beaded hide coat, never looked more stunning! Should we be surprised that a story about a character who received and could interpret dreams would be the first to be produced as an illustrated children's book and cherished among this First Nation community? When we can fully integrate both the stories of our Indigenous ancestors and our ancestors in the faith, Indigenous Christians will be walking on a good path toward flourishing and healing.

We will return to this theme of seeing ourselves in Scripture as integral to our flourishing and healing in chapter six. But before we can say more on this topic, we need to first share some hard truths with our Euroamerican brothers and sisters about the difficult trail that the government and citizens of both the United States and Canada have sent our peoples on. As we will see in the next chapter, our darkest experiences of settler colonialism also resonate with Scripture's stories and frame our interpretation of Scripture.

---

[45]See "The Story of Jospeh," Indigenous Spiritual Ministry of Mishamikoweesh, accessed March 4, 2025, https://mishamikoweesh.ca/resources/the-story-of-joseph.

5

NABOTH'S DESCENDANTS

Reading the Bible Along a Trail of Broken Treaties

IN SEASON ONE, EPISODE SIX of the Canadian sitcom *Acting Good*, the story centers on the annual Battle of the Bush, a wrestling show that visits the Rez every year. The final match in the yearly event has, since 1971, been an Indigenous wrestler versus "Mr. NDN Affairs." The episode opens with a brief montage of an announcer introducing Mr. NDN Affairs through the decades: "You know him, you hate him. You got all these treaty rights but he's still not treating you right! . . . He doesn't want you to get new glasses or your cavities filled! . . . He's about to put your community into third-party management. Let's tell him where to go. Let's give it up for Mr. NDN Affairs!" But in the present, the wrestler playing Mr. NDN Affairs flew to the wrong Rez and is unable to make the annual event. The community becomes distressed and sets about finding a suitable white man to play the part. Show regular Brady, the comically awkward white guy and goodhearted store clerk, is tasked with the role. But he is understandably nervous, not only to be in a wrestling match but to be the object of the entire community's hatred. Backstage, the Elder Agnes, another series regular, compels Brady, saying:

> You have to. Wrestling day has been a big deal in my family for a long time. And the most important part of it is telling Mr. NDN Affairs to . . . [buzz] off.[1] . . . Every year he loses. And for one night, we get to win. Our kids get to see a wrestler who is one of us beat the . . . [snot] out of the system that has taken everything from us. . . . Now get in that suit and get your . . . head kicked in.

Brady understands the assignment, puts on the mask, and transforms into Mr. NDN Affairs, resolutely stating, "Your funding request is denied!" Out in

---

[1]Danny has sensitive ears, so Chris edited the colorful language. Our apologies to the artistic intent of the showrunners.

the wrestling ring, the announcer prepares the crowd: "You know him, you hate him. He wants to take a dump on your sovereignty. Let's tell him where to go! Ladies and gentlemen, Mr. NDN Affairs!" The wrestling match commences. Quickly, Mr. NDN Affairs is in control, giving a hard clothesline to his opponent, knocking him down. "I could really feel the oppression behind that one!" the announcer comments. Mr. NDN Affairs then yells, "I own you! Now the government's really going to take care of you!" He pulls from his back pocket a roll of red tape and proceeds to immobilize his young opponent. "Try cutting through all this!" Mr. NDN Affairs mocks and then, turning to the crowd, gloats, "I'm going to break his back like I broke your treaty!" Intense booing ensues from the crowd. In dramatic fashion, the camera focuses in on the young Indigenous wrestler. The announcer's voice rings out, "Oh wait! Look at this! I can't believe it! He's busted through the red tape!" With the red tape broken, Mr. NDN Affairs gets body-slammed and pinned for the count.[2]

This is classic Indigenous humor, able to uphold the seriousness of a situation while providing a means of coping through laughing together. After all, if we're not laughing, we're crying. Mr. NDN Affairs's taunts encapsulate years of colonization that Indigenous people have endured, including the dispossession of their ancestral lands, broken treaties, and a bureaucratic system that has historically *not* acted in good faith. Moreover, ol' Mr. NDN Affairs and his kind have a long history of colluding with the church and missionaries. As Vine Deloria Jr. (Hunkpapa Lakota/Standing Rock Sioux) quips: "It has been said of missionaries that when they arrived they had only the Book and we had the land; now we have the Book and they have the land. An old Indian once told me that when the missionaries arrived they fell on their knees and prayed. Then they got up, fell on Indians and preyed."[3] These realities are not going away. We will not forget about them. And we will continue to rage against the colonial machine. So, we continue to wrestle with Mr. NDN Affairs, and the legacy of settler colonialism that he embodies, even in our reading of Scripture.

In this chapter, we consider how the colonial legacy of land theft, broken treaties, and the forced removal of Indigenous peoples from their ancestral

---

[2] *Acting Good*, episode 6, season 1, "Battle in the Bush," directed by Michael Greyeyes, November 21, 2022 on CTV Comedy Channel.
[3] Vine Deloria Jr., *Custer Died for Your Sins: An Indian Manifesto* (New York: Avon, 1969), 105.

lands can frame interpretations of land theft and forced relocation in the stories of Scripture. Moreover, we will propose that an Indigenous reading of Scripture can appreciate how Creator's commitment to healthy covenant relationships and Jesus' Jubilee commitment to reparations embolden our spirits as we maneuver in the ring. And as we dance through the medicine wheel of our Turtle Island hermeneutical approach, we may find ourselves like Jacob with the angel of the Lord (Gen 32:22-31), wrestling with Scripture itself: asking questions, complicating stories, and tussling about in ways that may make some readers uncomfortable. Even if we come out with a limp, it's worth it to get a win with Elder Agnes, even if it's only for one night.

In this chapter and the next, we will be discussing sensitive topics, especially so for Indigenous readers. Intergenerational trauma is a reality for our communities, and we ask that you care well for yourself as you read.

At times, these chapters may feel like short lessons in history rather than biblical interpretation. This is intentional, as many of these traumatic stories remain unknown to our non-Indigenous neighbors even as they haunt our communities' readings of Scripture. Returning back to our medicine wheel model of interpretation, these stories have affected the quadrants of our cultural traditions as well as our hearts and minds, and so there we will dance. Indigenous and non-Indigenous people do not share a common understanding of our historic relationships on Turtle Island that have brought us to the challenges we face today. Telling the hard truths of these experiences can be cathartic and even transformative for Indigenous and non-Indigenous people alike. It is our hope that in telling these stories we might *begin* to build toward a more common understanding of how Indigenous and non-Indigenous people have related to one another in our past in order to journey together toward a vision of reconciliation encountered in Scripture.

NABOTH'S VINEYARD

We begin first with a story of land dispossession in the Scriptures. Elaine Enns and Ched Myers call the story of Naboth's Vineyard in 1 Kings 21 "an archetypal parable of empire vs. indigeneity."[4]

---

[4] Elaine Enns and Ched Myers, *Healing Haunted Histories: A Settler Discipleship of Decolonization*, The Center and Library for the Bible and Social Justice Series (Eugene, OR: Cascade, 2021), 187.

> Now it happened sometime later that Naboth from Jezreel had a vineyard in Jezreel that was next to the palace of King Ahab of Samaria. Ahab ordered Naboth, "Give me your vineyard so it can become my vegetable garden, because it is right next to my palace. In exchange for it, I'll give you an even better vineyard. Or if you prefer, I'll pay you the price in silver." Naboth responded to Ahab, "Lord forbid that I give you my family inheritance!" So Ahab went to his palace, irritated and upset at what Naboth had said to him—because Naboth had said, "I won't give you my family inheritance!" Ahab lay down on his bed and turned his face away. He wouldn't eat anything. His wife Jezebel came to him. "Why are you upset and not eating any food?" she asked. He answered her, "I was talking to Naboth. I said, 'Sell me your vineyard. Or if you prefer, I'll give you another vineyard for it.' But he said, 'I won't give you my vineyard!'" Then his wife Jezebel said to him, "Aren't you the one who rules Israel? Get up! Eat some food and cheer up. I'll get Naboth's vineyard for you myself." (1 Kings 21:1-7)

Now, perhaps King Ahab truly was a sniveling pouter, like a spoiled child with too many toys who yet wants more because what he has no longer satisfies. Or perhaps instead King Ahab's refusal to eat was a temporary act of remorse. In either case, Naboth did not simply say, "No, I don't want to sell my vineyard." Naboth instead reminded the king of the ancestral laws of inheritance. Numbers 36:7 states, "the inheritance of the Israelites doesn't transfer from one tribe to another. The Israelites will each retain the tribal inheritance of his ancestral tribe." This command is itself predicated on the laws in Leviticus 25:23-28. Leviticus states, "The land must not be permanently sold because the land is mine. You are just immigrants and foreign guests of mine. . . . When one of your fellow Israelites faces financial difficulty and must sell part of their family property, the closest relative will come and buy back what their fellow Israelite has sold" (Lev 25:23, 25). Naboth takes seriously his ancestral and familial relationship with the land: "Naboth's commitment to his land in terms of the triangular covenant [of God, the people, and the land] is eclipsed by Ahab's commodification of land as an abstract asset whose value should be maximized."[5] This commodification of land in more present times intentionally seeks to break the relationships

---

[5] Matthew Humphrey, "A Pipeline Runs Through Naboth's Vineyard: From Abstraction to Action in Cascadia," in *Watershed Discipleship: Reinhabiting Bioregional Faith and Practice*, ed. Ched Myers (Eugene, OR: Cascade Books, 2016), 130.

between lands and people who belong to those lands, an intentional act that was and is part of the colonial project.

In the story, Queen Jezebel hatches a plot to have Naboth killed. Palestinian theologian Mitri Raheb notes that Ahab recognized himself as subject to the ancestral laws, but Jezebel as a non-Israelite has a different conception of royalty. "Jezebel's models were the imperial rulers, who were absolute sovereigns. It was the occupier-occupied relationship, where the law serves the empire and its policy of expansion."[6] With Naboth out of the way, Ahab happily takes possession of Naboth's vineyard (1 Kings 21:8-16). This does not go unnoticed by God, and his prophet Elijah is sent to deliver his judgment against Ahab, Jezebel, and their family. While Ahab does repent, the judgment is only deferred. The blood of Naboth, and the land to which he belongs, will receive its justice.

As descendants of nations who were dispossessed of their lands, Indigenous peoples today understand this story all too well.[7] While modern readers understandably condemn the actions of the wicked king and queen, it is less likely that Christians in North America actually recognize that their stories align more with Ahab and Jezebel—and in condemning them, they condemn themselves. After all, almost the entirety of the United States and Canada sits on contested land, paths littered with broken treaties or no treaties at all. Indigenous readers of this text see themselves and their ancestors in Naboth and his ancestors. And perhaps what is most frustrating for Indigenous followers of Jesus is that we have not seen the church live in the spirit of Elijah, who bravely speaks truth to power (1 Kings 21:17-26). Elijah spoke the words of Creator in defense of Naboth, but the same cannot always be said of the church speaking in defense of First Nations.

The spirit of Elijah's critique lives on in an 1888 affidavit written by an independent Indigenous Methodist evangelist named Arthur Wellington Clah (Coast Tsimshian) from what is now northern British Columbia. In his affidavit, Clah speaks out against the government's choice to give a parcel of his family's land to another group and local judges who told his people that

---

[6]Mitri Raheb, "The Bible and Land Colonization," in *The Land: Majority World and Minoritized Theologies of Land*, ed. K. K. Yeo and Gene L. Green (Eugene, OR: Cascade, 2020), 29.

[7]Naboth's story has been reflected and drawn on in Aotearoa as well. See Alistair Reese, "Te Papa: Naboth's Vineyard? Towards Reconciliation in Tauranga Moana: Executive Summary and Recommendations," University of Otago, 2018, https://hdl.handle.net/10523/8559.

they could not "build houses, or leave our things." It is into this historical situation that Clah reflects on Naboth: "I read in the Bible that God did not approve of Ahab taking the land from Naboth. So I don't think that God is pleased with the way the Government has taken our land."[8] Into the situation of land dispossession, Clah also speaks regarding the queen and her use of kinship language to describe the First Nations as "her children." He states: "Did you ever see a Christian take land from another Christian and sell it, not letting him know anything about it. We have heard that the Queen, that all the people in the west and in the interior across the Rocky Mountains are her children. She calls them such. Is that the way a mother treats her children, takes away their land and not tell them about it?"[9]

Today settler Christians must reckon with the reality that past Canadians and Americans have played the role of Ahab and Jezebel. The resulting commodification of land is very often the very lands that they own and that our churches sit on and own. While Indigenous folk see ourselves as Naboth's descendants, settler Christians have been unable to reckon with the reality that they may be Ahab's and Jezebel's descendants. As we wrestle with this story and other Scriptures, we are striving to take seriously that we are people built for covenant and community. The Old Testament covenant was in all iterations a triangular relationship between God, the people, and the land.[10] Naboth understood that his ancestral laws were rooted in the covenant with God. In the same way, Indigenous nations understand themselves to be in a sacred covenant relationship with the land and with Creator. Indigenous peoples carried this same sacred understanding into the treaty process in the United States and Canada. These treaties were done in ceremony before Creator. This is why, despite how often treaties have been dishonored, broken, and ignored—Indigenous communities are still willing to return to the terms of treaty.

---

[8] Arthur Wellington Clah, "Affidavit of A. W. Clah (An Indian)," in *Letter from Methodist Missionary Society to the Superintendent General of Indian Affairs regarding the British Columbia Troubles* (Toronto, 1889), 43.

[9] Susan Neylan, "'Eating the Angels' Food': Arthur Wellington Clah—an Aboriginal Perspective on Being Christian, 1857–1909," in *Canadian Missionaries, Indigenous Peoples: Representing Religion at Home and Abroad*, ed. Alvyn Austin and Jamie S. Scott (Toronto: University of Toronto Press, 2005), 103.

[10] For more on this, see H. Daniel Zacharias, "The Land Takes Care of Us: Recovering Creator's Relational Design," in Yeo and Green, *Land*, 69–97.

INDIGENOUS UNDERSTANDINGS OF TREATIES

First Nations on Turtle Island have long and storied histories of making, honoring, and adjudicating treaties with other Indigenous and non-Indigenous nations. Ray Aldred (Cree), who directs the Indigenous studies program at Vancouver School of Theology, identifies four basic principles or affirmations that undergird Indigenous treaties based on his interviews of Indigenous elders.[11] At the heart of Indigenous treaties are the affirmations that all people on the land should have the right to access and live in an interconnected manner with the land, to be sustained by the land's gifts, to seek a peaceful existence, and to live in their Creator-given, tribally specific identities.[12] Thus when Indigenous people first made treaties with early colonists and settlers, the understanding was that the Indigenous people would always have some relationship to the land they agreed to share with the newcomers. After all, the land Indigenous peoples agreed to share was *storied* land. The land held the stories of powerful divine encounters with Creator and various spiritual beings, contained the deeds and bones of their ancestors, and contained relationships with all kinds of more-than-human relatives, including plants, animals, and minerals, that provided for the sustained health and healing of its people. Thus, within Indigenous understandings, treaties involved agreements between more than two nations but also invoked the Creator and the land itself. "The treaty," writes Aldred, "meant that the newcomers and First Nations would live like relatives in the land, and the Creator would make sure that we kept up our relationships."[13] It is worth emphasizing again that for Indigenous peoples, ideally, treaties were understood to represent the beginning of long-lasting friendship and partnerships that would organically grow to the mutual benefit of both parties. Treaties are living and dynamic.

We can also learn valuable lessons about Indigenous understandings by tending to the oral traditions surrounding the wampum belt treaties preserved among Haudenosaunee elders. When the Haudenosaunee Confederacy first entered into a treaty with Dutch newcomers in 1613 on their lands

---

[11]Ray Aldred, "The Land, Treaty, and Spirituality: Communal Identity Inclusive of Land," *Journal of NAIITS* 18 (2019): 1-17. See also Raymond C. Aldred and Matthew R. Anderson, *Our Home and Treaty Land*, rev. ed. (Altona, MB: Friesen, 2024), in which the concept of treaty is a recurring theme throughout the work.
[12]Aldred, "Land, Treaty, and Spirituality," 2.
[13]Aldred, "Land, Treaty, and Spirituality," 8.

in present-day New York, the Haudenosaunee presented the Dutch with the two-row wampum belt to commemorate their agreement to live peacefully with one another. The two-row wampum belt, made of precious, refined wampum shells, consists of two rows of purple set against a background of white shells. One row represents a canoe, the other a ship traveling down the Hudson River, signifying their distinctive yet equal sovereign identities. Haudenosaunee elder Richard W. Hill Sr. explains that the two rows signaled "an agreement not to impose culture, belief, or laws on each other."[14] In 1701, the Haudenosaunee along with the Anishinaabe entered into a sacred agreement with the British recorded by the Nanfan Treaty or Dish With One Spoon wampum belt. Our elder, Uncle Adrian Jacobs (Haudenosaunee), explains that the central image of a dish with one spoon established an agreement "to share the land that feeds us all with the same spoon of access." No nation or people group is dominant in this scene, Jacobs continues; each is invited to enjoy the bounties of the land and waters, "free from racism" as "Martin Luther King Jr. dreamed of—the Beloved Community."[15] At the heart of Haudenosaunee treaty making lay the values of "kinship, dialogue, equity, and shared sovereignty"—values that were maintained and respected for too short a time between the Haudenosaunee Confederacy and the waves of newcomers, who misinterpreted these treaties as legal rights to own the land as property apart from sustained relationships of mutual respect and benefaction.[16]

Last, alongside the use of wampum belts, the Haudenosaunee Confederacy made use of a silver covenant chain to represent their treaty relationships with neighboring nations. "Silver is sturdy and does not break easily," according to Haudenosaunee elders. "It does not rust or deteriorate with time. However, it does become tarnished. So when we come together, we must polish the chain, time and again, to restore our friendship to its original brightness."[17]

---

[14] Daniel Coleman and Richard W. Hill Sr., "The Two Row Wampum-Covenant Chain Tradition as Guide for Indigenous-University Research Partnerships," *Critical Studies—Critical Methodologies* 19 (2019): 351, quoted in Mike Hogeterp, "Kinship and Two Row Covenant Chain Tradition: An Exploration of Responsibility and Hope," *Journal of NAIITS* 19 (2021): 102.

[15] Adrian Jacobs and Jennifer Henry, "Treaty: Medicine for Anxiety," *Journal of NAIITS* 16 (2018): 103.

[16] Hogeterp, "Kinship and Two Row Covenant Chain Tradition," 107.

[17] *Report on the Royal Commission on Aboriginal Peoples* (Ottawa, ON: Canada Communication Group, 1996), 1:657.

There is much we can learn from Indigenous oral traditions regarding the principles and values that undergirded some of the earliest treaties established on Turtle Island. It is unfortunate for the original stewards of Turtle Island that later treaty making conducted by the Royal Crown and the United States was driven more by the vices of ethnic superiority, the subordination and removal of "inferior barbarians," the accumulation of property and wealth, and the commodification of land and resources than by any vision of sustained friendship among sovereign nations. Space limits us from fully fleshing out treaty relationships across Canada and the United States, and so we will center on stories relating to Chris's tribe, the Choctaws.

BROKEN TREATIES, BROKEN HEARTS

In the United States, approximately 368 treaties were signed between US authorities and Indigenous leaders between 1777 and 1868. In Canada, the first nation-to-nation treaty was signed between New France and forty First Nations in 1701, and between 1760 and 1923, the British crown signed fifty-six treaties with First Nations—the most encompassing of these being the eleven numbered treaties that cover most of central and western Canada.[18] In the Canadian context, oral traditions accompanied the treaties along with details beaded into wampum belts, as the Indigenous peoples could not read the actual treaty documents. According to Suzan Shown Harjo (Cheyenne and Hodulgee Muscogee), who spent decades advocating for and contributing to US legislation concerning Indigenous repatriation of lands, hunting rights, and religious freedom, "most [US treaties] have been stretched to the breaking point, ignored, or all but forgotten."[19] For example, consider when the United States disregarded the Treaty of Fort Laramie (1868) when it stole the Black Hills in South Dakota from the Lakota. In 1874, US Colonel George Custer discovered gold around this sacred mountain range, known as *Paha* or *He Sapa* to the Lakota. Soon after, gold miners descended on the hills as ravenous locusts for "the yellow metal that makes the Wasichus [white people] crazy," without concern for or consent from the land's Lakota

---

[18]Michelle Filice, "Numbered Treaties," in *The Canadian Encyclopedia*, August 3, 2016, www.thecanadianencyclopedia.ca/en/article/numbered-treaties.

[19]Suzan Shown Harjo, ed., *Nation to Nation: Treaties Between the United States and American Indian Nations* (Washington, DC: Smithsonian Institution, 2014), 1.

caretakers.[20] Violent conflicts ensued, with the result that the Lakota were ultimately removed from these lands to smaller reservations. However, in 1980 the US Supreme Court ruled in *United States v. Sioux Nation of Indians* that the United States had illegally taken the Black Hills from the Lakota. The Lakota refused the settlement of $106 million, demanding that the United States return *He Sapa* to them. To this day, this money remains in an interest-bearing trust fund that may now be worth about $2 billion.

Some treaties were negotiated in good faith between tribal leaders and US commissioners but would never be ratified by US federal legislators. For example, eighteen treaties made in 1851–1852 between Northern California tribes and federal commissioners were never ratified by the US Senate, with the result that these tribes had no legal protection from the greedy prospectors and speculators who murdered and drove them from their lands during the California gold rush.[21] At the heart of most treaties was the unrelenting greed for land and resources. As many as one out of every ten US signatories of Indigenous treaties were at some point in their career bank directors, land office personnel, or land surveyors eager to turn a profit on cheap land.[22] Within the eyes of American and Canadian governments, Indigenous peoples were not making efficient and industrious use of the land according to European standards—that is, not farming or mining it to its full potential, squandering its potential to produce wealth.[23]

When we imagine how many of these treaties were signed, we should picture less a scene of a good-faith business deal and more a scene pulled from a mafia series such as *The Godfather* or HBO's *The Sopranos*, characterized by intimidation and trickery. Such was the case for the Choctaws, when the Treaty of Dancing Rabbit Creek was signed, which ceded the Choctaw's ancestral home in Mississippi for land in Indian Territory (present southeastern

---

[20]Black Elk and John G. Neihardt, *Black Elk Speaks: The Complete Edition*, ProQuest ed. (Lincoln: University of Nebraska Press, 2014), 68.
[21]Harjo, *Nation to Nation*, 3.
[22]Martin Case, *The Relentless Business of Treaties: How Indigenous Land Became U.S. Property* (St. Paul: Minnesota Historical Society, 2018), 36-37.
[23]A major component of making Indigenous peoples "civilized" was persuading them to settle in one place and adopt farming and cultivation practices. See, for example, Thomas S. Abler, "A Mi'kmaq Missionary Among the Mohawks: Silas T. Rand and His Attitudes Toward Race and 'Progress,'" in *With Good Intentions: Euro-Canadian and Aboriginal Relations in Colonial Canada*, ed. Celia Haig-Brown and David A. Nock (Vancouver: UBC, 2006), 72-86.

Oklahoma). While the Choctaws had presumed that President Andrew Jackson was their friend, having fought alongside him in the War of 1812 (and the coinciding US–Creek War of 1813–1814), Jackson aggressively sought the removal of all Indigenous peoples from east of the Mississippi River to the west.[24] US state legislators, emboldened by Jackson, passed aggressive bills that sought to impose their "foreign" laws on sovereign Indigenous peoples.[25] In fall 1830, after the majority of Choctaw leaders had refused to sign away their ancestral lands, Secretary of War John Eaton privately threatened Choctaw *mingos* ("chiefs"), including LeFlore, Mushulatubbee, Nittakaichee, and Folsom, saying that the Choctaws' refusal would invite war against the military of the United States.[26] Colonel John Coffee, who accompanied Eaton in his negotiations, described Eaton's coercive theatrics as persuasion at gunpoint. And so, on September 27, 1830, the Treaty of Dancing Rabbit Creek was signed behind the backs of many Choctaw leaders under the threat of violence, ceding ten million acres of land to the United States.[27]

SINGING SONGS OF LAMENT ALONG THE TRAILS OF TEARS

Following the Treaty of Dancing Rabbit Creek and many more like it, Indigenous peoples across the United States experienced their own traumatic exodus from their ancestral lands to unfamiliar territories and reservations. As a Choctaw reader of Christian Scripture, Chris can no longer approach biblical stories and references to the Babylonian exile of Judeans in the sixth century BCE found in 2 Kings, Jeremiah, Ezekiel, Lamentations, and the Psalms and not think about the Indigenous stories and responses to the American exile imposed on his people and so many others. Chris's fellow Choctaw theologian and Episcopal bishop Stephen Charleston remarks that American Christians have yet to grasp that the Trail of Tears represents a tragic story of "Christians cheating and oppressing Christians," given that many Choctaws believed in Jesus and sang newly composed Choctaw hymns along the trail. "On the Trail of Tears," Charleston writes, "my ancestors were,

---

[24]Christina Snyder, *Great Crossings: Indians, Settlers, and Slaves in the Age of Jackson* (Oxford: Oxford University Press, 2017), 138; James Taylor Carson, *Searching for the Bright Path: The Mississippi Choctaws from Prehistory to Removal* (Lincoln: University of Nebraska Press, 1999), 117.
[25]See Snyder, *Great Crossings*, 136; Carson, *Searching for the Bright Path*, 112-16.
[26]Snyder, *Great Crossings*, 140.
[27]Carson, *Bright Path*, 122-23.

quite literally, crying for a vision. They were being tested, driven out, sent into an unknown land as exiles by the waters of Babylon, longing for a sign from God in which they could hope."[28] Holding close to heart memories of forced relocation, the Trail of Tears, and "long walks," as they have come to be known, Indigenous readers of Scripture can relate all too well to the ancient Judean long walk to Babylon.

Beginning in 597 BCE, Judeans from the Southern Kingdom of Judah were marched in chains to Babylon in successive waves after King Jehoiachin of Judah submitted to King Nebuchadnezzar of the Chaldeans, who had laid siege to Jerusalem. Members of the royal house and the aristocracy were among the first to be exiled. It may be that the Babylonian king thought it strategic to first remove anyone who might inspire a revolt against his sustained control over Judah. However, the next king, Zedekiah, who was installed by Nebuchadnezzar himself, revolted nevertheless. In response, Nebuchadnezzar laid siege to Jerusalem again, this time with much more devastating results: the wall was breached, the king captured, the army dispersed, the temple destroyed, and Jerusalem and its inhabitants suffered great devastation (2 Kings 25; Jer 52). The destruction of Jerusalem in 586 BCE was followed by another exile of its citizens, which encompassed "the people who were left in the city" save for "some of the land's poor people [left] behind to work the vineyards and be farmers" (2 Kings 25:11-12). While there may have been several smaller deportations and voluntary migrations during this period, the last noted removal of people from Jerusalem to Babylon occurred in 582 BCE. Many of these Judeans were relocated just outside Babylon, likely grouped in ethnic enclaves by the irrigation canals (Ps 137). These Judeans were forced to endure the never-ending labor of removing salt from the canals to maintain and increase Babylon's agricultural economy.[29]

Of course, the experiences and reasons for forced removal of the North American tribes like the Choctaw are not directly analogous to those of the ancient Judeans under Babylonian rule. There certainly were no negotiated terms of removal or agreed-on articles and provisions between the vassal

---

[28]Steven Charleston, *The Four Vision Quests of Jesus* (New York: Morehouse, 2015), 67-68.

[29]John J. Ahn, *Exile as Forced Migration: A Sociological, Literary, and Theological Approach on the Displacement and Resettlement of the Southern Kingdom of Judah*, BZAW 417 (New York: de Gruyter, 2011), 83-85.

Judeans and their Babylonian conquerors. We have very little remaining documented evidence describing what Judeans experienced during their long walk to Babylon, and what we do have from archaeological remains comes from official Babylonian documents preserved on cuneiform tablets. This might not come as a surprise to Indigenous readers, given that our own accounts from ancestors' experiences on such trails were generally passed down through stories and songs shared among family, kin, and church relations. What was *written* in the 1830s about the removal of tribes from the southeastern United States largely comprised official reports and journal entries from non-Indigenous military officers and ministers. Many of our ancestors' stories were recorded in later interviews of families living in Oklahoma under the auspices of the Indian and Pioneer Interviews of Oklahoma during the 1930s.[30]

Stories from the Trail of Tears are still publicly shared today when introducing hymns that were composed and sung in our native tongues during the long walk. Many of these stories associated with hymns are gravely tragic. For example, in the Cherokee hymn "One Drop of Blood," the lyrics repeatedly celebrate Christ as our "governor" or "chief," but behind this simple, pious hymn lie traumatic memories.[31] The first time the chorus is sung, it is done slowly, like a dirge, and according to tradition conveys the weight of the suffering and of lives lost along the trail. The second time, the pitch of the voices is raised and the tempo increases in speed. This change in pitch and pace, according to tradition, reflects an urgent plea to fellow walkers to pick up their pace lest US soldiers murder them with bayonets for slowing down the march. This was an imminent threat and tragic fate of some Cherokee elders, women (especially those in childbirth), and young children.[32] When Chris heard this song and its accompanying story performed and told by the melodic chorus of Cherokee hymn singers from Tahlequah United Methodist Church in Oklahoma, he was viscerally shaken. The stories

---

[30] See the online database of The Indian-Pioneer Papers in the Western Histories Collections, University of Oklahoma, https://digital.libraries.ou.edu/whc/pioneer/.

[31] See esp. Justine Wilson, "Beyond the Equivalence Divide: Developing a Performative Theory of Biblical Translation" (PhD diss., Harvard University, 2018), 146-49, who discusses this hymn in more depth and includes interviews with elders.

[32] On the violence enacted against Cherokee women and children on the Trail of Tears, see Daniel S. Butrick, *Cherokee Removal: The Journal of Rev. Daniel S. Butrick, May 19, 1838–April 1, 1839* (Park Hill, OK: Trail of Tears Association, Oklahoma Chapter, 1998), 6-32.

and songs can be multiplied, but it is enough to pause and wonder whether seemingly innocuous and pious psalms recorded in the Bible may have also served as containers or vehicles for responding to and processing traumatic experiences of Judeans along their journey to Babylon. Would Judean grandmothers share the stories of their long walk to Babylon to their children as they taught them the psalms they remembered in their hearts? Of course, this is beyond the reach of anyone to know, but listening to Indigenous hymns written and sung along the trail certainly raises a compelling question of how the Psalms may have functioned among Judean deportees removed from a liturgical setting of the Jerusalem temple.

Again, it is unsurprising that we lack any direct evidence for how the Babylonians coordinated the series of forced removal of Judeans from Jerusalem to Babylon. While the so-called Weidner cuneiform texts mention rations of oil and grain that were provided for the forced migration of Jehoiachin and his court in 597 BCE, it remains unclear how generous the Babylonians were in their portions because we do not know how large the royal entourage was.[33] And while the Al-Yahudu texts, which comprise receipts and contracts dating from 572–477 BCE, reference Judeans engaging in business transactions, it still remains unclear what such texts actually indicate about the lived experiences of Judeans in exile.[34] It is also unclear how many Judeans were involved. Estimates for the total number of Judeans forced to migrate over this period have ranged as high as seventy thousand or eighty thousand people.[35] If the time it took for Judeans to travel from Babylon back to Jerusalem is any indicator (Ezra 7:9), the journey may have taken at least four months. Whether in the low or high tens of thousands, it is a bureaucratic nightmare to begin to orchestrate any such mass deportation, as the US military discovered for themselves. Even though so much uncertainty clouds what we can know about this critical period of biblical history, our minds must *imagine* something when telling this story. And what we imagine is influenced by what we

---

[33] Daniel L. Smith-Christopher, *The Religion of the Landless: The Social Context of the Babylonian Exile* (repr., Eugene, OR: Wipf & Stock, 2015), 35.

[34] See Tero Alstola, *Judeans in Babylonia: A Study of Deportees in the Sixth and Fifth Centuries BCE*, Culture and History of the Ancient Near East 109 (Leiden: Brill, 2020), 253-55.

[35] Alstola, *Judeans in Babylonia*, 31-32. And yet, in contrast to the Indigenous experience of forced migration along the Trail of Tears, in which the majority of any given tribe was forced to relocate, biblical scholars seem to largely assume that the majority of Judeans remained in their land and were not forced to migrate to Babylon (see Smith-Christopher, *Religion of the Landless*, 31).

know and have experienced. So what difference might it make to linger with stories of Native American removal to imagine Judean removal? I invite us to sit just a little longer with some difficult stories from Chris's own tribe again.

After the signing of the Treaty of Dancing Rabbit Creek in 1830, the US War Department set out to deport thousands of Choctaws from Mississippi to Cantonment Towson in southeastern Oklahoma, along the Red River. Massachusetts congressman Edward Everett's reaction to the project is telling of the magnitude of the project that was set before the government: "Whoever heard of such a thing before? . . . Ten or fifteen thousand families, to be rooted up, and carried hundred, aye, a thousand miles into the wilderness! . . . It is an experiment on human life and human happiness of perilous novelty!"[36] Fort Towson was about 375 miles west of the Choctaw Nation; however, migrants had to travel along circuitous rivers and longer, rugged paths that extended their journeys. The first deportees set out first by steamboat along the Mississippi River south from Memphis, Tennessee, or north from Vicksburg, Mississippi, to Arkansas Post. From there the Choctaws would then walk the remaining 230 miles to Fort Towson in Indian Territory.[37] The austere budget of merely $7–9 a head and strict rules around spending bound both the hands and purses of US officers, who refused to hire sufficient numbers of doctors, medicine, and wagons to aid in the transport of so many vulnerable lives.[38] These preparations hardly proved sufficient to sustain the Choctaws in their removal. One wonders how much the Babylonian commanders budgeted and prepared for the forced removal of the Judeans and whether the rations of oil and grain were sufficient for the traveling convoys of men, women, elders, and children.

As difficult and tragic as the first removals were, the second round in 1832 was all the worse due to a historic outbreak of *vibrio cholerae* that plagued the United States. *V. cholerae* is a nasty and easily transmittable virus that infects the upper small intestine. Without going into disturbing details, it is an excruciatingly painful, humiliating, and frightening way to die. The outbreak hit both Memphis and Vicksburg just as the second wave of Choctaw migrants arrived—two thousand in Memphis and seventeen hundred in

---

[36]Claudio Saunt, *Unworthy Republic: The Dispossession of Native Americans and the Road to Indian Territory* (New York: Norton, 2020), 111.
[37]Saunt, *Unworthy Republic*, 127.
[38]Saunt, *Unworthy Republic*, 127.

Vicksburg. Overcrowded steamboats became incubators for *V. cholerae*. One federal agent wrote, "Scarce a boat landed without burying some person." Fourteen died among a party of 455 while traveling aboard the steamboat *Reindeer*. It remains unknown just how many Choctaw died during this second round of removal. Reports from federal officers observed that the Choctaw "suffered dreadfully with the Cholera" and that the "woods were filled with the graves of its victims." Another wrote, "Death was hourly among us, and the road lined with the sick." Upon arrival at Fort Towson, the joy of being reunited with kin was short lived. The summer of 1833 was marked by floods that destroyed their newly planted crops and constructed homes. According to one estimate, by fall 1833, approximately 20 percent of Choctaw who were forced to migrate to Indian Territory had died.[39]

In her 1930 recorded account, Mrs. Effie Oakes Fleming detailed what was passed on to her by her Choctaw grandmother, who walked the Trail of Tears when she was eight. Her grandmother shared that everyone was made to walk in those days, even the little children. Apparently, babies too tired to walk and without parents to carry them were at risk of being taken by drivers of the ox wagons and swung against a tree until they were dead and left unburied. Her grandmother saw two toddlers killed this way. With this fearful vision haunting her, Mrs. Fleming's grandmother carried her four-year-old brother Joel, even to the point that she thought she would die from exhaustion. But she hung on to him. Joel survived, thanks to his sister, and eventually grew up to serve on the supreme court of the Choctaw Nation.[40]

Sitting with these stories, one wonders about the multitude of individual stories of trauma, horror, unspeakable grief, impossible endurance, and death-defying resilience that Judean forced migrants faced in their own long walk to Babylon. One can imagine that these stories, although lost to us, lived on in the family stories of Judeans as they wept by the irrigation canals of Babylon. Studies on the exile of Judeans to Babylon often comment on the communal lament of Psalm 137 as an exemplary piece of poetry that

---

[39] Saunt, *Unworthy Republic*, 146, 149, 153, 155. Saunt also notes that the Muscogee/Creek fared just as poorly. About 16 percent, or 2,459 of the 3,000 Muskogee who had migrated, perished in this same period.

[40] Oral history from Effie Oakes Fleming, June 12, 1937, "Family Stories from the Trail of Tears," Indian-Pioneer History Collection, ed. Lorrie Montiero, https://ualrexhibits.org/tribalwriters/artifacts/Family-Stories-Trail-of-Tears.html#Overview.

poignantly responds to tragic sorrow of the exile.[41] Psalm 137 seems to have been composed between 587 and 582 BCE and reflects the concerns of a first-generation migrant who was caught up in the first removal (597 BCE) and had been resettled "by the irrigation canals of Babylon" (Ps 137:1, translation ours). The psalm reads:

> Alongside Babylon's streams [or irrigation canals],
>   there we sat down,
>   crying because we remembered Zion.
> We hung our lyres up
>   in the trees there
>   because that's where our captors asked us to sing;
>   our tormentors requested songs of joy:
>   "Sing us a song about Zion!" they said.
> But how could we possibly sing
>   the Lord's song on foreign soil?
> Jerusalem! If I forget you,
>   let my strong hand wither!
> Let my tongue stick to the roof of my mouth
>   if I don't remember you,
>   if I don't make Jerusalem my greatest joy.
> Lord, remember what the Edomites did
>   on Jerusalem's dark day:
>   "Rip it down, rip it down!
>   All the way to its foundations!" they yelled.
> Daughter Babylon, you destroyer,
>   a blessing on the one who pays you back
>   the very deed you did to us!
>   A blessing on the one who seizes your children
>   and smashes them against the rock!

The well-known psalm invites us down beside the captive Judeans, who think on their ancestral homeland as they labor to desalinate the canals that nourish Babylonian soil. Indigenous eyes might notice and appreciate the presence of Grandmother Willow in Psalm 137:2, standing beside the migrants, listening to their cries and perhaps crying herself. The Judeans' grief is amplified when

---

[41]On the complex genre of Ps 137, see Ahn, *Exile as Forced Migration*, 40-66, 78-79.

a traditional song is requested of them by their overseers.[42] The psalmist's rhetorical question regarding the impossibility of singing the Lord's song in foreign soil deeply resonates with the Indigenous insight that our identities, both physical and spiritual, are bound to the land and soil we inhabit. One wonders what Choctaw songs were no longer sung or were lost not long after their removal from their ancestral lands.

The psalmist charges his audience to not forget Jerusalem, just as our Choctaw elders surely charged their young not to forget their ancestral land or *Nanih Waiya*—the sacred mound site from which, according to some ancient stories, the Choctaws first emerged from the ground. The psalm then shifts to cursing the Babylonians and the Edomites, even going as far as to call for the vivid execution of Babylon's babies, perhaps recalling the communal grief over the loss of life of so many children within their own community during the destruction of Jerusalem (see Is 47:8; Jer 31:15).[43] Such unspeakable loss was certainly known by the Cherokees, whose own traumatic loss of life is commemorated in the oral stories told around the hymn "One Drop of Blood." Indeed, of all the Muskogee/Creek babies born between 1830 and 1833, only a quarter seem to have survived.[44] And certainly one cannot read this curse against Babylon's children and not call to mind the horror that Mrs. Fleming's grandmother witnessed of young children's heads being bashed against trees. What meaning would Psalm 137:9 have had for Mrs. Fleming and her grandmother? I imagine Mrs. Fleming's grandmother knew something about the space of trauma and anger from which this verse arose for the psalmist.

During his travels interviewing Indigenous ministers for this book, Chris had the pleasure of meeting Reverend McKinney, a member of the Choctaw Nation and moderator of the Dakota Presbytery of the Presbyterian Church (USA). During the Presbyterian Church (USA)'s 2022 Indigenous Peoples' Day, Rev. McKinney eloquently preached on Psalm 137. In preparing for his sermon, Rev. McKinney recalled: "I thought about the hymns we love. They are powerful medicine for our weary souls." Native hymns, Rev. McKinney continued, "connect us with the past, with those who lived through unimaginable atrocities designed to eradicate us as people." Native people "may live in the poorest areas

---

[42] Ahn, *Exile as Forced Migration*, 90.
[43] Ahn, *Exile as Forced Migration*, 95.
[44] Saunt, *Unworthy Republic*, 155.

of the country and our churches may be falling to pieces around us," Rev. McKinney observed, "but we will continue to sing the songs that have sustained our people through the generations."[45] True to his word, Rev. McKinney closed the worship service with the old Choctaw hymn "The Christian's Resolution," which was sung by some Choctaw as they rose many mornings during the long walk to Indian Territory to steel their resolve in their faith in Jesus and hope that God would be with them along the trail. And indeed, the Choctaw continue to sing to this day and will continue to sing of Creator, who walked beside the ancient Judeans along the trail to Babylon, who walked beside their own ancestors along the trail to Indian Territory, and who continues to walk beside them and present-day migrants along the *Hina Hanta*, the Bright Path.

CREATOR HONORS TREATIES

Creator, as revealed throughout Scripture, is a treaty maker and faithfully abides by the terms of Creator's treaties (e.g., Lev 26:44; Deut 4:31; 7:9; Judg 2:1; Ps 105:8-10; Is 54:10) despite the unfaithfulness of Creator's human covenant stakeholders. Creator provides Original Instructions to Adam (Gen 2:15). Creator establishes a covenant with Noah and all living creatures instructing them to multiply and not murder, while also promising not to flood the earth again (Gen 9:5-17). Creator instructs Abraham to "walk with me and be trustworthy" (Gen 17:1) and to circumcise every male, promising the land of Canaan and many descendants to Abraham (Gen 15:18-21; 17:1-22). Creator establishes a covenant containing ordinances, promises, and warnings, which Moses consecrates and seals in a ceremony in which he dashes the blood of animals on the book of the covenant and the Israelites (Ex 24:3-8). According to the prophets Jeremiah and Ezekiel, Creator will establish a new, everlasting covenant of peace, which will be written on the hearts of the people despite their nation's failure to uphold the previous covenant (Jer 31:33; 32:40; see also Ezek 16:59-62; 37:25-26). Followers of Jesus will interpret these promised peace treaties as fulfilled in the new covenant established by Jesus, consecrated and sealed with his own blood, as commemorated by the wine

---

[45] Mike Ferguson, "During Wednesday's PC(USA) Chapel Service, a Native American Pastor Retraces a Recent Blessed Journey Undertaken by a Father and His Son," Presbyterian News Service, October 12, 2022, https://pcusa.org/news-storytelling/news/during-wednesdays-pcusa-chapel-service-native-american-pastor-retraces-recent-blessed-journey.

shared among his followers at the Last Supper (Mt 26:28; Mk 14:24; Lk 22:20). Followers of Jesus are a covenant people who commemorate their identity as treaty people every time they participate in the Eucharist.

In the eyes of our treaty-making Creator, broken treaties have consequences. To illustrate this point, Richard Twiss (Sicangu Lakota/Rosebud Reservation) turns to an underappreciated story in Scripture in which Creator punishes the land of Israel with three successive years of famine during the reign of David on account of an ancient broken treaty.[46] The Lord informs David that his predecessor, Saul, had tried to destroy the Gibeonites in order to secure their coastal lands for Israelite resettlement (2 Sam 21:2, 5). Saul's colonizing aggression violated an ancient peace treaty with the Gibeonites and merited the Lord's wrath (2 Sam 21:1). About four hundred years prior, during the time of Joshua's conquest of Canaan, the Gibeonites cleverly brokered a treaty with Joshua, whereby they pretended to be poor refugees from a foreign land in need of Joshua's protection (Josh 9). Little did Joshua know that the Gibeonites were actually inhabitants of the land who wanted to spare themselves from Joshua's conquest after hearing about his devastating victories over the cities of Jericho and Ai. Despite the Israelites' military aims to conquer the inhabitants of the land, they honored their oath and let them live. In order to reconcile with the remaining Gibeonites, David abided by the Gibeonites' demand to deliver seven of Saul's sons to them to be hanged during the opening days of the barley harvest (2 Sam 21:9). It was only after the ritual execution of Saul's sons, and after David had properly gathered and reburied the bones of Saul's family within their family tomb, that the Lord begins to listen to requests on behalf of the land (2 Sam 21:14). Twiss observes that even though Creator did not establish this covenant, Creator nevertheless enforced it, even over the span of four hundred years. Moreover, God refused to answer Israel's prayers for relief and health for the land because their previous leader had violently broken a peace treaty in his greed to acquire more land for his people. Twiss wonders why it is such a stretch for North American Christians to consider that Creator might *not* be "blessing" their nations and land because of their own history of broken treaties with Indigenous peoples.[47]

---

[46] Richard Twiss, *One Church, Many Tribes: Following Jesus the Way God Made You* (Bloomington, MN: Chosen Books, 2000), 181-86.
[47] Twiss, *One Church, Many Tribes*, 183-86.

While Joshua's conquest was the paradigm for European colonization, Randy Woodley has observed how Abraham's own way of entering and dwelling within the Promised Land provides a refreshing juxtaposition to Joshua's military campaign into the land following the directives laid out in the covenant just mentioned. "Abraham," Woodley writes, "enters the same land of Canaan, with the same promise given by God that was given to Joshua to inherit the land, and he is a perfect guest at every turn."[48] Upon Abram's return from a successful battle against kings who had sacked Sodom and kidnapped his nephew Lot, Abram met with the king of Sodom and King Melchizedek of Salem. As a good guest in the land, Abram humbly accepts Melchizedek's blessing in the name of "El Elyon (God Most High)"—a name of divinity not yet attested or attributed to the Lord in the biblical account. Abram doesn't seem to cringe at the evocation of this foreign name but even goes so far as to acknowledge that he has sworn an oath to this God Most High, maker of heaven and earth, whom he identifies as his own "Lord" (Gen 14:22).

In a later story, as a humble foreigner in the land of the Philistines, God's favor for Abram—now Abraham—is recognized by Abimelech, the king of the Philistines, and the two agree to deal faithfully with each other regarding their land claims (Gen 21:22-24). This treaty is put to the test when Abimelech's servants seize a well that belongs to Abraham, and so Abraham establishes another covenant with Abimelech, accompanied by a gift of seven ewe lambs, to recognize Abraham's ownership of the well (Gen 21:25-34). Finally, with the death of his wife Sarah, Abraham consults with the Hittites to purchase a piece of land to bury his family, recognizing that he is "an immigrant and a temporary resident with you" (Gen 23:4). Throughout the negotiation process, Abraham, as a good guest, "bowed before the local citizens" (Gen 23:12; see also Gen 23:7). Abraham's story provides a witness to a vision of hospitality and being a good guest in the land that resonates with Indigenous values and points toward what peace or shalom can look like in sharing land. Indigenous followers of Jesus invite Christians to be more like Abraham than Joshua.[49]

---

[48] Randy Woodley, *Mission and the Cultural Other: A Closer Look* (Eugene, OR: Cascade, 2022), 41.
[49] In the prelude/appendix, we will return to the Joshua story and the ambiguity and complexity of interpreting the Israelite conquest from an Indigenous perspective. Moreover, Indigenous readers of the Bible must wrestle with the numerous passages that prohibit making treaties with the people of the land, which were intended to forestall the Hebrews from honoring other gods (Ex 34:11-12; Deut 7:12; Judg 2:2).

JESUS' JUBILEE VISION FOR #LANDBACK

Jesus' Jubilee vision, discussed in chapter three, has surprising and underappreciated ramifications for restoring Indigenous lands, as illustrated in the story of Jesus' encounter with a rich young man (Mk 10:17-31; Mt 19:16-30; this person is called a rich young ruler in Lk 18:18-30). In Mark's version, a man runs up and kneels before Jesus and asks, "Good Teacher, what must I do to obtain eternal life?" (Mk 10:17). After Jesus affirms that only God is good and runs through the latter six of the Ten Commandments, the man proudly responds, "Teacher... I've kept all these things since I was a boy" (Mk 10:20). Jesus looks upon the man, loves him, and tells him, "You are lacking one thing. Go, sell what you own, and give the money to the poor. Then you will have treasure in heaven. And come, follow me" (Mk 10:21). Upon hearing this, the man is "dismayed" and leaves saddened, for, like many citizens in the United States and Canada, "he had many possessions" (Mk 10:22).

Ched Myers convincingly argues that we should imagine that this man had accrued his wealth in a manner similar to how many others accumulated wealth in the region: "land acquisition from those defaulting on debt."[50] Promissory notes found in the Judean Desert dating from the first century CE indicate that borrowers typically put their property and future possessions up as collateral for loans from large estate owners, and interest rates could range from 12 percent to 20 percent if the loan was paid back by an agreed-on time.[51] For many Galilean farmers living at subsistence levels, a drought, diseased harvest, or simply bad luck could plunge them into debt, leading them to forfeit their landholdings to those like the wealthy individual speaking to Jesus. According to historian Martin Goodman, "the only logical reason [for Jewish aristocratic families] to lend was thus the hope of winning the peasant's land by foreclosing on it when the debt was not paid off."[52] That Jesus asks whether the rich man had defrauded his neighbor (Mk 10:19) leads us to further wonder whether this man's wealth came from acquiring land from defaulting creditors. When Jesus instructs the rich man to sell his

---

[50] Enns and Myers, *Healing Haunted Histories*, 278.
[51] G. Anthony Keddie, *Class and Power in Roman Palestine: The Socioeconomic Setting of Judaism and Christian Origins* (Cambridge: Cambridge University Press, 2019), 103.
[52] Martin Goodman, *The Ruling Class of Judea: The Origins of the Jewish Revolt Against Rome, A.D. 66–70* (Cambridge: Cambridge University Press, 1987), 57.

possessions and give to the poor, it is possible to envision Jesus as effectively promoting a Jubilee return of land and wealth to the poor. A Turtle Island hermeneutic lifts up Jubilee Jesus as supporting #landback. According to Myers, "Jesus clearly commands the wealthy to repatriate land that has been stolen. This is a hard word to settlers: redistribution is our precondition for discipleship."[53]

It brings Jubilee joy to our hearts when we encounter stories of Christian communities following Jesus' landback teachings by investing in relationships with local Indigenous peoples and giving back church-owned property and land. Rev. Dr. Allen Buck (Cherokee) has been involved as a liaison and consultant in several landback procedures underway among United Methodist and Presbyterian Church (USA) communities. In 2018, the Oregon-Idaho Conference of the United Methodist Church returned a 1.5-acre parcel of land along the Wallowa River in Oregon to the Nez Perce tribe. In 1877, the Nez Perce were removed from their ancestral land along the Wallowa mountain range in violation of the 1855 Treaty of Walla Walla, which had secured 7.5 million acres of their once vast territory across Oregon, Idaho, and Washington. Although a tiny fraction of their vast homeland, this return of land was marked by a ceremony filled with moving speeches from elders, drumming, and a commemorative walk to the river, where a ceremonial stone was returned to the river that had traveled between the leadership of Nez Perce and the Oregon-Idaho Conference, symbolizing the relationship between the two.[54] In 2021, the United Methodist Church also transferred the deed of a closed United Methodist Church in Wallowa built in 1910 to the Nez Perce. Reflecting on his experience with the Nez Perce during these transfers of land, Rev. Allen Buck shared with Chris, "My theology has become grounded in giving it all away. If we are decolonizing, it always involves giving back."[55]

In Canada, one of the Truth and Reconciliation Commission's calls to action involves repudiating the Doctrine of Discovery. This work of repudiation has

---

[53] Enns and Myers, *Healing Haunted Histories*, 279. Enns and Myers poignantly reimagine this story as a meeting between "Indigenous Jesus" and "powerful settler official" (281-82).
[54] Greg Nelson, "Wallowa Lake Ceremony Honors Return of Land to Nez Perce," Oregon-Idaho Conference of the United Methodist Church Greater Northwest Area, August 8, 2018, www.umoi.org/newsdetail/wallowa-lake-ceremony-honors-rightful-return-of-land-to-nez-perce-11627405.
[55] Allen Buck, interview, March 11, 2024.

resulted in landback restorations. For example, in 2017 a 10.5-acre plot owned by Emmanuel United Church in Waterloo was given to the White Owl Native Ancestry Association for their food sovereignty program, named Wisahkotewinowak, a collective led by David Skene (Red River Métis) and others.[56] Rev. Jodi Spargur in British Columbia has been involved with some landback initiatives and is documenting some of these stories both online and in her ongoing PhD work.[57]

Land back is also harmony back and has implications for restoring all kinds of imbalanced relationships. Circling back to the story of Jesus' encounter with the rich young man, an Indigenous reading can recognize how the young man's attachment to his possessions is indicative of both an imbalance and brokenness of relationships, both within himself and with those around him. According to Terry LeBlanc (Mi'kmaq), "as the young man hears Jesus' admonition, we have a very clear sense that he is so fixed on his wealth that he is left relationally isolated."[58] LeBlanc juxtaposes the relatively broken response of the rich young man with that of Zacchaeus the tax collector, whose response to his encounter with Jesus leads to actions aimed at restoring relationships. Zacchaeus's own wealth seems to have been generated in part by exploiting people by collecting an excessive amount of money from them in order to cover their taxes and his own service fees. Zacchaeus, though, has a change of heart about his illicitly gained wealth when Jesus publicly honors him by being his guest for the evening (Lk 19:1-10). As the crowd in Jericho begins to question Jesus' taste in hosts, Zacchaeus publicly announces that he will give away half of his possessions to the poor and four times the amount of whatever he had defrauded anyone (Lk 19:8). Is this not a biblical case for reparations and land back? Jesus declares that this lost "son of Abraham" has been saved and found—in other words,

---

[56] Emily McFarlan Miller, "Churches Return Land to Indigenous Groups as Part of #LandBack Movement," Religion News Service, November 26, 2020, https://religionnews.com/2020/11/26/churches-return-land-to-indigenous-groups-amid-repentance-for-role-in-taking-it-landback-movement/. *Wisahkotewinowak* is a Métis word that means "the first green shoots that come up from mother earth after a fire has gone through the land."

[57] Jodi Spargur, "Imagination for Land-Based Repair," *Repair Café* (blog), July 4, 2024, https://open.substack.com/pub/spargur/p/imagination-for-land-based-repair?r=21fl8m&utm_campaign=post&utm_medium=web.

[58] Terry LeBlanc, "Toward an Indigenous Eschatology: Caution, Circle Ahead," in *Indigenous People and the Christian Faith: A New Way Forward*, ed. William H. U. Anderson and Charles Muskego (Wilmington, DE: Vernon Press, 2020), 241.

relationships within the family of Abraham have been restored and are in the process of healing. Land back and similar forms of reparations are not just about returning to others what is due but returning to harmonious relationships with our kin from our broken and isolated selves.

For churches that are #landback-curious, our elder Adrian Jacobs (Haudenosaunee) has argued for and even drafted a "token lease payment" for churches established on lands historically marred by broken and unfulfilled treaties with First Nations peoples. This spiritual covenant acknowledges Indigenous interest in land occupied by the church, commits to a token ninety-nine-year "lease" payment to the ancestral steward of the land, and recognizes that the church property is held in trust until such a time that the land can be returned to the Indigenous nation or the church becomes "decommissioned" and repurposed to the local Indigenous community. "The church," Jacobs dreams, "could be the pressure of conscience that exerts itself among the powers of this world to do more than offer empty apologies for past injustice and impotent efforts to make things right."[59] So what's to prevent us from giving generously? Perhaps what's holding some of us back is that we become beholden to a mindset that is driven by competition and a fear of scarcity as opposed to a mindset of abundance, generosity, and—dare we say it again—Jubilee? It should be noted, dear reader, that previous versions of this chapter included instructions, including a QR code, for how you could give generously and directly to Danny's Canadian bank account, but they were removed by our cautious editor, Rachel.

CONCLUSION: WHOSE PROMISED LANDS?

As we close this chapter on Indigenous interpretations of Scripture with respect to treaties and dispossession of ancestral lands, we acknowledge that wars are currently being waged over competing claims to land believed to be the ancestral inheritance to particular nations and ideologies. All this talk about ancestral lands, treaties, reparations, and #landback raises the question: Who does land belong to, and to whom is land promised? How many ancestors must be buried in the soil for a land to be one's birthright? Who has the right to supersede or absolve treaties and make new ones? These are

---

[59]Adrian Jacobs, "A Spiritual Covenant with Churches and First Nations," *Journal of NAIITS* 19 (2021): 8-9.

all complicated questions. For a response to any geopolitical situation to be satisfying, it must be nuanced to the particular stories and treaties of a land and its people, including its more-than-human persons. We make no claims to attempt to solve these questions to everyone's satisfaction. But we can briefly name and share a few more Indigenous stories and principles that provide helpful ingredients to walking forward in a good way together.

First, as we introduced in chapter three, the principles of harmony and right-relationships that respect the dignity and care for the flourishing of both human and more-than-human creation must rest at the center of land claims. There is enough land, there are enough resources—if only we return to the essential principles of sustainability and sharing. Even where land is being given back to Indigenous peoples where treaties have been broken, harmony doesn't find its fulfillment unless relationships between Indigenous and non-Indigenous peoples are restored. We don't just want land back; we want relationships back. We want to see settlers living in a good way with the land too.

Second, the concept of promised land and the story of Exodus has a troubled legacy among Indigenous peoples. When Spanish and English explorers, colonists, and settlers arrived on Turtle Island, they declared that they had discovered a "New World," an "empty land" (*terra nullius*), which they could mythologize as a new promised land that was their destiny to colonize and civilize for Christ. Christian politicians and preachers such as Puritan minister Cotton Mather portrayed white colonists as "the chosen people" who had a divine claim on American soil, and Indigenous peoples as disposable and despicable Amalekites and Canaanites.[60] Robert Warrior (Osage) has famously contended that Native North Americans, like the Canaanites, have faced the brunt and violent ends of stories of promised lands that celebrate the conquest and decimation of Canaanite/Indigenous peoples. "America's self-image as a 'chosen people,'" Warrior argues, "has provided the rhetoric to mystify domination."[61]

---

[60]See, for example, Cotton Mather's sermon "Souldiers Counselled and Comforted. A Discourse Delivered unto Some Part of the Forces Engaged in the Just War of New-England Against the Northern & Eastern Indians," September 1, 1689.

[61]Robert Alan Warrior, "Canaanites, Cowboys, and Indians: Deliverance, Conquest, and Liberation Theology Today," in *Native and Christian: Indigenous Voices on Religious Identity in the United States and Canada*, ed. James Treat (New York: Routledge, 1996), 99.

Sarah Augustine (Pueblo, Tewa), a cofounder of the Coalition for Dismantling the Doctrine of Discovery, argues that Deuteronomy 6:10-12 provides scriptural justification for the colonization of Indigenous land. Here the Lord reminds the Israelites that he has brought them to a land promised to their ancestors full of "large and wonderful towns that you didn't build, houses stocked with all kinds of goods that you didn't stock, cisterns that you didn't make, vineyards and olive trees that you didn't plant" (Deut 6:10-11). Augustine reflects, "I am from the people who built the cities of clay on the crest of cliffs, mesas, that were seized by the Spanish; the people who originally lived in homes with good things in the river valley of what is now called the Rio Grande."[62] Dismantling and repudiating the Doctrine of Discovery is the hard work of "restorying" the land, of unforgetting, of recognizing that peoples existed in the lands before the arrival of the colonies and that the Indigenous peoples still care for and belong to these lands.[63] The effects of colonization are not in the past but a present reality, and so the work of decolonization, like land back, is an ongoing work.

No matter how imperfectly implemented in the past, we lift up an Indigenous vision of upholding treaties as an ideal worth striving toward. Treaties form ongoing relationships with other nations to share in the abundance of the land and waters so that all may prosper in harmony. Again, an Indigenous reading of Scripture appreciates the Jubilee vision of Leviticus 25:23, where Creator declares, "the land is mine. You are just immigrants and foreign guests of mine." This sentiment was echoed even by King David during the coronation ceremony of his son Solomon, when he blessed Creator, acknowledging that "everything come from you" and that all things already belong to Creator, on whose lands the Hebrews and their ancestors were merely "aliens and transients" (1 Chron 29:14, 15, NRSV). A decolonizing, Indigenous reading of Scripture would privilege the deep humility at the heart of these passages that discourage national forces from encroaching on the sovereignty of other nations while still preserving one's own—an ambitious and sometimes ambiguous process of negotiation.

---

[62]Sarah Augustine, *The Land Is Not Empty: Following Jesus in Dismantling the Doctrine of Discovery* (Harrisonburg, VA: Herald, 2021), 119-20.
[63]On unforgetting, see Patty Krawec, *Becoming Kin: An Indigenous Call to Unforgetting the Past and Reimagining Our Future* (Minneapolis: Broadleaf Books, 2022).

Third, as we will discuss more in chapter seven, at the heart of respecting treaties and land claims is the preservation and maintenance of Indigenous sovereignty—that is to say, the right to self-determine how best to live out Creator's vision and covenant established with one's ancestors on the land. Any path toward harmony between Indigenous and non-Indigenous nations must respect and incorporate Indigenous peoples as stakeholders in shared visions of mutual flourishing on our shared and sometimes unceded lands. To honor and make attempts at making good on broken treaties and promises, to give land back, to offer reparations, and to restore relationships, all contribute to supporting Indigenous sovereignty and fall into step with the Bright Path of the Jesus Way.

In closing, consider the choice of Scripture that closes Martin Scorsese's *Killers of the Flower Moon*. This film, developed in close consultation with the Osage nation, dramatically introduced millions of people worldwide to the true story of how white settlers conspired to murder Osage people systematically in order to acquire their headship rights to land that contained lucrative oil in the 1920s. Just before the credits roll, Scorsese himself reads out Genesis 4:10: "The LORD said, 'What did you do? The voice of your brother's blood is crying to me from the ground.'" When Chris finished the movie, he couldn't help but appreciate the deep resonance of Indigenous insight and perspective that echoed from Genesis to the Osage nation: the land remembers. Our ancestors' blood still cries out for justice as our hearts cry out for healing. It's fortunate that our ancestors and Creator have not left us without tried-and-true wisdom and even some wrestling moves to use against ol' Mr. NDN Affairs as trails toward healing and wholeness, as we will discuss in the next two chapters.

6

FROM BABYLON TO BOARDING SCHOOLS

Reading Scripture and Sharing Truths
for Reconciliation and Healing

CHRIS IS FOND OF TELLING his undergraduate students that no one wakes up in the morning and says, "You know what, I want to be the bad guy in someone's story today." Of course, this is a generalization; and exceptions such as Danny, who recites this mantra when editing Chris's contributions to his book, prove the rule. Canadian and US Christians are fond of identifying themselves with the heroes of biblical stories. They are the Israelites whose destiny holds the key to God's plan, the Davids and Joshuas who overcome all their enemies against great odds, the Josephs and Daniels who persevere and thrive within a majority culture that is pitted against their values, or the persecuted faithful in exile. But does anyone ever stop to consider whether they themselves or their society are the Pharaohs or the Babylonian rulers, or at least the Egyptians or Babylonians who benefit from the exploitation of Hebrew labor, wealth, and resources?[1] Certainly, for many First Nations people, the policies and actions of the United States and Canada toward their nations mirror the policies and actions of the Egyptians and Babylonians to the Hebrews.

This chapter continues the work of chapter five in exploring difficult stories from our peoples' recent history that are still not well understood by our non-Indigenous neighbors and what difference these stories make in how we interpret Scripture. As mentioned at the beginning of chapter five, we ask

---

[1] At least our friend Anna Robbins has! See Anna Robbins, "We Are Babylon: Transforming Postcolonial Crocodile Tears into Collective Repentance. Laing Lecture, Feb 23, 2016 London School of Theology," *Evangelical Quarterly* 88 (2017): 195-207.

Indigenous readers to care well for themselves, especially as this chapter discusses the experiences of residential and boarding school students. We invite readers whose own traumatic experiences or family stories resonate with the narratives shared below to take time to care for themselves and, if necessary, seek out help, counseling, ceremony, or a friend to talk and pray with.

As a Sixties Scoop survivor, Shari Russell (Anishinaabe/Saulteaux), the director of NAIITS: An Indigenous Learning Community, can't help but read the story of Moses in light of her own experiences of wrestling with her identity of being an Anishinaabe *kwe* (woman) raised within a non-Indigenous family apart from her tribal community, with whom she would later reconnect. From the late 1950s through the 1980s, Canadian social workers apprehended thousands of First Nations children, seizing them from their homes to be adopted or placed in foster homes. The term "Sixties Scoop," as well as "Eighties Scoop" and/or "Millennium Scoop" has become associated with this event. It comes from the testimony of a British Columbia social worker who tearfully described the all-too-common practice of social workers systematically "scooping" up newborns from their Indigenous mothers in these decades and adopting them out—for the most part to middle-class non-Indigenous families across Canada and even to Canadians abroad. These social workers, who were not trained to appreciate or recognize functioning Indigenous lifeways, thought they were protecting and rescuing children from Indigenous families they interpreted to be too poor or uncivilized to properly care for them. However, these social workers did not account for the physical, psychological, cultural, and spiritual devastation they would bring on countless children's lives. By 1977, First Nations children made up 20 percent of children in the care of Canadian social services, even though they made up only 5 percent of the Canadian population.[2] Russell, along with her brother and sister, was scooped at an early age.

Not all adoptive Canadian homes were loving and supportive; some were abusive, and almost all of them directly or indirectly contributed to cultural genocide. In general, these homes and families, no matter how loving, were not prepared to raise First Nations children in ways that dignified or reconnected these children to their life-giving Indigenous heritages. Indeed, that was the

---

[2] H. Philip Hepworth, *Foster Care and Adoption in Canada* (Ottawa, ON: Canadian Council of Social Development, 1980), 111.

point of the removals within the broader legacy of Canadian assimilationist policies: to sever the link between Indigenous children and their families, land, languages, spirituality, and traditions so that they might die to their "sinful" Indian natures, to be reborn as good Christian citizens. In 1982, associate chief judge E. C. Kimelman reviewed ninety-three adoption cases and found that there had been no attempt to place these children in Indigenous homes and that about half were even sent out of the country. Kimelman gravely concluded that "cultural genocide has taken place in a systematic and routine manner."[3]

As Russell grew up and became more aware of her Anishinaabe identity, she began to wrestle internally with what it meant to be Indigenous and with her status as living within a privileged culture that stigmatized her heritage as deficient and inferior. Auntie Shari describes this internal duality, in the words of W. E. B. Du Bois, as *double consciousness:* "two souls, two thoughts, two unreconciled strivings; two warring ideals in one dark body, whose dogged strength alone keeps it from being torn asunder."[4] When Auntie Shari reads the story of Moses in Exodus 2, she recognizes Moses' own double consciousness of wrestling with what it means to be a Hebrew while growing up as a prince of Egypt. Moses' own internal conflict turns deadly when he murders an Egyptian soldier for beating a Hebrew slave (Ex 2:12). Soon after, Moses, flying high from his self-assured heroism, comes on two Hebrews fighting among themselves and imagines that his elevated status entitles him to play peacekeeper. However, Moses misjudges his acceptance among the Hebrews, whose sarcastic rebuff of Moses' intervention signals to Moses not only that his murder has become public knowledge but that he doesn't properly belong among them (Ex 2:13-14). And so, Moses runs away with a broken identity that is neither Egyptian enough nor Hebrew enough. Auntie Shari observes that this internal conflict that drove Moses to harm others and exile himself resonates with children of the Sixties Scoop.[5] As Raven Sinclair (Cree, Assiniboine, Saulteaux) has observed from her work researching and

---

[3]Edwin C. Kimelman et al., *No Quiet Place: Final Report to the Honourable Muriel Smith, Minister of Community Services* (Winnipeg, MB: Manitoba Community Services, 1985), 328-29.
[4]W. E. B. Du Bois, "Of Our Spiritual Strivings," in *The Souls of Black Folk: Essays and Sketches* (Amherst and Boston: UMass Amherst Libraries and University of Massachusetts Press, 2018), 1-12.
[5]For another account of a Sixties Scoop survivor and her journey of healing, read our friend Jigaabiikwe Diane Campeau's account, "From Soul Wounds to Soul Healing: Decolonizing Trauma Healing Practices," *Journal of NAIITS* 18 (2020): 11-27.

documenting in film stories surrounding the Sixties Scoop, some scoop children have exhibited "destructive and harmful behaviors to themselves, their adoptive family, and their environment."[6]

What do we do with this history? Indigenous communities carry these stories in our bodies and spirits. Canadian and US attempts to assimilate and civilize Indigenous children by forcibly removing them from their families frame our interpretations of Scripture. Pivoting from the Sixties Scoop, we discuss the history and legacy of Indian residential schools in the United States and Canada as another federally organized and church supported attempt to civilize and christianize Indigenous children, to "kill the Indian in the child." When we carry these histories and encounter the story of Daniel's experience in Babylonian boarding school, fresh ways of interacting with these ancient stories come to light for both Indigenous and non-Indigenous readers of Scripture. Indigenous people return to these traumatic stories not just to commemorate and honor the suffering of our ancestors and to understand our own intergenerational trauma but also *to heal*. As trauma-informed counselors know well, having one's story of pain acknowledged and reconnecting with one's Indigenous heritage in a holistic manner are essential steps in the journey toward healing the internal conflicts that still traumatize Indigenous people. Raven Sinclair posits, "Perhaps by reconnecting with their birth culture, the individual provided for themselves vital cultural mirrors necessary for self-validation; a cultural reframing from which to review and re-perceive their experiences."[7] As we trace biblical and Indigenous stories, this chapter will also consider what pathways forward might look like for reconciliation and conciliation between Indigenous and non-Indigenous as we attempt to walk gently toward healing and right-relationships.

INDIAN RESIDENTIAL SCHOOLS AND BOARDING SCHOOLS FROM TURTLE ISLAND TO BABYLON

In May 2021, the Tk'emlúps te Secwépemc Language and Culture Department announced its preliminary findings, identifying up to 215 possible unmarked burials on the grounds of the Catholic-run Kamloops Indian Residential

---

[6]Raven Sinclair, "Identity Lost and Found: Lessons from the Sixties Scoop," *First Peoples Child & Family Review* 3, no. 1 (2007): 73.
[7]Sinclair, "Identity Lost and Found," 75.

School (British Columbia) with the help of ground-penetrating radar and ceremonial Knowledge Keepers. The Truth and Reconciliation Commission of Canada had spent about seven years (2008–2015) collecting extensive reports and oral histories documenting the tragic histories of abuse, cultural genocide, and deaths of First Nations children that occurred in residential schools, including the memorial list of the known names of children who never returned home from residential schools.[8] The Kamloops announcement sent shock waves across Turtle Island and brought widespread international attention to the history and legacy of Indian residential schools and boarding schools in both Canada and the United States. This news exposed the wider/whiter society to the stories and trauma that Indigenous communities have lived with for generations as they refused to forget the children who never returned home—their blood cried out from the ground (Gen 4:10). In June 2021 in the United States, the first Native American secretary of the interior, Deb Haaland (Pueblo Laguna), announced the Federal Indian Boarding School Initiative, which would investigate, identify, and report on the number and locations of Indian boarding schools and of burial sites of Native children at these schools.[9]

This history is tragic and complex.[10] And it is not just history but continues as present reality. Our people carry stories of trauma, including those shared and recorded and those that live only in the haunting memories of

---

[8]"Memorial," National Centre for Truth and Reconciliation, https://nctr.ca/memorial/. See also *Canada's Residential Schools: Missing Children and Unmarked Burials*, The Final Report of the Truth and Reconciliation Commission of Canada (Montreal, QC & Kingston, ON: McGill-Queens University Press, 2016). The TRC documentation was also followed up by *Final Report on the Missing and Disappeared Indigenous Children and Unmarked Burials in Canada: Executive Summary* (Office of the Independent Special Interlocutor for Missing Children and Unmarked Graves and Burial Sites associated with Indian Residential Schools, 2024).

[9]Much of this section is adapted from Chris's portion of a coauthored essay: Melodie Bergquist-Turori, T. Christopher Hoklotubbe, and Shari Russell, "In Their Own Lands: Indigenous Interpretations of Scripture in Diaspora," *Oxford Handbook of the Bible, Race, and Diaspora*, ed. Mitzi Smith, Raj Nadella, and Luis Menendez-Antuna (Oxford: Oxford University Press, forthcoming).

[10]While the stories shared below emphasize the overwhelming negative experiences that many Native children endured while in boarding schools, some others have expressed a measure of appreciation for their education, even if it was a mixed experience. For example, Basil Brave Heart writes about his education at the Holy Rosary Mission in Pine Ridge, SD, "This type of education helped a lot of us integrate hands-on lessons as well as academic learning. The vocational education that was part of our curriculum provided the skills we later used in life to build our homes, work on our cars, and do practical things like that. For some time now I've come to really appreciate the quality of education that was provided at the Holy Rosary Mission." See Brave Heart, *The Spiritual Journey of a Brave Heart* (self-published, 2011), 50. It is impossible to concisely summarize

survivors. As Danny traveled across Canada, almost all of his interviewees were survivors of the residential schools or the Scoops, or children of survivors. As we discussed these realities, the language of trauma and intergenerational trauma was almost always used, as was the language of healing. Dean Shingoose (Anishinaabe, Cote First Nation), a chaplain serving in Alberta, was a Sixties Scoop survivor who spoke about how reconnecting with his culture and people was an essential part of his healing process.[11] Chief George "Crow" Cote, from Cote First Nation in Saskatchewan, spoke about how learning about the residential schools and hearing stories from his grandparents and family helped them all to make sense of the challenges the family had faced.[12] Rev. Tony Snow (Nakota, Stoney Nakoda First Nation) in Calgary sees as part of his work the creating of "safe spaces for people to share their stories and begin to heal. It's an essential part of our collective recovery."[13] Willard Martin, an elder of Nisga'a First Nation, summed up what many interviewees stated: "Healing from this trauma requires acknowledging the past and working together as a community. It's a difficult journey, but it's necessary for our future."[14] Our communities hold stories of resilience and growth that were essential for navigating and negotiating a colonizing society, and are essential for striving for healing from the colonial systems.

Chris's own great-grandfather, Edwin Hoklotubbe, was orphaned at a young age and attended Jones Academy in southeastern Oklahoma. Edwin later learned about taking care of poultry in a federally run boarding school, Chilocco Indian Agricultural School in north-central Oklahoma. In both Canada and the United States, thousands upon thousands of Indigenous children were removed from their homes and sent to one of about 139 federally supported schools in Canada from 1828 to 1997, or to one of about 523 US Indian boarding schools between 1869 and the 1960s.[15] By the 1930s,

---

the over 150 years of complicated and evolving histories of Indian boarding schools here. Readers are encouraged to further examine the resources referenced in this section.

[11]Dean Shingoose, interview by Danny Zacharias, September 27, 2022.
[12]George Cote, interview by Danny Zacharias, October 19, 2022.
[13]Tony Snow, interview by Danny Zacharias, October 21, 2022.
[14]Willard Martin, interview by Danny Zacharias, October 15, 2022.
[15]See the digital map of boarding schools in the US: "Interactive Digital Map of Indian Boarding Schools," National Native American Boarding School Healing Coalition, accessed March 4, 2025, https://boardingschoolhealing.org/digitalmap/. See the digital map of boarding schools in Canada: "Residential Schools in Canada Interactive Map," The Canadian Encyclopedia, last

Christian churches in Canada extensively ran its residential school system, with the Roman Catholic Church operating forty-three of the seventy-eight schools running at the time, Anglicans operating twenty, the United Church of Canada thirteen, and the Presbyterians two.[16] In the United States, Christian denominations, including the Methodists, Orthodox Friends, Presbyterian, Episcopalians, Catholics, Hicksite Friends, Baptists, Reformed Dutch, Congregationalists, Unitarians, and Lutherans, operated about 115 schools.[17] By 1926, the US Indian Office estimated that nearly 83 percent of school-age Native children attended a boarding school.[18]

US officials such as Carl Schurz, who served as the secretary of the interior from 1877–1881, justified this assimilationist policy on the economic grounds that it cost a "little less than a million dollars to kill an Indian in war," whereas it cost only $150 a year to educate a Native student at a boarding school.[19] According to David Wallace Adams, the aims of these residential schools were fivefold: (1) to provide a rudimentary education; (2) to enculturate Indian children in Western values of individualism, private property, and self-sufficiency, training them in agricultural and industrial trades as well as homemaking; (3) to promote patriarchal household and family structures; (4) to convert students to Christianity; and (5) to train students to become productive US citizens.[20] These aims could be easily summed up by the oft-quoted statement of Captain Richard Henry Pratt, who founded the Carlisle Indian School in 1879, which was a prototype for off-reservation Indian boarding schools in the United States: "kill the Indian in him and save the man."[21] To achieve these "civilizing" aims, Pratt argued that it was essential to

---

edited August 6, 2021, www.thecanadianencyclopedia.ca/en/article/residential-schools-in-canada-interactive-map.

[16] *Annual Report of the Department of Indian Affairs, 1931*, 60.

[17] Brett Lee Shelton and Michael Johnson, *Trigger Points: Current State of Research on History, Impacts, and Healing Related to the United States' Indian Industrial/Boarding School Policy* (Boulder, CO: Native American Rights Fund, 2019), https://narf.org/nill/documents/trigger-points.pdf, 7. For statistical information regarding Indian residential schools in Canada, see Daniel Schwartz, "Truth and Reconciliation Commission: By the Numbers," CBC, June 2, 2015, www.cbc.ca/news/indigenous/truth-and-reconciliation-commission-by-the-numbers-1.3096185.

[18] David Wallace Adams, *Education for Extinction: American Indians and the Boarding School Experience, 1875–1928*, 2nd rev. ed. (Lawrence: University of Kansas Press, 2020), 31.

[19] Carl Schurz, "Present Aspects of the Indian Problem," *North American Review* 133, no. 296 (1881): 17.

[20] Schurz, "Present Aspects of the Indian Problem," 24-29.

[21] Schurz, "Present Aspects of the Indian Problem," 56.

quarantine Indigenous children.²² This same mentality was operative in Canada. Canadian Prime Minister John A. MacDonald stated:

> When the school is on the reserve, the child lives with its parents, who are savages, and though he may learn to read and write, his habits and training mode of thought are Indian. He is simply a savage who can read and write. It has been strongly impressed upon myself, as head of the Department, that Indian children should be withdrawn as much as possible from the parental influence, and the only way to do that would be to put them in central training industrial schools where they will acquire the habits and modes of thought of white men.²³

As Danny speaks on this issue with mostly non-Indigenous congregations, he poses a simple question that we'll pose now: *What would you think and how would you feel toward a government and a religion that systematically came after your children?* In the reading that follows, we focus on stories from boarding school survivors from the United States as we discuss the book of Daniel.²⁴

The opening stories of Daniel resonate with Indigenous peoples on Turtle Island insofar as they tell of children being forcibly removed from their ancestral land and placed in residential schools where they would be educated and civilized in a manner that served the economic, political, and religious interests of the dominating society. In the aftermath of the fall of Jerusalem and the trail of tears to Babylon, the opening story focuses on four exceptionally bright young Israelite men of noble birth, Daniel, Hananiah, Mishael,

---

²²K. Tsianina Lomawaima, *They Call It Prairie Light: The Story of Chilocco Indian School* (Lincoln: University of Nebraska Press, 1994), 5.

²³"Official report of the debates of the House of Commons of the Dominion of Canada," May 9, 1883, 1107-8.

²⁴Some helpful resources for learning about the history and experiences of First Nations peoples in Canadian residential schools include J. R. Miller, *Shingwauk's Vision: A History of Native Residential Schools* (Toronto: University of Toronto Press, 1996); John S. Milloy, *A National Crime: The Canadian Government and the Residential School System, 1879–1986* (Winnipeg, MB: University of Manitoba Press, 1999); Roland Chrisjohn, Sherri Young, and Michael Maraun, *The Circle Game: Shadows and Substance in the Indian Residential School Experience in Canada*, rev. ed. (Penticton, BC: Theytus Books, 2006); Aimée Craft and the Truth and Reconciliation Committee of Canada, *A Knock on the Door: The Essential History of the Residential Schools from the Truth and Reconciliation Commission of Canada* (Winnipeg, MB: University of Manitoba Press, 2016); and the National Centre for Truth and Reconciliation hosted by the University of Manitoba, www.nctr.ca, which includes the official publications coming out of the Truth and Reconciliation Commission of Canada.

and Azariah, who were brought to the palace to be taught "the literature and language of the Chaldeans" for three years to eventually serve within the king's court (Dan 1:4). King Nebuchadnezzar's selection of promising Israelites from royal or noble lineages shares some similarities with many of the first children who were sent to Carlisle Indian School and whose parents were chiefs and leaders of their tribes, including Luther Standing Bear (Sicangu and Oglala Lakota). Luther Standing Bear remembers that when his father, a chief among the Sicangu, was approached by "sweet talking" white men who were looking for volunteers to attend Carlisle, Luther was among the first to volunteer to prove to his father that he was "honored with a brave son." While the story of Daniel does not recount what the young men experienced while being forcibly removed from Jerusalem to Babylon, Luther Standing Bear recounts the unsympathetic gazes of curious white townsfolk and the hateful jeers that met them at each new stop between South Dakota and Pennsylvania—"the conquerors looking upon the conquered." And so the "civilizing process" to kill the Indian to save something worthwhile to the interest of the state began—in the words of Luther Standing Bear, "killing us as it went."[25]

One of the first strategies of assimilation that the palace master, Ashpenaz, imposed on Daniel and his friends was to give them proper "civilized" names that would be easily recognizable to the dominant culture: "Daniel he called Belteshazzar, Hananiah he called Shadrach, Mishael he called Meshach, and Azariah he called Abednego" (Dan 1:7). Like the palace master, US agents, ministers, priests, and nuns gave children new, "Christian" names, or in the case of some Canadian residential schools, children were fully dehumanized by simply being assigned a number for a name.[26] Again, it is worthwhile to listen to Luther Standing Bear:

> Almost immediately our names were changed to those in common use in the English language. Instead of translating our names into English and calling Zinkcaziwin, Yellow Bird, and Wanbli K'leska, Spotted Eagle, which in itself would have been educational, we were just John, Henry, or Maggie, as the case

---

[25]Luther Standing Bear, *Land of the Spotted Eagle* (Lincoln: University of Nebraska Press, 1978), 231-32, 236.
[26]See the memoir by Bev Sellars, *They Called Me Number One: Secrets and Survival at an Indian Residential School* (Vancouver, BC: Talonbooks, 2013).

might be. I was told to take a pointer and select a name for myself from the list written on the blackboard. I did, and since one was just as good as another, and as I could not distinguish any difference in them, I placed the pointer on the name Luther. I then learned to call myself by that name and got used to hearing others call me by it, too.[27]

Among many Indigenous peoples, names are sacred; entire ceremonies are devoted to the process of giving names with spiritual significance. For example, among the Hopi, a name is given days after a child is born during a sunrise ceremony, in consultation with elders and family. The naming ceremony imparts a sense of destiny or a life for the child to live up to within the community. The callous practice of ascribing new names to Native Americans without much concern about their cultural meaning and significance was both disrespectful and disorienting for many children. Luther Standing Bear goes on to decry the school's policy of forbidding him and others from speaking their native languages under the threat of punishment—a policy that was standard among most residential schools.[28] It is not hard to imagine that Daniel and his friends would have been forced to speak the language of their captors and were only free to speak their ancestral Hebrew "heart language" when they were alone together.

In an attempt to maintain his purity, Daniel is determined not to "pollute himself" by eating "the king's rations or the royal wine" provided by Ashpenaz (Dan 1:8). Instead, Daniel persuades Ashpenaz to serve him and his friends only "vegetables to eat and water to drink" (Dan 1:12) and, after ten days, to test them by comparing their health and appearance against the other boys in court eating the royal rations. Daniel's refusal of the colonizer's food is a symbolic act of resistance against the presumed power and patronage of the Babylonian king.[29] It is in fact Creator, the faithful God known to Daniel's ancestors, whose power and patronage is ultimate. Anathea Portier-Young posits that this story would have been especially empowering to ancient Judeans who were refusing pressure from the Seleucid ruler Antiochus IV Epiphanes (reigned 175–164 BCE)

---

[27]Sellars, *They Called Me Number One*, 233-34.
[28]Sellars, *They Called Me Number One*, 234.
[29]Anathea Portier-Young, *Apocalypse Against Empire: Theologies of Resistance in Early Judaism* (Grand Rapids, MI: Eerdmans, 2014), 181. So also Daniel Smith-Christopher, "The Book of Daniel," in *New Interpreter's Bible* (Nashville: Abingdon, 1996), 7:40-42.

to eat defiling pork as recounted in the Maccabean literature (e.g., 1 Macc 1:63).[30]

Tragically, in contrast, thousands of Native children who attended off-reservation residential schools in the late nineteenth and early twentieth centuries would find their school "masters" less persuadable than the Babylonian palace master when it came to preserving their ancestral customs and purity concerns. It is an ironic inversion to the Daniel story that vegetables and fruit were generally withheld from the children and reserved for the priests. St. Joseph's Boarding School in Chamberlain, South Dakota, is an example, according to multiple accounts solicited by Denise K. Lajimodiere (Turtle Mountain Band of Chippewa). In contrast to the royal rations presented to Daniel, food was meager for Native children, comprising cereal, sandwiches, potatoes, coffee, and meat (which in many schools was rare or spoiled).[31] Luther Standing Bear had a similar experience at Carlisle:

> Of all the changes we were forced to make, that of diet was doubtless the most injurious, for it was immediate and drastic. White bread we had for the first meal and thereafter, as well as coffee and sugar. Had we been allowed our simple diet of meat, either boiled with soup or dried, and fruit, with perhaps a few vegetables, we should have thrived. But the change in clothing, housing, food, and confinement combined with lonesomeness was too much, and in three years nearly one half of the children from the Plains were dead and through with all earthly schools. In the graveyard at Carlisle most of the graves are those of little ones.[32]

Whereas Daniel's self-imposed meager diet of vegetables and water sustained and fattened him and his friends, the impoverished diets of Native children, who were forbidden to maintain their ancestral ways in the Babylon of boarding schools, depleted their spirits and left them lean and susceptible to illness.

In Daniel 3, the Babylonian king, Nebuchadnezzar, demands that everyone worship and bow before a golden statue made in his image or suffer the absurd and cruel punishment of being thrown into a fiery furnace (Dan 3:1-6). Hananiah, Mishael, and Azariah are soon identified as not conforming

---

[30]Portier-Young, *Apocalypse Against Empire*, 182.
[31]Denise K. Lajimodiere, *Stringing Rosaries* (Fargo: North Dakota State University Press, 2019), 33-34, 52.
[32]Standing Bear, *Land of the Spotted Eagle*, 234.

themselves to these "civilized" religious practices endorsed by the state and stubbornly maintaining their ancestral spirituality, which prohibits the worship of such images (Dan 3:7-18). Then the three friends are bound and thrown into the furnace, which for an extra measure of vindictiveness was heated up seven times more than normal such that the flames even killed the guards who tossed the friends into the fire. But miraculously, the three friends are unaffected, and a divine figure is seen to be present in solidarity with them in vindication of their loyalty to their ancestral religious values (Dan 3:19-28). And of course, there is the punishment of Daniel being thrown into the lion's den for not exclusively worshiping the Persian king Darius in Daniel 6.

Like the Babylonian and Persian kings, those who operated Indian boarding schools had a cruel and evil flair for the absurd when it came to doling out punishments to Native children who sought to maintain their ancestral customs. Basil Brave Heart, who attended the Holy Rosary Mission School on Pine Ridge Reservation in South Dakota (now renamed Red Cloud Indian School), describes the following punishments for speaking Lakota:

> We were not allowed to speak our language and our mouths were washed with soap if we did. This was done to some of us but not to everyone. Another punishment for some was to hold a rubber band between our front teeth and pull it ourselves and snap it back to hit the lips. Another was to be put in a corner facing the corner, or to be put in a dark closet and left for some time.[33]

In *Stringing Rosaries*, Denise K. Lajimodiere records the testimonies of boarding school survivors who detailed the traumatizing indignities they endured as children. Survivors recounted being sexually abused by those who supervised them, including priests, nuns, and older students; being made to kneel on broomsticks; being burned on their heads by kerosene to kill off potential lice; being beaten with leather straps, wooden paddles, and by gangs of undersupervised children; being punished for wetting the bed by having their faces rubbed in urine; receiving insufficient medical treatment; and lacking meaningful emotional connections with healthy adults.[34] The

---

[33]Brave Heart, *Spiritual Journey*, 43.
[34]Lajimodiere, *Stringing Rosaries*, 13-14, 24-26, 35, 44-46, 53-55, 64, 66, 77, 79, 105, 112, 124, 127-28, 149, 188-92, 215-16, 218, 271. Some children were beaten for wetting the bed (55, 64, 105, 166). See also the chapter "Illness and Death," in Brenda J. Child, *Boarding School Seasons: American Indian Families, 1900–1940* (Lincoln: University of Nebraska Press, 1998), 55-68.

punishments detailed by Lajimodiere are mirrored in the hundreds of survivor testimonials gathered during Canada's Truth and Reconciliation Commission.[35] Similar to Daniel's fate in the den of lions, one survivor of the St. Joseph's Catholic boarding school in Chamberlain, South Dakota, was locked in the pantry cellar for three days for cracking an egg.[36] Readers of Daniel might wonder whether and where the fourth person with the appearance like "one of the gods" (Dan 3:25) might have been present in solidarity amid the unusual punishments these Native survivors endured.

The burns and gouges sustained from the furnaces and lions' dens of boarding schools had lasting effects on residential school survivors and their children. Ursula Running Bear, who studies public health and whose parents and grandparents attended Indian boarding schools, has analyzed data detailing the mental-health disorders and the use of health services among Plains Indians to understand how childhood trauma resulting from boarding school experiences has adversely affected this demographic. Running Bear and her colleagues observed that the assessed quality of life of those Plains Indians who had attended boarding schools was significantly lower than those who had not.[37] Those who had attended boarding schools were 44 percent more likely to report chronic physical health conditions, including tuberculosis and risks of cancer.[38] "I believe every single one of my brothers and sisters have some form of post-traumatic stress disorder," one Chippewa boarding school survivor told Lajimodiere.[39] Whenever she is in institutional spaces, she has flashbacks of her boarding school experience.

Children and grandchildren of boarding school survivors have also found themselves caught in intergenerational cycles of physical abuse, arrested emotional development, and addictions. Reflecting on her parents' and grandparents' experiences, Lajimodiere recognized that "their only parenting

---

[35]*The Survivors Speak: A Report of the Truth and Reconciliation Commission of Canada* (Truth and Reconciliation Commission of Canada, 2015).
[36]*Survivors Speak*, 34.
[37]Ursula Running Bear, Janette Beals, Carol E. Kaufman, Spero M. Manson, and the AI-SUPERPFP Team, "Boarding School Attendance and Physical Health Status of Northern Plains Tribes," *Applied Research Quality Life* 13 (2018): 633-45.
[38]Ursula Running Bear, Zaneta M. Thayer, Calvin D. Croy, Carol E. Kaufman, Spero M. Manson, and the AI-SUPERPFP Team, "The Impact of Individual and Parental American Indian Boarding School Attendance on Chronic Physical Health of Northern Plains Tribes," *Family & Community Health* 42, no. 1 (2019): 1-7.
[39]Lajimodiere, *Stringing Rosaries*, 56.

model was strict military-style corporeal punishment ... combined with a total lack of love and caring experience there, along with the absolute forbiddance of tribal cultural traditions."[40] Eddie, Chris's great-uncle, could not help but wonder to what extent his own father's binge drinking and physical abuse of his wife and children resulted from trauma experienced in the boarding schools exaggerated by his experience in World War II. But what model of parenting did his own father experience other than the military discipline shown to him at boarding school?

REPENTANCE, (RE)CONCILIATION, AND RESURGENCE

In both the aftermaths of Hananiah's, Mishael's, and Azariah's perseverance within the fiery furnace (Dan 3) and Daniel's survival of the lion's den (Dan 6), each of the rulers responsible for these indignities recognized their mistake, honored and recognized the powerful authority of the Israelites' God (Dan 3:28-29; 6:25-28), and made some effort toward setting matters right. King Nebuchadnezzar gives Hananiah, Mishael, and Azariah promotions (Dan 3:30), and King Darius punishes those who conspired against Daniel and restores Daniel to his position (Dan 6:24, 28). It is also true that these leaders all fall back into their old ways in one way or another later on. After extolling the praise of Daniel's God and promoting the young Hebrew men in Daniel 2, Nebuchadnezzar still demands the incineration of Hebrews in Daniel 3. And as our modern histories have shown, Indigenous peoples are still gracious and willing to work with their persecutors and hope for the best from them, just as Daniel will interpret another dream for Nebuchadnezzar in Daniel 4.

Like the Babylonian and Persian kings, on behalf of the Canadian government the Canadian Prime Minister Stephen Harper apologized to Indigenous survivors and former students of Indian residential schools. Harper's formal statement recognized the generational harm that the government caused in removing children from their families and cultures and in placing them in institutions where children often experienced abuse and neglect. The formal apology asked for forgiveness and recognized that the attitudes and beliefs that inspired the residential schools have no place in Canadian society. It acknowledged the ongoing work of healing and reconciliation that has been

---

[40]Lajimodiere, *Stringing Rosaries*, 267.

underway among First Nations people and has materialized in the 2007 Indian Residential Schools Settlement, the Truth and Reconciliation Commission of Canada, and the ongoing work of truth and reconciliation in Canada. Like Nebuchadnezzar's waffling back and forth between praising the young Hebrew men and seeking their demise, the Canadian government after the apology has done well in some areas but in others has continued its colonizing ways.[41]

On October 25, 2024, President Joe Biden traveled to the Gila River Indian Community in Laveen Village, Arizona, and issued a long-overdue formal apology on behalf of the United States for the Indian boarding school program. Recognizing that apologies without action ring hollow, the president highlighted his administration's accomplishments and commitments to support Indigenous peoples, including improving tribal consultation in federal decision making and making significant federal investments in tribal communities.[42] This apology came as a response to the first recommendation of a historic two-volume investigative report into boarding schools led by Deb Haaland and the assistant secretary of Indian affairs, Bryan Newland (Bay Mills Indian Community).[43] These historic reports identify Indian boarding schools, marked and unmarked burial sites, the names and tribal affiliations of students, and religious institutions that

---

[41] Stephen Harper, "Statement of Apology to Former Students of Indian Residential Schools," Government of Canada, June 11, 2008, www.rcaanc-cirnac.gc.ca/eng/1100100015644/1571589171655. It should be noted that the apology and its immediate results saved the Canadian government billions of dollars, as a small settlement was agreed to as opposed to the avalanche of cases from residential school survivors. While Indigenous leaders accepted the apology, it was with some reservation, as right actions are to follow an apology. In the case of Stephen Harper, some have pointed to laws enacted after the apology as evidence that his apology rang hollow. See Shauna MacKinnon, "Fast Facts: The Harper 'Apology': Residential Schools and Bill C-10," Canadian Centre for Policy Alternatives, January 24, 2012, https://policyalternatives.ca/publications/commentary/fast-facts-harper-apology-residential-schools-and-bill-c-10.

[42] See "Remarks by President Biden on the Biden-Harris Administration's Record of Delivering for Tribal Communities, Including Keeping His Promise to Make This Historic Visit to Indian Country," The White House, October 25, 2024, https://bidenwhitehouse.archives.gov/briefing-room/speeches-remarks/2024/10/25/remarks-by-president-biden-on-the-biden-harris-administrations-record-of-delivering-for-tribal-communities-including-keeping-his-promise-to-make-this-historic-visit-to-indian-country-lavee/; see also Kevin K. Washburn, "The March of Co-management—The Biden-Harris Administration's Expanding Work with Tribes," *U Iowa Legal Studies Research Paper no. 2023-25* (July 2023), http://dx.doi.org/10.2139/ssrn.4502951.

[43] Bryan Newland, "Federal Indian Boarding School Initiative Investigative Report," vols. 1-2, US Department of the Interior Indian Affairs, 2022–2024, www.bia.gov/sites/default/files/dup/inline-files/bsi_investigative_report_may_2022_508.pdf; www.bia.gov/sites/default/files/media_document/doi_federal_indian_boarding_school_initiative_investigative_report_vii_final_508_compliant.pdf.

operated schools. These reports call for federal actions and policies to invest in remedies against the present-day impacts from boarding schools, repatriate the remains of children and former school sites to tribes, and ensure that American citizens are educated about this dark period of US history.

The United States trails behind the historic steps that Canada took in the Indian Residential Schools Settlement Agreement and its payment of billions of dollars in reparations to Indigenous survivors, the subsequent Truth and Reconciliation Commission and the vision it cast for all sectors of society in the 94 Calls to Action.[44]

The tragedy of juxtaposing the stories in the book of Daniel with stories from First Nations who experienced residential schools is that the biblical stories of Daniel's resistance, survival, and relative flourishing in Babylon were certainly known to the Christians who operated these boarding schools. One can only imagine how the experience of thousands of Native children would have been different had Christian bureaucrats, priests, ministers, and nuns entertained the idea that *they* might be the Babylonians with respect to these displaced children under their care. What a shameful missed opportunity in both biblical interpretation and Christian imagination. As Willie Jennings has argued, it was the failure of theological and social imagination by the colonizers to envision God's work in a "new world" and the failure of the colonizers to see themselves as anything other than the Israelites conquering the Promised Land.[45] This hard work of Christian imagination and honesty could have changed countless Indigenous lives.

It's not just governments that stand in need of repentance but Christians too. While it is a common refrain among people to excuse those of the past by saying such things as, "They held beliefs common to their time," or "They did not know what was happening," these excuses are invalid in light of the evidence. The architects of the residential and boarding schools knew exactly what they were doing and why they were doing it. And in Canada, the government knew of the appalling conditions through a study it commissioned and then

---

[44]Truth and Reconciliation Commission of Canada, "Truth and Reconciliation Commission of Canada: Calls to Action," www.trc.ca. See also the dashboard of sorts by the CBC, tracking progress on the Truth and Reconciliation Commission of Canada calls to action, www.cbc.ca/news interactives/beyond-94/.

[45]See Willie James Jennings, *The Christian Imagination: Theology and the Origins of Race* (New Haven, CT: Yale University Press, 2010).

later ignored by Dr. Peter Bryce.[46] This excuse is even more empty as we think about Christians who were involved in the running of these schools and advocating these policies, as we hold to the same scriptural teachings on the dignity of all humanity. Indeed, there were some notable Christian voices through this period that spoke prophetically against the government and church. In Mi'kmaq territory, missionary Silas Rand is a notable example who advocated on behalf of the Mi'kmaq, but these voices were few and often ignored.[47]

Yet another common response is to balk at the idea that the present generation is in any way accountable or responsible. Our friend Anna Robbins, the president of Acadia Divinity College (who also happens to be Danny's favorite boss besides his wife), has eloquently composed a biblical case for why modern evangelical Christians ought to adopt a collective posture of repentance.[48] White evangelical Christians, in our experience, have seemed allergic to the idea that they might have anything to repent of when they were not individually responsible or involved, to say nothing of any sort of ongoing responsibility or perhaps even (dare we say it) reparations. This is ironic, as these same Christians often have no trouble with the idea that the sin of Adam and Eve has pervasive and lasting effects on themselves and their society, which invites a posture of repentance. But we get it; the very concept of collective guilt and repentance goes against modern Euroamerican notions of individual responsibility and fairness.

However, as Robbins shows, the stories of Scripture are replete with calls for group repentance.[49] The prophets Jonah, Ezekiel, and Amos call entire nations to repentance, and Israel itself is called to repent and engage in rituals of collective repentance during the annual ceremony of Yom Kippur (Lev 16:29-34).

---

[46]Peter H. Bryce, *The Story of a National Crime: An Appeal for Justice to the Indians of Canada* (Ottawa, ON: James Hope & Sons, 1922), https://archive.org/details/storyofnationalc00brycuoft. Bryce's work is also discussed throughout the well-documented work by Milloy, *National Crime*.

[47]On Rand, see Dorothy May Lovesey, *To Be a Pilgrim: A Biography of Silas Tertius Rand, 1810–1889, Nineteenth Century Protestant Missionary to the Micmac*, Baptist Heritage in Atlantic Canada 13 (Hantsport, NS: Lancelot, 1992); Bridget C. J. Graham, "From Missionary to Linguist: An Account of Silas Tertius Rand, 1810–1889" (MA thesis, Dalhousie University, 2017); H. Daniel Zacharias, "250+ Years of Baptists in Mi'kma'ki," *Journal of NAIITS* 16 (2018): 79-93.

[48]Anna Robbins, "No Reconciliation Without Repentance: Accepting Collective Responsibility For Historical Sin," *Journal of NAIITS* 13 (2015): 119-34.

[49]See also Joel Kaminsky, *Corporate Responsibility in the Hebrew Bible* (Sheffield: Sheffield Academic Press, 1995).

Even passages such as Ezekiel 18, which on the surface seems to represent a theological shift from ancestral, corporate guilt to individual responsibility for sins (i.e., Ezek 18:4: "only the one who sins will die"), actually leaves the ancient Hebrew notion of national guilt intact. According to Hebrew Bible scholars such as Christopher Wright and Joseph Blenkinsopp, Ezekiel is challenging his audiences to recognize that their present experience of displacement and hardships under Babylonian dominance can't simply be blamed on their parents but that they too bear responsibility insofar as they *continue* to disobey Creator's instructions as their parents had.[50] Robbins declares:

> We are called to repent then, of the atrocities that the church and the government visited on Aboriginal people, not only because of the sins of those who went before, and because we have benefitted from past exploitations, but because we ourselves are guilty. We also must own *our* responsibility for perpetuating sinful actions against Indigenous people, through neglect or offense. Repentance is necessary because we are guilty; repentance is possible because we may yet be forgiven.[51]

A posture of repentance that recognizes the gravity of the depravities committed against Indigenous peoples makes way for reconciliation between churches and Indigenous peoples. But what can reconciliation look like?

In 2022, the pope visited Canada to officially apologize to First Nations peoples for the evil harms committed by the Catholic Church, which operated 66 out of Canada's 139 residential schools. While this happened much later than what was desired in the Truth and Reconciliation Commission Call to Action 58, this was nonetheless an important moment for Indigenous peoples, especially those who were still devoted Catholics. While the Catholic dioceses in Canada have set a goal to spend around $80 million by 2027 toward efforts in healing and reconciliation, both First Nations leaders and church leaders recognize these as the "first step in a long journey of reconciliation."[52] The

---

[50]Christopher Wright, *The Message of Ezekiel* (Leicester, UK: Inter-Varsity Press, 2001), 188; Joseph Blenkinsopp, *Ezekiel* (Louisville, KY: Westminster John Knox, 1990), 82.
[51]Robbins, "No Reconciliation Without Repentance," 128-29.
[52]Nicole Winfield and Rob Gillies, "Pope's Apology to Indigenous Peoples for Abuse at Residential Schools Insufficient, Canada Says," PBS News Hour, July 28, 2022, www.pbs.org/newshour/world/popes-apology-to-indigenous-peoples-for-abuse-at-residential-schools-insufficient-canada-says. See also Nicole Winfield and Peter Smith, "Pope Apologizes for 'Catastrophic' School Policy in Canada," Associated Press, July 26, 2022, https://apnews.com/article/pope-francis-canada-apology-visit-137ad23719603e9d370257f257ec0163.

Catholic Church ran the largest number of residential schools in Canada. All of the other church parties to the settlement agreement have responded to the Truth and Reconciliation Commission and continue in their work of reconciliation to one degree or another. Most of the churches that fall outside the denominations that ran the residential and boarding schools have not seen any immediate need to enter into reconciliation efforts, and others who are more conscious of the issue have often struggled to understand their responsibilities toward the ongoing work of reconciliation.

If reconciliation presumes a right relationship to return to, what if there was no relationship to begin with? The reality is that there are places and spaces on Turtle Island that have no relationship to reconcile to. For example, while there are the numbered treaties across Canada, as well as the Peace and Friendship treaties in the Atlantic provinces, most of the lands on the west coast of Canada are not governed by treaties.[53] Instead, in the absence of treaties, Canadian Parliament simply declared itself sovereign over such lands and its peoples, along with all Indigenous peoples and lands, through the 1875 Indian Act.[54] In such spaces where no original treaty exists, there is no right relationship to try to return to. In such cases, the work of *conciliation* or building new relationships is what is needed. Mark Charles (Diné) states:

> Conciliation does not happen without truth telling. Conciliation without truth is trying to bring health without a comprehensive diagnosis. Truth telling requires the deeper examination of the existing narratives and the unearthing of the dysfunction surrounding those narratives. The broken system and the dysfunctional theological imagination that the broken system emerges from must be exposed.[55]

As much as people often desire a neat and tidy story, or simply want "the ten simple steps to reconciliation," the reality is much more complicated.[56]

---

[53]Michelle Filice, "Numbered Treaties," in *The Canadian Encyclopedia*, August 3, 2016, www.the canadianencyclopedia.ca/en/article/numbered-treaties; Sarah Isabel Wallace, "Peace and Friendship Treaties," in *The Canadian Encyclopedia*, last edited February 17, 2023, www.thecanadian encyclopedia.ca/en/article/peace-and-friendship-treaties.

[54]See Bob Joseph, *21 Things You May Not Know About the Indian Act: Helping Canadians Make Reconciliation with Indigenous Peoples a Reality* (Port Coquitlam, BC: Indigenous Relations, 2018).

[55]Mark Charles and Soong-Chan Rah, *Unsettling Truths: The Ongoing, Dehumanizing Legacy of the Doctrine of Discovery*, ProQuest ed. (Downers Grove, IL: InterVarsity Press, 2019), 15.

[56]For more on the realities and difficulties of reconciliation in Canada, see Jody Wilson-Raybould, *True Reconciliation: How To Be a Force for Change* (Toronto: McClelland & Stewart, 2022).

Moving from reconciliation toward healing, which encompasses the restoration and resurgence of what was lost in the residential and boarding school experiences, Indigenous people can find encouragement in Daniel's prophetic message to never give up one's allegiance and fidelity to one's ancestral customs and understanding of the divine. Daniel models a kind of faithful code-switching, that is, a deft balancing act of negotiating the cultural demands of his Jewish faith within the Babylonian court, a survival strategy familiar to Indigenous peoples negotiating the maintenance of their Native heritage within the contexts of Canadian and US churches, institutions, and society.[57] Following the angel Gabriel's encouragement to Daniel that "the people who acknowledge their God [in keeping their ancestral covenant and customs] will stand strong and will act" (Dan 11:32), Native readers of Daniel can regard their efforts to revitalize their ancestral ways and faith as providing a stable foundation for their healing and flourishing. Lajimodiere shares that the survivors she spoke with "expressed that an individual way for each to heal their *soul wound*, both personally and as tribes, would be through either a governmental apology, therapy, or a return to American Indian spirituality, including language and ceremony."[58] One such survivor, Roger White Owl (Hidatsa, Ojibwe), shared with Lajimodiere: "Healing from the hurts of boarding school is hard to do. What's necessary for us to do to get better is we need to forgive, to get rid of that hatred. Once you can forgive, then you can truly heal. To help heal the reservation would be a return to our ancestral ways . . . that were given to us by the Creator."[59]

Reflecting on his own road to recovery, Basil Brave Heart writes:

> Through all of this, the teachings my grandmother gave me were strong, to not hold resentments or prejudice or hate against anyone because it would poison you. To hate was not what the sacred pipe taught. My grandma told me to practice compassion and forgiveness so I could live my life without carrying the burden of hate and resentment.[60]

---

[57] See also Robert D. Miller, "Daniel and Friends at Carlisle Indian School," *Stellenbosch Theological Journal* 7, no. 1 (2021): 12-13, who summarizes the message of Daniel as follows: "Keep the traditions, trust in the Lord, and code-switch as much as necessary."

[58] Lajimodiere, *Stringing Rosaries*, 14, emphasis original. On the notion of "soul wounds," see Eduardo Duran, *Healing the Soul Wound: Trauma-Informed Counseling for Indigenous Communities*, 2nd ed. (New York: Teachers College Press, 2019).

[59] Lajimodiere, *Stringing Rosaries*, 47-48.

[60] Brave Heart, *Spiritual Journey*, 47.

It cannot be stressed enough that within our communities, ancestral wisdom, and spiritual ceremonies, Indigenous peoples have an abundance of good medicine at hand for healing our soul wounds.[61]

Reflecting on what reconciliation might look like between Indigenous peoples and missionaries in light of Indian residential schools, Patty Krawec (Anishinaabe) poetically brings together an Anishinaabe story with the Gospel of Matthew. After describing Herod's slaughter of Israelite children, the Gospel of Matthew recalls the prophet Jeremiah's lament (Jer 31:15; cf. Mt 2:18):

> A voice is heard in Ramah,
> > weeping and wailing.
> It's Rachel crying for her children;
> > she refuses to be consoled,
> > because her children are no more.

In the Anishinaabe story about how humans overhunted the deer despite their ancient promise to take care of one another, the deer, like Rachel, refused to be comforted and left humans without a reliable source of meat. Native people too, Krawec states, can refuse to be comforted in light of stories of (sexual) abuse, forced labor, and cultural genocide that occurred at some of these boarding schools. Just as Herod slaughtered Israelite children because he felt that his authority was threatened, so too did the Christian church harm Indigenous children. But what does sincere repentance and reconciliation look like? In her Anishinaabe story, the people take a season to reflect on their role in breaking a harmonious relationship with the deer and take full responsibility for their harm, eventually reconciling with the deer. And so Krawec holds out hope for reconciliation and peace. The truth can be taught, policies can change, sovereignty can be respected, land can be restored.[62]

In the United States, organizations such as the National Native American Boarding School Healing Coalition are leading the way in educating the public, advocating for new federal and state policies, and making resources available to promote healing.[63] Within the scope of theological institutes,

---

[61]See esp. Shelton and Johnson, *Trigger Points*, 62-79.
[62]Patty Krawec, "Refusing to Be Comforted: What Rachel's Lament Teaches Us About the Work of Repairing Relationships," Sojourners, December 20, 2021, https://sojo.net/articles/refusing-be-comforted-krawec.
[63]See the National Boarding School Healing Coalition website, www.boardingschoolhealing.org. Allies are invited to donate to this organization to support their work.

NAIITS: An Indigenous Learning Community—the first accredited theological institute that is Indigenous designed, developed, delivered, and governed—is working alongside of Indigenous counselors and ministers to develop trauma-informed, asset-based pastoral care and counseling courses that recognize the legacy of boarding schools.[64] And while a few Indian boarding schools still exist today, including Sherman Indian School (Riverside, CA), Red Cloud Indian School (formerly Holy Rosary, Pine Ridge, SD), St. Joseph's Indian School (Chamberlain, SD), Chemawa Indian School (Salem, OR), and the Jones Academy (Hartshorne, OK), they are generally operated by the Bureau of Indian Education, tribal members and nations, and repentant allies who seek to promote Indigenous culture and heritage. If the one with "the appearance of a god" (Dan 3:25) was difficult to identify amid the furnaces of the boarding schools, then this divine figure is certainly dancing in solidarity amid the renewed circle dances, medicine wheels, and long walks toward healing, reconciliation, and resurgence of our cultures.

THE WRITING ON THE WALL FOR WITHHOLDING NATIVE ARTIFACTS

An Indigenous reading of Daniel also notices the story's concern over the Babylonians' pillaging and boastful display of Judean sacred artifacts, which resonates with Indigenous concerns over Canada's, Britain's, and the United States' pillaging and display of their own sacred artifacts and ancestral remains. Returning to the opening chapter of Daniel, it's easy to miss how the second verse notes how the Babylonians pillaged the vessels of the temple of Jerusalem and stored them within the treasury of Babylon's gods (Dan 1:2). In his commentary on Daniel, Daniel Smith-Christopher states that these temple goods, now placed on display, served as a symbol of "the Jew's subordinate position in relation to Babylonian imperial and religious power."[65] The temple vessels, turned trophies of war, were removed from their proper

---

[64]See www.naiits.com. On the trauma-informed training that is being used within NAIITS, see, for example, Michelle Oberwise Lacock and Carol Lakota Eastin, "We Hold Our Stories in Blankets," in *Women Out of Order: Risking Change and Creating Care in a Multi-cultural World*, ed. Jeanne Stevenson-Moessner and Teresa Snorton (Minneapolis: Fortress, 2009), 93-114.

[65]Smith-Christopher, "Book of Daniel," 38-39. Smith-Christopher's commentary is exemplary among commentaries on Daniel in that as a non-Indigenous scholar, he incorporates into this reflection insights gleaned from reading Daniel with Lakota Christians and traditionalists on the Rosebud Reservation in South Dakota.

ceremonial settings and served a new purpose. They now served to display the glory and power of Babylon's gods and empire as they sat in a subordinate position within Babylon's temple.

The story of these sacred vessels continues in Daniel 5, where King Belshazzar, the son of King Nebuchadnezzar, in a drunken state orders for the vessels from the Jerusalem temple to be used for serving wine to his royal entourage (Dan 5:1-2), thereby relegating their status even further, from sacred use to ordinary use. From these consecrated cups, the royal party drinks and praises the Babylonian gods, whom they toast for making Babylon great. And just then, the record scratches and the script of this party scene suddenly turns to horror, as detached human fingers begin writing on the palace walls an elusive message: "MENE, MENE, TEKEL, and PARSIN" (Dan 5:25). The reaction of King Belshazzar is meant to be both graphic and humorous. Despite a number of differences between English translations of Daniel 5:6, the Hebrew indicates that Belshazzar crapped his pants.[66] When it becomes clear that none of the king's wise men can interpret the writing on the wall, Daniel is called in. Daniel wastes no time chiding the Babylonian king for his hubris—after all, the king should have learned to walk gently after witnessing how the God of the Judeans had stripped the sanity from his own father, the previous ruler, for his excessive pride (Dan 5:17-22; 4:28-37). On account of the king's flagrant disregard for the sacredness of Judean temple vessels and not honoring the true Creator, Daniel explains that the ghastly fingers spelled the doom of the king and his kingdom, which would soon be given to the Persians (Dan 5:23-25). That very night, King Belshazzar is killed, and Darius the Mede will reign.

The script didn't change for imperial British, US, and Canadian powers as they discovered, desecrated, stole, and acquired sacred Indigenous ceremonial instruments and regalia, funerary objects, and items of cultural patrimony that should never have been alienated from a tribe's designated caretaker. This even includes the bodily remains of our ancestors. These sacred items of Indigenous culture were then displayed and stored in museums, libraries, and academic institutions across Turtle Island and in museums in Europe for exhibition and study, and sometimes simply for "safekeeping" where no one but museum staff has access. Recalling how the Babylonians displayed the temple vessels in a

---

[66] See Al Wolters, "Untying the King's Knots: Physiology and Wordplay in Daniel 5," *Journal of Biblical Literature* 110 (1991): 117-22.

parade-like fashion, Smith-Christopher juxtaposes this image of imperial power to how Methodist minister Colonel Chivington paraded the corpses and body parts from the 150 Cheyenne men, women, and children he and his soldiers massacred at Sand Creek in 1864. "A society based on injustice must find ways to sustain its existence," Smith-Christopher reflects. "It must appear to be more civilized, more advanced, more cultured than those conquered, who must, therefore, be portrayed as bloodthirsty, disrespectful of the land, heathen."[67] This barbaric story of Chivington, juxtaposed with Smith-Christopher's insights, can only be reconciled by the diseased imagination of early settlers, who viewed Indigenous peoples as subhuman and barriers to their manifest destiny.

In 1990, US Congress passed the Native American Graves Protection and Repatriation Act, ending, as Smith-Christopher would put it, "a centuries-long 'Belshazzar's feast.'" This act required federal agencies and institutes receiving federal funds, including museums, universities, and seminaries, to return Native American remains and cultural artifacts to their home tribes. Smith-Christopher exhorts settler Christians to reflect on how they might benefit from the privileges of their society's own "Belshazzar feasts" and "involve themselves in prophetic delivery of God's judgment on the gluttony of the hundreds of 'Belshazzar's feasts' that have victimized so many people over the centuries."[68] The return of Native American artifacts and remains is a slow-going, costly, and complicated affair, with many museums, universities, and religious institutions making little to no progress in identifying and processing tribal claims on their ancestral artifacts. Nevertheless, this is important decolonizing and just work, and we remain hopeful, as many artifacts have been returned and are in the process of being returned home.[69]

READING RESILIENCE AND ALLYSHIP IN DANIEL

It is necessary to recognize that the stories of residential schools are far more complex and nuanced than space allows to discuss. For example, K. Tsianina

---

[67] Smith-Christopher, "Book of Daniel," 84-85.
[68] Smith-Christopher, "Book of Daniel," 85.
[69] For example, see Sangita Chari and Jaimie M. N. Lavalle, *Accomplishing NAGPRA: Perspectives on the Intent, Impact, and Future of Native American Graves Protection and Repatriation Act* (Corvalis: Oregon State University Press, 2013); Logan Jaffe, Mary Hudetz, Ash Ngu, and Graham Lee Brewer, "America's Biggest Museums Fail to Return Native American Human Remains," ProPublica, updated January 11, 2023, www.propublica.org/article/repatriation-nagpra-museums-human-remains.

Lomawaima (Muscogee/Creek, unenrolled), who has researched and interviewed elders who had attended boarding schools, observes that "the schools were not monolithically destructive or successful in their assimilative goals, but the harsh reality is—for some people, they were."[70] It is also important that we do not characterize Indigenous peoples as simply victims without agency in these narratives.[71] Indigenous students, families, and their communities sometimes found resourceful and resilient ways to make schools work for them, learn valuable trades, meet future spouses, build meaningful lives, and/or simply survive.[72] When Cameron Eggie (Cree) reflects on Canada's history of residential schools, which both his grandparents navigated, he recalls the words his grandfather Alexander Bear told him before he died: "You don't get to be angry on our behalf." Eggie's grandparents made a new life for themselves despite the hardships they faced. As Eggie's aunt shared with him, "They took our identity, but they couldn't take all of it, and we created a new one."[73] When Chris thinks of a Daniel figure among those who attended Indian boarding schools, one who found favor in the court of a colonizing king and triumphed over repeated adversity, the achievement and legacy of Jim Thorpe (Osage), one of the greatest athletes of the twentieth century, comes to mind. After attending Carlisle Indian School, where he was captain of the football and basketball teams, Thorpe went on to win gold medals in the decathlon and pentathlon events at the 1912 Summer Olympic games in Stockholm.[74]

Many boarding school and Sixties Scoop survivors, like the character of Daniel, were able to take advantage of the difficult situations they were put in

---

[70]Clifford E. Trafzer, Jean A. Keller, and Lorene Sisquoc, eds., *Boarding School Blues: Revisiting American Indian Educational Experiences* (Lincoln: University of Nebraska Press, 2006), xi. See Lomawaima, *They Call It Prairie Light*.

[71]See Adams, *Education for Extinction*, 250-65. Adams lists the following examples of documented resistance among Native boarding school students: running away, passive resistance (i.e., not working, not engaging in the classroom, keeping silent, going through the motions, etc.), nicknaming officials with insulting Indian names, acts of cultural maintenance (i.e. braiding one's hair according to Lakota customs), manipulating the Indian school bureaucracy (i.e., transferring from school to school), self-medicating (i.e., ingesting hallucinogenic substances), and letter writing.

[72]See Shelton and Johnson, *Trigger Points*, 25.

[73]Cameron Eggie, interview, April 18, 2024.

[74]Child, *Boarding School Seasons*, 3. See also David Maraniss, *Path Lit by Lightning: The Life of Jim Thorpe* (New York: Simon & Schuster, 2022). Thorpe is held in such high esteem among many Natives that the *T* in T. Christopher Hoklotubbe was almost Thorpe, but his parents decided to give him another dignified name, Thomas, after his father.

and through their uncanny resilience to apply their diaspora education and skills to better their own lives and to advocate on behalf of Indigenous causes. One unexpected outcome of boarding schools was that as Native children from tribes across Turtle Island were brought together, a pan-Indian identity began to emerge.[75] This pan-Indian sentiment is captured beautifully by Native American singer, songwriter, and boarding school survivor Mitch Walking Elk (Arapaho) in his song "Indians":

> I'm Captain Jack, the Modok, Tecumseh, the Shawnee
> My people are the Hopi and Passamaquoddy....
> They put me in the boarding school and they cut off all my hair
> gave me an education, but the Apache's still in there.[76]

For modern Christians aspiring to be allies to Indigenous peoples, Smith-Christopher suggests that the Babylonian palace master Ashpenaz in the story of Daniel may be an "apt role model of resistance." He states, "Ashpenaz emerges from the power elite to have sympathy for those who suffer and resist. But like Ashpenaz, the faithful among the elite must be aware that their faith borders on treason; hence identification with, let alone sympathy for, the 'exiled' peoples may have its cost." If the book of Daniel is to remain a powerful witness to a life of resistance, may it continue to challenge readers to resist "the enticements of financial power and control over the destiny of others—such as powerful nations over the developing world—and to the enticements of luxury that come from the abuse of underpaid laborers in struggling societies."[77]

CONCLUSION: ENVISIONING THE BRIGHT PATH BEYOND BABYLON

Reading stories of Moses and Daniel from the perspective of First Nations peoples is a powerful reminder that nations, churches, educational institutions, and social welfare programs, even with the most "Christian" and "civilized" of intentions, may be more Egyptian or Babylonian than the pious Hebrew

---

[75]Lomawaima, *They Call It Prairie Light*, 129; Sally McBeth, *Ethnic Identity and the Boarding School Experience of West-Central Oklahoma American Indians* (Washington, DC: University Press of America, 1983), 141.
[76]Mitch Walking Elk, "Indians," Shaiela, 1988, cited in Child, *Boarding School Seasons*, 8.
[77]Smith-Christopher, "Book of Daniel," 45.

heroes they would like to identify with. It is only with and alongside Indigenous eyes that we can prophetically interpret the Bible as addressing our shared contexts of living in modern nation states, whose wealth and power have derived overwhelmingly from the theft of land, cultures, and childhoods of Indigenous peoples now living in diaspora in their own lands.

The grand arc of the stories that make up Christian Scripture is one of reconciliation. The reconciling work of Christ returns us to a state of right-relationship with Creator that our first parents had in the Garden of Eden, and our own work of repentance as Christians leads us to the new covenant relationship brought about by the work of Christ. In 2 Corinthians 5, Paul writes that there is something exciting at work within those who are in Christ, a new creation in which followers of Christ will be able to live in covenant harmony with Creator and one another. Paul then elaborates: "All of these new things are from God, who reconciled us to himself through Christ and who gave us the ministry of reconciliation. In other words, God was reconciling the world to himself through Christ, by not counting people's sins against them. He has trusted us with this message of reconciliation" (2 Cor 5:18-19).

If Indigenous and non-Indigenous followers of Christ have been commissioned to preach a message of God's reconciliation of the world to himself through Christ, the question remains, What does this reconciliation *actually look like* on Turtle Island? We can only begin to answer these questions in productive ways once we've spent time listening to the truths of our elders regarding how our historic relationships have been severed, and in some cases a relationship has not yet been established in earnest.

In closing, we want to share with you a story and vision from Megan Murdock Krischke (Wyandotte), who directs Native InterVarsity campus ministry. Not long ago, when Krischke was visiting Haskell Indian Nations University in Lawrence, Kansas, and praying over the campus, she experienced a powerful vision akin to Ezekiel's vision of the resurrection of the dry bones (Ezek 37). As she prayed, she suddenly saw Haskell's quad filled with Native children in school uniforms, presumably from the darker days of Haskell's past. What was extraordinary about this vision was that each time Krischke closed her eyes, she could see a young boy from that crowd standing beside her, looking up at her expectantly. This vision stayed with Krischke for some time, and she occasionally asked friends about their interpretation of the matter. Eventually, a young woman with the prophetic intuition of Daniel asked Krischke whether she had ever asked Jesus how she should respond to the boy's presence. She had not. Krischke shares what happened next:

> When I did, Jesus told me to take his hand and walk him home. So I returned to the image in prayer, took the boy's hand and told him I was going to take him home. The final image that came to me in prayer was of the two of us walking hand in hand into the sun sitting on the horizon. I came away from that time of prayer with a deep sense of assurance that the boy made it home and was welcomed into loving arms.[78]

Reflecting on her personal mystical experience, Krischke recalled how God gave prophetic words of healing to the prophet Ezekiel to speak over the bones of his ancestors, calling on sacred breath from the four directions to breathe new life into them and causing them to stand (Ezek 37:9-10). Creator then tells Ezekiel to speak Creator's words over them: "The LORD God proclaims: I'm opening your graves! I will raise you up from your graves, my people, and I will bring you to Israel's fertile land. . . . I will put my breath in you, and you will live. I will plant you on your fertile land" (Ezek 37:12, 14). Krischke's and Ezekiel's visions are operative today as some First Nations continue to walk in strength, others revitalize their ways, and still others are in the midst of coming back to life. Indeed, some literal graves are being opened as the remains of Indigenous children who died at boarding schools are finally brought home, reburied, and prayed over in their ancestral lands. We believe that Creator's Spirit, the fourth man in the fire, still dances among our peoples, in solidarity with the practices and processes of truth telling, healing, reparations, and repatriations. As old ways are recovered and new ways are brought into existence, Indigenous resilience and sovereignty is basking in the light of the sun on the horizon and being animated by the breath of the Spirit.

---

[78] Megan Murdock Krischke, "5th Sunday of Lent," *Unbound: The Intersections of Faith and Justice*, February 19, 2023, https://justiceunbound.org/5th-sunday-of-lent-2.

7

READING WHILE RED(BONE)

Come and Get Your Love and Ceremony

IN 2014, THE CINEMA-VIEWING WORLD was (re)introduced to one of the greatest rock songs of the 1970s in the opening title scene to the Marvel blockbuster *Guardians of the Galaxy*. In this scene, Star-Lord, played by Chris Pratt, is about to enter a mysterious temple to loot a forgotten treasure. To pump himself up, he hits play on his '80s Walkman headphones. Then a drumbeat drops and a familiar baseline fills the theater. You may be hearing it already. The joyful anthem is "Come and Get Your Love." And while the song may be well known as a rock classic on Turtle Island, the band is less known among younger audiences. The group behind the hit, Redbone, was the first Native American band to have a top-five hit on the Billboard Hot 100. Redbone is Cajun slang for "mixed blood" and reflects the diverse family heritage of Pat and Lolly Vegas (Yaqui, Shoshone, and Mexican). The song itself is a raucous invitation to discover and claim the universal love we all deeply desire. In a recent interview, Pat Vegas explained: "The song has a deeper meaning of a spiritual, religious and universal love. When we say in the song 'Come and get your love, get it from the main vine,' that connects to Mother Earth. We are all longing for love."[1]

On February 22, 1974, Redbone was invited to play this song on Burt Sugarman's Midnight Special, which they opened with Tony Bellamy (Yaqui, Mexican), one of the guitarists, performing a "fancy dance" dressed in full regalia.[2] For many TV viewers, this was the first powwow dance they had ever

---

[1] Sandra Hale Schulman, "Why 'Come and Get Your Love' Now? After 46 Years 'The Time Has Come,'" Indian Country Today, August 3, 2020, https://ictnews.org/news/after-46-years-redbone-releases-come-and-get-your-love-video.

[2] Redbone, "Come and Get Your Love (Live on Midnight Special)," YouTube, June 9, 2010, 4:46, https://youtu.be/OnJqFrVD3uE?si=xgZCDob8PZHlKNxF.

seen. In 2020, forty-six years after the song's initial debut, a fresh music video was released. The video incorporates mixed-media visuals as it follows an Indigenous man's quest to find love across time, place, and even outer space.[3] It's a colorful pastiche of past, present, and futuristic artwork mixed with playful satire that tells a familiar hero's journey in which the protagonist's quest for love and identity takes them to the furthest reaches of the unknown territory only to find themselves returning home, in this case to the protagonist's rich heritage, to find the love that was always there. This song encapsulates Indigenous joy. This song encapsulates Indigenous life at its best and celebrates the assets inherent in Indigenous identity. And surprisingly, this song resonates deeply with the heartbeat-drumbeat of Turtle Island hermeneutics, grounded as it is in an asset-based theology. A resonance that is unapologetically, authentically, and joyfully Indigenous and Christian. Hail! *Hail!*

So what does it look like to be authentically Indigenous? Moreover, what does it look like to be authentically Indigenous *and* a follower of Jesus? Indigenous peoples for generations have struggled with these existential questions. Euroamerican colonization and Christian missionaries have demonized Indigenous cultures, worldviews, and ways of being. This feeling is captured well in the following twisted sentiment that has been felt by many of our Indigenous people: "Jesus loves you, but he doesn't *like* you." For too long, Indigenous people have been measured and policed in their identity, whether by federal agents, Christian missionaries and educators, or one another. The toxic result is always the same: we are left to feel we are lacking something, never enough. Never civilized enough. Never ceremonial enough. Never Christian enough. Never Indigenous enough. Part of this insecurity arises from our collective history of being denied legal rights in both the United States and Canada to practice our ceremonies, dances, prayers, and rituals by our respective federal governments, and being told that such practices were sinful and idolatrous by Christian missionaries and educators.

In his book *Rescuing the Gospel from the Cowboys*, Richard Twiss (Sicangu Lakota/Rosebud Reservation) recounts his experiences of being disinvited from Christian spaces and having to constantly justify his facilitation of dancing, drumming, and wearing of his traditional regalia against charges of

---

[3]Redbone, "Come and Get Your Love (Official Music Video)," YouTube, August 3, 2020, 3:31, https://youtu.be/BA4rSO-h9Io?si=26l1fDCg-jckMOpO.

"syncretism."[4] Twiss, along with many others who composed the NAIITS community in its earliest inception, tirelessly and patiently argued for a seat at the theological table within Christianity, particularly within evangelical spaces, to address and deconstruct characterizations of the Indigenous Christian movement as inappropriately syncretistic.[5] These questions around syncretism continue into the present and are among the first concerns Chris and Danny address with non-Indigenous Christian groups. And while we continue to be sympathetic and patient with our friends, it can be discouraging and exhausting to address this topic repeatedly when compelling responses are readily available.[6] When non-Indigenous groups ask us to justify the relevance of our identity and cultural practices to our faith, how often we would like to offer the same challenge to *them*. If only they would look in the mirror and recognize that their own expressions of Christianity reflect modern Euroamerican expressions of the faith.[7] If they would only consult any work on global and historical expressions of Christianity, they would find that our faith has never existed in a cultural vacuum.[8] Christianity has always syncretized to some degree to the host culture. Moreover, cultures are complex, dynamic, and ever-developing networks of creativity that are always negotiating the traditional with the new. Charges of syncretism function more as rhetorical bludgeons, often used by the dominant culture to describe and judge something it doesn't like or approve of—whereas describing a cultural mixing as "contextualization" is reserved for those approaches that the dominant culture approves or at least tolerates. And yet these concerns do not just come from non-Indigenous Christians.

---

[4] Richard Twiss, *Rescuing the Gospel from the Cowboys: A Native American Expression of the Jesus Way* (Downers Grove, IL: InterVarsity Press, 2015).
[5] Numerous essays in *Journal of NAIITS* have wrestled with this issue. See, for example, the inaugural essay of the journal: Richard Twiss, Terry LeBlanc, and Adrian Jacobs, "Culture, Christian Faith and Error," *Journal of NAIITS* 1 (2003): 5-35.
[6] See Twiss, *Rescuing the Gospel*; Casey Church, *Holy Smoke: The Contextual Use of Native American Ritual and Ceremony* (Cleveland, TN: Cherohala, 2017).
[7] See Frank Viola and George Barna, *Pagan Christianity? Exploring the Roots of Our Church Practices* (Carol Stream, IL: Tyndale House, 2010).
[8] On the diversity of worship, see *Journal of NAIITS* 21 (2023), focused on ethnomusicology. See also Global Ethnodoxology Network, www.worldofworship.org. For the diversity of the global church, see the important works of Lamin O. Sanneh, *Whose Religion Is Christianity? The Gospel Beyond the West* (Grand Rapids, MI: Eerdmans, 2003); Sanneh, *Disciples of All Nations: Pillars of World Christianity*, Oxford Studies in World Christianity (Oxford: Oxford University Press, 2008); Sanneh, *Translating the Message: The Missionary Impact on Culture*, 2nd ed. (Maryknoll, NY: Orbis Books, 2009).

Indigenous Christians too have shamed those in the NAIITS community for not leaving behind their "pagan" traditions in order to follow Christ according to more Euroamerican sensibilities.

Turtle Island hermeneutics invites Indigenous readers to read Scripture as their whole, holy selves, recognizing and living into how Creator made them in his image, with the roles and responsibilities that entails. It is a dark legacy of settler-colonial theology that caused so many Indigenous people to doubt their inherent and sacred dignity and the assets of their ancestral heritages. One of the founders of NAIITS, Wendy Petersen, shares a story of feeling a deep, unnamed heaviness while participating in a talking circle composed of First Nations men and women at a church in Winnipeg. Confused and concerned, Wendy turned to her Christian friend beside her, "a physically beautiful Cree woman working on a seminary masters degree," as Wendy describes her, and asked her a pointed question: "When you are all alone, and you look into a mirror, what do you see?" The Cree woman's response shocked and grieved Wendy as it does us: "I see a no-good dirty Indian."[9] This Cree woman, despite pursuing a theological degree, had not yet received a gospel message of love so penetrating as to heal this deep soul wound that has scarred so many in our communities. To this Cree woman and to anyone else who needs to hear it, we sing, "Come and get your love." Well, to be more accurate—Danny sings, Chris croaks.

In this chapter we will discuss how a Turtle Island hermeneutics is driven by the assumption that within our own Creator-inspired ancestral traditions and ceremonies, we have good medicine and assets in place to heal, inspire, and empower us to live in harmony. We will explore Indigenous ceremonial lifeways for Indigenous readers to appreciate the ways in which ceremony guides and informs the stories and legislation in Scripture. Scripture and ceremony can come together in beautiful ways within the hearts of Indigenous followers, with ceremonial experiences reframing how Indigenous people read Scripture and vice versa. However, particular Scripture passages from the apostle Paul, including Galatians 4:8-11 and 2 Corinthians 5:17; 6:17 have sometimes been weaponized by settlers to compel Indigenous people to consider their ceremonies as idolatrous and wrong. Leveraging our fancy

---

[9]Wendy Petersen, Cheryl Bear-Barnetson, and Linda Martin, "Ways of Knowing Self: Reclamation of Real Indigenous Identity," *Journal of NAIITS* 9 (2011): 33.

degrees in New Testament studies, we dig deeper into Paul's life and theology to propose some more fruitful and life-giving ways to think about the place and possibilities of Indigenous ceremonies in the lives of Indigenous followers of Jesus. In the spirit of Redbone, we contend that Creator was already present and is already waiting for us to circle back *home* in our Indigenous lifeways, inviting us to come and get our love.

CIRCLING BACK: ASSET-BASED THEOLOGY

We've grounded this book in an interpretive approach we've called Turtle Island hermeneutics, introduced in chapter one. In various ways we've danced through our medicine wheel of interpretation as we've discussed biblical passages guided by themes relevant to Indigenous experiences. As discussed in the first chapter, an asset-based theological foundation underpins our hermeneutical approach and theologically justifies our circling back into our lifeways and cultural traditions in this chapter. Asset-based theology chooses to root itself in Genesis 1 rather than Genesis 3. In Genesis 1, we see the beauty and goodness of the creation, of which we are a part. This should be our starting place, in contrast to Genesis 3 and its narration of the fall of humanity. Grounding ourselves in the true beginning of our shared story chooses to focus on the good. Rather than seeing Indigenous culture and heritage as deficits to condemn and root out, they are seen as places to find assets to walk in a good way as Jesus-followers.

An unmentioned component of asset-based theology that is relevant for this discussion is its time orientation. It is well recognized that Indigenous worldviews almost always have a past-present time orientation, whereas modern Western societies have a present-future orientation.[10] The future orientation of Christian theology has been especially prevalent (and sometimes catastrophic) in the last two centuries especially, with the rise of dispensationalism and Zionism. This orientation to the past and present does not ignore the future or deny its reality but recognizes that the future remains in some ways unknowable until it arrives.[11] In some Indigenous languages, such

---
[10]See Randy S. Woodley, *Shalom and the Community of Creation: An Indigenous Vision*, Prophetic Christianity (Grand Rapids, MI: Eerdmans, 2012), 112-14.
[11]Even the work of futuring and the burgeoning discipline of theo-futures anticipates possible futures through deep and thorough analysis of the past and present. For the work of theo-futures, see Futuring Hub, https://futuringhub.ca/.

as Lakota, verbs have only present-tense forms.¹² As Terry LeBlanc has often shared when teaching, the past is ever present right in front of us as Indigenous peoples, and we walk into the future, as it were, backward, with the wisdom of the past and present guiding our steps into an unknown future. It is our memories of life at its best, which has oftentimes been life in ceremony, that hold the seeds for imagining how to live into life at its best in the future. This past-present orientation is part of asset-based theology because it is the past that holds the stories of our collective assets.

A CELEBRATION OF BIBLICAL CEREMONY

A life of ceremony characterizes traditional Indigenous lifeways across Turtle Island. Tink Tinker (wazhazhe/Osage) helpfully describes ceremony as about "structured ways of building and maintaining relationships . . . of balance with all our relations, including human and other-than-human relatives and those relatives that live in . . . the spirit world."¹³ Some ceremonial practices are similar across many nations, but First Nations have different ceremonies that characterize their communities and may conceive of similar/identical ceremonies in different ways. Individuals may also create and practice their own personal ceremonies or adapt what may be a common component of their life in a more ceremonial way.¹⁴ For some Indigenous people, defining their spirituality is not to point primarily to beliefs or a worldview but to point to a life characterized by ceremony. Ceremony is an embodied practice of an individual and community that integrates our lives with the life of Creator and the sacred, reinforcing our worldview(s) and our sense of belonging in the circles of relationships that we are part of. Though *ceremony* may not be

---

¹²For Paul Sneve (Lakota), this Lakota time orientation helped him cut through sacramental discussions on the nature of the Eucharist in Western theology. The Lakota language naturally re-calls and re-presents the Eucharist as present in the sacrament without arguments over consubstantiation. See Paul Sneve, "Anamnesis in the Lakota Language and Lakota Concepts of Time and Matter," *Anglican Theological Review* 95 (2013): 487. Sneve also notes that when the missionaries first came, Lakota also had no gender pronouns, nor did they distinguish between physical and spiritual matter. These components of the language could have been seen as assets to utilize in the explanation of Christianity, but Christianity had to be discussed only in English.

¹³Tink Tinker, "The Irrelevance of euro-christian Dichotomies for Indigenous Peoples: Beyond Nonviolence to a Vision of Cosmic Balance," in *Peacekeeping and the Challenge of Violence in World Religions*, ed. Irfan A. Omar and Michael K. Duffey (Malden, MA: Wiley-Blackwell, 2015) 209.

¹⁴For example, many Indigenous scholars intentionally imbue their work with ceremonial significance. See Shawn Wilson, *Research Is Ceremony: Indigenous Research Methods* (Black Point, NS: Fernwood, 2008).

the word that non-Indigenous people use, most lives are characterized to a greater or lesser degree by ceremonies, rites, rituals, and rhythms.[15] Part of culture building and cultural perpetuity is the habitual practice and adaptation of these actions. Typically, the reason that Euroamerican people have not recognized that their lives actually fall into these rhythms is that they have not had significant crosscultural encounters, which aid in seeing one's life from an external perspective. This in turn aids in seeing the aspects of one's life and helps to evaluate how the ceremonies, rituals, and rhythms of one's life embody one's values.

The life of the Christian church is also marked by significant ceremony. Even evangelicalism, the seemingly least ceremonial branch of world Christianity, is marked by ceremonial weekly (or twice a week) gatherings, by baptism as a marker of entry into the spiritual community, by a weekly/monthly/quarterly symbolic meal (Communion), and quite often by a childhood rite of passage (child baptism or child dedication). To this we add sacred holidays such as Easter and Christmas, and some denominations include footwashing as a ceremonial practice. While we can of course find scriptural support for some of these Christian ceremonies, there is no direct prescription for things such as child dedication. Arguably, even our most central ceremony of the Eucharist does not actually have a prescription for frequency. Danny was nurtured in the conservative Plymouth Brethren tradition, which celebrated the Lord's Supper weekly. While he deeply valued this practice, and in some ways wishes his Baptist denomination would practice Communion more frequently than once a month, the reality is that the Bible does not prescribe frequency. We see in Acts 2:42 that the early church devoted themselves to "the breaking of bread," but this does not denote frequency, and in this case it is not altogether clear whether this is speaking of a more formalized Communion ceremony or simply eating together. Likewise, in 1 Corinthians 11:23-34, Paul gives instruction on the Eucharist that does not prescribe frequency but rather provides instruction for *whenever* they come together to eat (1 Cor 11:26, 33) and share in the Eucharist ceremony. We will return to the Eucharist later in the chapter, but here it is enough to note that while a strict prescription is not dictated by the

---

[15]See the short but helpful book by Dru Johnson, *Human Rites: The Power of Rituals, Habits, and Sacraments* (Grand Rapids, MI: Eerdmans, 2019).

Scriptures, nonetheless the assumption that this central ceremony is part of the regular rhythm of the believing community is assumed.

Yet, for many Christians (non-Indigenous and some Indigenous) the issue is not the recognition that Christian life is marked by ceremony but that Indigenous followers of Jesus are "adding to" their Christian practice ceremonies that are foreign to the Scriptures. Should not those old ceremonial practices be renounced and forgotten? Isn't this what Paul means when he says, "So then, if anyone is in Christ, that person is part of the new creation. The old things have gone away, and look, new things have arrived!" (2 Cor 5:17), or "Come out from among them and be separated, says the Lord" (2 Cor 6:17), or Paul's exhortation, à la the KJV, to "put off the old man" (Col 3:9; see Rom 6:6; Eph 4:22)? We suggest that this type of response is both simplistic and incorrect. Christian practice is always encased in cultural expression. In fact, as Frank Viola and George Barna have documented well in *Pagan Christianity*, most modern expressions of Christian ritual, ceremony, worship, preaching, and church structure are only a few centuries old and largely European.[16] While it is true that certain practices may cease (or be resisted) after conversion, it is not the case that cultural practice is forsaken. After all, for Paul "new creation" was not about the destruction of what came before but the renewal of it.[17] For Indigenous people, the reality has been that we were often forced to adopt Euroamerican culture at conversion because of an assumption that European culture was civilized and Christian. But as Richard Twiss states, "When we come to Christ, Jesus does not ask us to abandon one sin-stained culture only to embrace another sin-stained culture."[18]

The Scriptures, as well as archaeological study on Israel and the early church, attest to numerous cultural and ceremonial practices that were not prescribed by God but nonetheless contributed to shared religious life. These

---

[16] Viola and Barna, *Pagan Christianity?*.

[17] N. T. Wright's important work *Surprised by Hope* (London: SPCK, 2007) reminds us that the new-creation teaching applies to all of creation, of which we are a part. The new heavens and new earth, like us, will not be destroyed and replaced but renewed. This pattern of new creation is predicated on Jesus himself as the firstfruits of new creation (1 Cor 15:20-23). In the same way that breath and spirit reanimated Jesus and renewed his body into something greater, so too is our life, born anew, a new creation.

[18] Richard Twiss, Terry LeBlanc, and Adrian Jacobs, "Culture, Christian Faith and Error," *Journal of NAIITS* 1 (2003): 28.

practices are not condemned by God. For instance, there are numerous sacred sites in the Old Testament that are not formally established by God. There is the Oak of Moreh, a sacred tree (Gen 12:4-9); a sacred grove, the Oaks of Mamre (Gen 13:18; Gen 18:1, 10); and the Palm of Deborah (Judg 4:4-5).[19] The law of Moses legislated numerous feasts and festivals for the Israelite faith, all of which conformed to the rhythms and cycles of the land.[20] But the Scriptures also attest to Israel celebrating New Moon festivals, something that most ancient Near East cultures practiced—it was not unique to Israel. The law of Moses acknowledges these feasts (Num 10:10) and prescribes an offering as well (Num 28:11-15). While not discussed at length, they are matter-of-factly referenced in the New Testament as well (Col 2:16). The New Moon celebration is even envisaged as part of the eschatological future (Is 66:22-24). We also have Jesus celebrating Hanukkah (John 10:22-23). While Christians are familiar with Hanukkah due to its proximity to Christmas or their love of Adam Sandler's Hanukkah Song,[21] this celebration is not a prescribed feast in the law of Moses but arose during the time of the Maccabean revolt in the intertestamental period. This feast was modeled on the Feast of Tabernacles and celebrated the reconsecration of the temple in 164 BCE, involving ceremony and numerous rituals with lights, branches, and song. These components of the festival are the very things that Jesus plays on and integrates into the teachings about himself.[22]

To reiterate, Jesus fully participated in a Jewish religious festival and ceremonies that are not prescribed in the Hebrew Bible.[23] Why would he do so? Because he was Jewish, and this celebration arose from their common history and common life together. As Indigenous peoples celebrate feasts and

---

[19]As Israel tumbled more and more into covenant disobedience, these sacred sites were condemned by God (see Ezek 6:13; Jer 3:6).

[20]See H. Daniel Zacharias, "Graceland: The Land as Relational Gift in the Bible," *Journal of NAIITS* 17 (2019): 170-72.

[21]*Saturday Night Live*, "Weekend Update: Adam Sandler on Hanukkah—SNL," YouTube, August 6, 2013, 4:16, https://youtu.be/KX5Z-HpHH9g?si=74r0k-cdthNIsYrB.

[22]See Gary M. Burge, *Jesus and the Jewish Festivals*, Ancient Context Ancient Faith (Grand Rapids, MI: Zondervan, 2012), chap. 5.

[23]It is important to recognize that the notion of the Hebrew canon continues to be debated and that some Christian traditions, such as the Catholic and the Orthodox, include the Apocrypha in their Old Testament canon. Most scholars agree that the modern Hebrew Bible (and Protestant Old Testament) is what was considered the Hebrew Bible in the first century. See James A. Sanders, "Canon: Hebrew Bible," in *Anchor Bible Dictionary*, ed. David Noel Freedman (New York: Doubleday, 1992), 1:840.

ceremonies within their communities, they do so in recognition of their common history and life together as well—a history in which Creator has been central, and a life that has encountered Jesus and the good news. We also see the early Jewish Christians continuing in their traditional Jewish practices. While boldly proclaiming that the resurrected Jesus was Israel's and the world's Messiah and meeting on Sundays, Jewish believers were still part of synagogue and temple life (Acts 2:46; 3:1; 5:20-22; 9:20; 13:5, 14-15; 18:26; 19:8; 21:26-30). The belief that in the gospel "the old things have gone away and new things have arrived" and "come out and be separate" did not change early Jewish Christian engagement with their cultural heritage, even as they were emerging as a new community centered on Christ. We will say more about this, centering our gaze on Paul, below.

The importance of ceremony for Indigenous peoples coupled with what is seen in the Scriptures helps Indigenous followers of Jesus to embrace their cultural expressions in their discipleship. Colonialism and its legacy have continued its reactionary condemnation of Indigenous cultural expression in the church, but the apostle Paul's perspective likely would have been what is stated in Romans 14:5-6:

> One person considers some days to be more sacred than others, while another person considers all days to be the same. Each person must have their own convictions. Someone who thinks that a day is sacred, thinks that way for the Lord. Those who eat, eat for the Lord, because they thank God. And those who don't eat, don't eat for the Lord, and they thank the Lord too.

Like the Israelites who used many instruments in the worship of God, including tree-made rattles (sistrums, 2 Sam 6:5) and skin-drums (timbrel/tambourine, Ex 15:20; Ps 150:4), so too do Indigenous followers make use of their cultural instruments. Like the feasts and festivals of Israel that arose in rhythm with the cycles of the land, as well as the unprescribed New Moon feasts and festivals such as Hanukkah, Indigenous peoples celebrate the feasts and ceremonies that mark the rhythms of their lands and communities. Casey Church (Potawatomi), among many others, incorporates biblical passages into his ceremonies and justifies the practice of smudging, the burning of some of the sacred medicines (sage, sweetgrass, cedar, and tobacco), by pointing to the ancient Hebrew practice of burning incense over the ark of the covenant (e.g., Ex 30:1-6, 34-36; Lk 1:8-10), as well as the continued practice of candle lighting and incense burning in other traditions of the global church up to the present.[24]

A CELEBRATION OF INDIGENOUS CEREMONY

During our travels and conversations with Indigenous followers of Christ, we heard many stories about how meaningful it was to participate in Indigenous ceremonies as Christians. Rev. Clarence Yarholar (Muscogee/Creek), who has worked as a counselor for the Kickapoo Nation, talked frequently about how many of his patients benefited from participating in their tribe's ceremonies as part of their path toward healing. Although Clarence grew up observing traditional ceremonies and rituals with his father, he eventually stepped away from the traditional path, thinking it was incongruent with Christianity. Over twenty-five years ago, while Yarholar was mourning the passing of his mother, he heard the Spirit instruct him, "Do what you know that helps you reconnect." And so Yarholar built his first sweat lodge and over time experienced healing and restored balance through the prayer ceremonies conducted within. "When we cleanse ourselves with a ritual," Yarholar explained to Chris, "it convinces me that my old being is gone and I get to try again, I get to rediscover it in a new angle, how spirituality keeps me balanced."[25] It was Yarholar who first walked Chris through praying toward the four directions and gave him cedar to smudge with during his morning prayers. Chris was deeply touched by this teaching and his time with Yarholar, an experience that remains foundational to Chris's own path toward revitalizing ceremony in his own life.

Ted Hernandez (Wiyot), an Indigenous follower of Christ who has served as chairperson of the Wiyot tribe in Northern California, shared with Chris how meaningful it was to participate in the return of ancestral land of Tuluwat Island around the Humboldt Bay to his people and the revitalization of Wiyot ceremonies. On February 26, 1860, six neighboring settlers, who lusted after Wiyot land, murdered at least sixty sleeping women, children, and elders while the men were away gathering preparations for their World Renewal Ceremony. "On the day of the massacre, our ceremonies went to sleep," Hernandez

---

[24]Church, *Holy Smoke*, 89-90.
[25]Clarence Yarholar, interview, January 9, 2023.

sorrowfully explained.²⁶ In 1992, then Wiyot chairperson, Cheryl Seidner, with her sister councilwoman Leona Wilkinson and with support from the Eureka United Church of Christ, organized an annual prayer vigil to commemorate the 1860 massacre. Hernandez credited the Indian Island Prayer vigil with creating "a climate of healing . . . for both Indian and non-Indian community members," and inspiring Seidner with a vision to raise funds to purchase their land back. In 2000, the Wiyot tribe purchased 1.5 acres of Tuluwat Island from the city of Eureka. In 2004, the city council returned 45 more. With the return of land, the ceremonies could awaken again. In 2006, Hernandez, with the support of Cheryl Seidner, held a coming-of-age ceremony for his daughter—a ceremony that had not been performed for over 150 years.²⁷ Hernandez recalled his gratefulness for cousin tribes among the Yurok and Hoopa for sharing their ceremonial knowledge so that they might observe proper protocol as best they could. He also greatly appreciated the community of women who participated in the design of his daughter's ceremonial dress, which included Leona Wilkinson, Irene Carlson, Joycelyn Teague, Rosario Hernandez, Michelle Hernandez and her sisters, and Cheryl Seidner, who incorporated design notes taken from her visit with the National Museum of the American Indian's Cultural Resource Center in Maryland.²⁸ Hernandez shared:

> When we did her ceremony, it was like that ceremony woke up that part of DNA inside me. That ceremony woke up the Wiyot ceremonial life. Creator will never leave you behind to figure things out on your own. Creator sent us people to help us relearn what we needed to know. This world has no balance, because we don't follow the way Creator wants us to go. Once ceremonies return, the healing can begin, balance can be brought back.²⁹

After a decade spent cleaning up the contamination on the island, the Wiyot council felt called to "wake up" the World Renewal Ceremony and observed the dance, prayers, and rituals in 2014. Hernandez recalled how meaningful it was to see the tears in elders' eyes as they witnessed the return of the

---

[26] Ted Hernandez, interview, February 9, 2024.
[27] David Helvarg, "Island of Resistance: The Wiyot Reclaim Their Land and Culture from a Dark Past," *American Indian* 21, no. 1 (2020), www.americanindianmagazine.org/story/wiyot.
[28] Helvarg, "Island of Resistance."
[29] Hernandez, interview.

ceremony. "Once we started our ceremonies, Creator continued to give things back," Hernadez explained. "If we follow what He wants us to, He gives it back to us."[30] And indeed, Creator continued to give back. In 2019, the city council of Eureka held an official signing ceremony to mark the transfer of the remaining 202 acres that the city owned of Tuluwat Island to the Wiyot.

As Ted Hernandez sees it, the same Creator who walked alongside the Wiyot people in the return of their land and the reawakening of their ceremonies is the one who incarnated in Jesus. For Hernandez, Jesus is a ceremonial person, a medicine man who knew well and observed proper ceremonial protocols and his responsibilities to his community. Hernandez continued:

> I see Jesus' teachings in the ceremonies. We share, we eat together as a family, as one. We all do our prayers together. There is no hatred, no anger. When you come to ceremony, you come with a clean heart and mind. . . . You might come to ceremony being angry, but you leave the anger behind before you go into ceremony. You may think, 'I don't want to dance with this person,' but you do dance, and after the end of it, you become friends again. It's your choice to walk in this new way.[31]

For Indigenous followers of Christ, a return to ceremony opens up opportunities to walk in a new way where they might experience healing and an affirmation of their whole selves. To follow a ceremonial Jesus means to follow him into the round dance, recognizing Jesus' footprints in the dusty steps of our brothers and sisters. As exemplified in these stories, Indigenous ceremonies need not be seen as incongruent with the Christian walk. Indeed, followers of Christ see their own ceremonies and what they experience in them reflected in the life of Jesus and in the stories of Scripture.

FREEDOM AND SOVEREIGNTY IN CHRIST: AN INDIGENOUS READING OF GALATIANS

How then do Indigenous followers of Jesus determine what ceremonies and rituals to maintain—whether from their Indigenous or Christian traditions? Christians have long turned to Paul's letter to the Galatians to help them think through the nature and purpose of Mosaic law, sacraments, and the essence

---

[30]Hernandez, interview.
[31]Hernandez, interview.

of the Christian faith. Martin Luther found Galatians especially helpful to justify his critiques against what he perceived to be excesses and legalism of sixteenth-century Catholic religious practices, in particular the sale of indulgences. In *The Freedom of a Christian* (1520), Luther goes to great lengths to explain how Christians are free and liberated from a relationship of bondage to sin and any superstitious idea that rituals and ceremonies ultimately set us in a right-relationship with Creator. Too often modern Christians interpret their freedom in Christ to justify their own suspicion toward or judgment against rituals and ceremonies, especially those belonging to spiritual traditions other than their own. But even Luther recognized that "we cannot live without ceremonies and works."[32] We suggest that a close reading of Galatians can help us unpack some problematic interpretations of Scripture that have inhibited the freedom, or we might say the sovereignty, that Indigenous followers of Christ should enjoy.

Paul is especially spicy in his letter to the Galatians. Paul writes this letter to followers of Christ in central Asia Minor or modern-day Turkey, whose ethnic heritage descended from the Gauls (Celtic people) who had migrated to the region centuries prior. Within the Roman imperial gaze, the Gauls were prototypical "barbarians"—a prejudice Indigenous people can relate to.[33] Apparently, other followers of Christ had been badmouthing Paul's gospel message, arguing that for the Gauls to be authentic followers of Jesus and to actually belong to the community, they must properly observe the Jewish rituals and ceremonies of the Messiah's heritage, especially the rite of circumcision. Paul proceeds to lay out a feisty defense of his legitimacy as an apostle and of his controversial gospel that Gauls do not need to observe Jewish ceremonies and rituals to be in right relationship with Creator. In doing so, Paul must explain how non-Jewish people can be found to be in a covenant relationship with Creator apart from following the very ceremonies, rituals, and works Creator laid out in the covenant with the Jewish people. Ultimately, Paul argues that the Gauls who put their faith in the Jewish Messiah are adopted into Abraham's family (Gal 4:5) and thereby become

---

[32]Martin Luther, *The Freedom of the Christian*, trans. and ed. Mark Tranvik, Luther Study Edition (Minneapolis: Fortress, 2008), 93.
[33]See Brigette Kahl, *Galatians Re-imagined: Reading with the Eyes of the Vanquished* (Minneapolis: Fortress, 2010), 31-33.

equal heirs to all the promises of blessings Creator made to Abraham's offspring (Gal 3:15-18). While it's well and good for Jews to observe Jewish laws and ceremonies, it's unnecessary for the Gauls.

With utter frustration toward those challenging his teachings, which he received from a vision from Jesus (Gal 1:11-12), Paul wishes that his opponents would simply castrate themselves if they truly believe that circumcision is universally essential and pleasing to Creator (Gal 5:12). Paul is so angry in part because he knows how this other gospel creates disharmony in ethnically diverse gatherings. He himself witnessed this disharmony years prior in Antioch when Peter, Barnabas, and many other Jews stopped eating with non-Jews due to the pressure exerted on them by Jewish believers associated with James's (Jesus' brother) community in Jerusalem (Gal 2:11-14). And yet in the heat of his argument, Paul makes a lot of ambiguous and confusing statements—as we all tend to do when we feel under attack and lash out. These texts about the meaning and value of ceremonies and rituals in Galatians can be weaponized against contemporary Indigenous followers of Jesus wishing to observe their own ancestral ceremonies and rituals.

In Galatians 4, Paul seems to categorically dismiss and discourage the Gauls from returning to anything resembling their previous ceremonial life lest they slip back into pagan idolatry. Paul writes:

> At the time, when you didn't know God, you were enslaved by things that aren't gods by nature. But now, after knowing God (or rather, being known by God), how can you turn back again to the weak and worthless world system [*stoicheia*, i.e., "elemental principles"]? Do you want to be slaves to them again? You observe religious days and months and seasons and years. I'm afraid for you! Perhaps my hard work for you has been for nothing. (Gal 4:8-11)

It's not clear what Paul means by "elemental principles" (*stoicheia* in Greek), both here and just before this passage when he also describes the Gauls as previously being enslaved to "the *stoicheia* of the world" (Gal 4:3).[34] *Stoicheia* could possibly refer to the basic building blocks of the universe as the Greeks understood it (i.e., the elements of fire, air, water, and earth) or divine beings

---

[34] Chris's own interpretation of this passage grew out of an independent study he supervised for Grant Showalter-Swanson (PhD candidate at Garrett-Evangelical Theological Seminary). Chris is grateful to Grant for their enlightening conversations and for Grant's work identifying helpful resources on this passage.

associated with heavenly bodies (i.e., sun, moon, clouds, stars).[35] Paul is probably using this ambiguous turn of phrase to describe divine beings that many Greeks presumed to organize and govern aspects of the earth, skies, and broader cosmos, from which the Gauls' ancestral religious practices originated—thus simultaneously referencing divine beings and ancestral customs or laws as the "basic building blocks" of Gallic spirituality.[36]

Paul then turns his attention to the perceived threat that some Gauls are observing ceremonies and rituals associated with the turning seasons, presumably in honor of these "elemental principals." Paul here seems to be following a recognizable one-two punch polemical trope that other contemporary Jews made against the ceremonies of their neighbors.[37] Strangely enough, Paul seems to conflate the enslaving conditions of previously practiced Gallic ritual observances with Jewish ritual observances, as just before this Paul said that "scripture locked up all things under sin" (Gal 3:22) and how "we"—does he mean to include the Gauls?—were imprisoned under the law (Gal 3:23). Again, the central problem Paul is addressing is that Gauls want to practice *Jewish* ceremonies and ritual observances, not *Gallic* ceremonies and ritual observances. But to dissuade Gauls from being circumcised, Paul argues that this is just as bad as if they were slipping back to the old superstitions they practiced before they came to trust in Christ. But now Paul seems to have backed himself in a corner as appearing to be against ceremonies in general, yet we know this is an incomplete picture given Paul's continuing Jewish practices as evidenced in Acts.

Perhaps it's the case that Paul worries that in engaging with Jewish ceremonies the Gauls might slip back into their former Celtic ceremonial lifeways or idolatrous practices of venerating the Roman emperor and so turn away from Christ.[38] And yet, if this is what Paul means, it is inconsistent with

---

[35]Nancy Elizabeth Bedford, *Galatians* (Louisville, KY: Westminster John Knox, 2016), 113.
[36]See Neil Martin, *Galatians Reconsidered: Jews, Gentiles and Justification in the First and the Twenty-First Centuries* (London: Apollos, 2022), 124; Craig Keener, *Galatians: A Commentary* (Grand Rapids, MI: Baker Academic, 2019), 330-33; Emma Wasserman, "Gods and Non-gods in Galatia: Reconsidering Paul's *Stoicheia*," in *The Social World of Ancient Jews and Christians: Essays in Honor of L. Michael White*, ed. Jaimie Gunderson, Tony Keddie, and Douglas Boin (Atlanta: SBL Press, 2022), 19-41.
[37]See Wasserman, "Gods and Non-gods," 24-25, who cites Epistle of Jeremiah 60-69; Philo, *Questions and Answers on Genesis* 4.51.
[38]Martin, *Galatians Reconsidered*, 49-50.

Paul's broader encouragement of followers of Christ to observe rituals and ceremonies such as baptism and the Lord's Supper, which never present any concern for Paul as slippery slopes into pagan ritual practices or Jewish practices, even though baptism and ritual meals were part of both Jewish practice and some pagan practices. Moreover, as we have already observed, Colossians 2:16 explicitly forbids looking down on followers of Christ for observing a Jewish "festival, a new moon, or sabbaths." Sometimes it is okay to recognize that some passages are difficult to interpret and to recognize that Paul, like every person, continued to expand his thinking and work out his theology through the years.

Whatever we make of Paul's ambiguous argument in Galatians, our goal is to disarm arguments that would weaponize this type of passage to discourage Indigenous followers of Christ from honoring Creator in ceremonial and ritual forms derived from their ancestral heritage. What is certain from Paul's letter to the Galatians is that particular cultural and ceremonial aspects of Judaism are not expected for non-Jews. And we are confident that a modern extension of this teaching is that Euroamerican cultural practices should not be expected of non-Euroamerican believers today. What is *ultimately* vilified in Paul's passing argument composed in the heat of the moment is the idolatrous worship of beings that are not gods (Gal 4:8). And while Paul may seem to throw Jewish ceremonies and rituals under the bus here as part of a slippery-slope argument (that is, if Gentiles observe Jewish festivals and ceremonies, they risk slipping back into an enslavement to pagan deities and practices), this should be interpreted more as a reactionary punch against his opponents rather than a fully developed theory about the nature of ceremonies and rituals. The threat that animates Paul's impassioned argument here is a colonizing gospel message that demands that Gauls observe an encultured Jewish ceremonial and ritual legal system that impinges on the Gauls' sovereignty in Christ. In contrast to most Western missionaries in the modern period, Paul argues against a culturally insensitive imposition of his own culturally rooted version of the gospel on the Indigenous people of Galatia. The question remains, then, if Paul is against others imposing Jewish ceremonial and ritual practices on the Gauls, what ceremonial and rituals are *appropriate* for Gauls to observe? To this Paul might answer, "What spiritual fruit do such ceremonies produce?"

Paul's turn to the "fruit of the Spirit" as an essential strategy for evaluating behavior builds on his thematic emphasis throughout Galatians that Christ has called the Gauls to "freedom" (Gal 5:13). As Paul declares, "Christ has set us free for freedom. Therefore, stand firm and don't submit to the bondage of slavery again" (Gal 5:1). Paul's proclamation of sovereignty here echoes back to his prior story (Gal 2:1-10) of how "false brothers and sisters" once slipped into a council meeting in Jerusalem in order to "spy on our freedom, which we have in Christ Jesus" (Gal 2:3-4). Spiritual freedom here is expressed in the refusal of Titus, Paul's partner in ministry, to be circumcised. According to Paul, these Torah-abiding Christians wanted "to make us slaves" insofar as they wanted Gentile followers of Christ to conform themselves to the Jewish Torah and be circumcised (Gal 2:4). Reflecting on this passage, Cheryl Bear (Nadleh Whut'en, Bear Clan) states, "First Nations people are continually subjected to circumcision, not of the flesh, but of their culture."[39] But if the Gauls are to embody some sense of sovereignty in their spirituality and behavior, how are they to discern what they should do? "Be guided by the Spirit," Paul recommends, "and you won't carry out your selfish desires" (Gal 5:16). But how do we know what is of the Spirit? "The fruit of the Spirit," Paul continues, "is love, joy, peace, patience, kindness, goodness, faithfulness, gentleness, and self-control" (Gal 5:22-23).

Indigenous followers of Christ can embrace their sovereignty/freedom in Christ by not allowing themselves to be enslaved to the idea that proper Christian ceremonies and rituals are those that simply replicate Western, Euroamerican expressions of the faith. Instead, Indigenous followers of Christ should be free to explore how their ancestral ceremonies and rituals can express devotion to Christ and bear spiritual fruit within their lives and community. It may even be that Indigenous followers of Christ determine that there are elements of their culture they would like not to participate in. For example, pastor Christina Dawson (Nuu-Chan-nulth) in Vancouver shared with Danny that there were a number of taboos in her community that caused her fear. But since becoming a follower of Christ, she has experienced freedom from these taboos and fears.[40] When these discussions

---

[39] Cheryl Bear-Barnetson, *Introduction to First Nations Ministry* (Cleveland, TN: Cherohala Press, 2013), 114.
[40] Christina Dawson, interview, September 22, 2022.

are had between Indigenous and non-Indigenous believers, a colonizing and paternalistic perspective is often not far away. But this work of discernment, this exercise of freedom in Christ, belongs to Indigenous believers. Fellow followers of Christ should be slow to judge, resist the urge to cast the colonial gaze, and adopt a posture of support and curiosity when encountering the spiritual journey of others. What is good medicine, useful, or fruitful in a given ceremony may not always be readily apparent to outsiders. As Richard Twiss wisely observes, "the dynamics of spiritual growth over time cannot be easily, cleanly identified and quantified, or categorized for accuracy."[41] Fruit needs time to mature before it can be properly harvested and evaluated. In the end it may be that an Indigenous follower of Christ finds wholeness and beauty in Euroamerican Christian church conventions, in traditional ceremonies, or in the adaptation of ceremonies (more on this below). As mentioned above, in perhaps one of Paul's more developed thoughts on rituals, he admonishes Christ-followers in Rome to not pass judgment on those who abstain from meat sacrificed to idols or who hold particular days more sacred than others (Rom 14:2-3; 5-6). We are to welcome others since they have already been welcomed by Creator (Rom 14:1, 3).

It is important to recognize that it is only in relatively recent history that it has been legal for Indigenous people on Turtle Island to openly observe their ancestral ceremonies and rituals. In 1883, the US Congress outlawed dancing (i.e., the Sun Dance, stomp dances), ceremonies, and medicine men through The Code of Indian Offenses, threatening to imprison Native Americans for practicing traditional ceremonies.[42] Native Americans found some relief from these oppressive laws in 1934, when the newly appointed commissioner of Indian affairs, John Collier, provided some protections against the government interfering in Native ceremonies and expressions of faith, though the use of eagle feathers remained a federal offense, and Sun Dancers in Pine Ridge were arrested as late as 1971.[43] In 1978, the American Indian Religious Freedom Act was passed by Congress during the presidency of Jimmy Carter, guaranteeing that Indigenous ceremonies and rituals would be protected

---

[41]Twiss, *Rescuing the Gospel*, 33.
[42]Lee Irwin, "Freedom, Law, and Prophecy: A Brief History of Native American Religious Resistance," in *Native American Spirituality: A Critical Reader*, ed. Lee Irwin (Lincoln: University of Nebraska Press, 2000), 295.
[43]Irwin, "Freedom, Law, and Prophecy," 302-3.

under the First Amendment, an outworking of President Carter's Baptist faith.⁴⁴ In 1993, the Religious Freedom Restoration Act compelled the government to "not substantially burden religious exercises without compelling justification," with specific rights, such as protections to use peyote, articulated in the 1994 Native American Free Exercise of Religion Act.⁴⁵

Likewise in Canada, the racist legislation known as the Indian Act, which came into effect in 1876 (and is still in effect today), banned the Sun Dance of the Plains people, banned the traditional governance systems and imposed a band council system, restricted the wearing of particular dress and regalia, and in a later 1884 amendment banned the potlatch of the west coast First Nations. The potlatch varied in its practice among the west coast nations, but it invariably involved feasting, dancing, theatrical demonstrations, tribal business, and gift giving, which served as a mechanism for wealth redistribution within the community. This last tradition was banned not only because of its cultural and religious significance but because "the Victorian idea of progress, which encouraged the individual accumulation of material goods, was the direct antithesis of the values implicit in the potlatch."⁴⁶ While many of these bans have since been excised from the Indian Act (for instance, the potlatch ban was repealed in 1951), we as yet have not been ex(or)cised from the Indian Act itself.

Indigenous struggles for religious sovereignty represent one of many efforts of First Nations people to reinstitute, defend, and expand Indigenous sovereignty, which include the right to self-determine their own governance, education system, land use, health care, economy, and social services, including adoption policies.⁴⁷ Of note in light of chapter five's discussion about treaties, Indigenous people across Turtle Island continue to fight for their rights for self-determination in governance that was guaranteed to them in treaties with the United States and Canada. Despite Canada's supposed

---

⁴⁴Irwin, "Freedom, Law, and Prophecy," 295.
⁴⁵Irwin, "Freedom, Law, and Prophecy," 305.
⁴⁶Brian Titley, *A Narrow Vision: Duncan Campbell Scott and the Administration of Indian Affairs in Canada*, ProQuest ed. (Vancouver, BC: University of British Columbia Press, 1986), 163.
⁴⁷See Rebecca Nagle's podcast, *This Land*, which powerfully chronicles the fight to maintain Indigenous sovereignty of land in Oklahoma (season 1) and how lawsuits on behalf of evangelicals trying to adopt Native children have been sponsored by powerful corporate interests with the aim of overturning federal Indian law and Indigenous sovereignty, https://crooked.com/podcast-series/this-land/.

commitment to the United Nations Declaration on the Rights of Indigenous Peoples (UNDRIP) as a framework for reconciliation and Indigenous rights, the Canadian government still spends more money in litigation fighting lawsuits for treaty violations and land claims. This despite the fact that Indigenous rights have time and again been upheld in Canada. This includes the Marshall decisions, in which the Supreme Court upheld fishing rights of the Mi'kmaq, and the landmark Supreme Court ruling that upheld Native title as an ancestral right protected by section 35(1) of the Constitution Act in Canada.[48] The ruling was upheld as recently as 2014 in *Tsilhqot'in Nation v. British Columbia*.[49]

South of the Canadian border, in a recent landmark ruling, *McGirt v. Oklahoma*, issued by the US Supreme Court in 2020, the court determined that the crimes of Jimcy McGirt (Seminole) were committed on land that falls under the jurisdiction of the Creek as opposed to the state of Oklahoma.[50] This ruling effectively recognizes that the territories that were once assigned to relocated tribes in Oklahoma, including Chris's tribe, the Choctaws, by treaties as reservations never lost their status and remain under Native sovereignty. Over a century ago, the Dawes General Allocation Act (1887) redistributed tribal landholdings to individual Native families with the aim of "civilizing" them through the experience of owning private property. This also freed up a vast amount of tribal land for white settlers to occupy. Since then, the state of Oklahoma has been acting in violation of treaties guaranteeing the sovereignty of tribes to govern their lands, which comprise 40 percent of Oklahoma, with respect to tribal laws, taxation, policing, and the administration of justice in their courts. In his written opinion in *McGirt*, Justice Gorsuch writes, "On the far end of the Trail of Tears was a Promise. . . . If Congress wishes to break the promise of a reservation, it must say so."[51] Sovereignty is an asset to Indigenous peoples and as such can inform a

---

[48] Gérald A. Beaudoin, "Delgamuukw Case," in *The Canadian Encyclopedia*, last edited January 11, 2019, www.thecanadianencyclopedia.ca/en/article/delgamuukw-case.
[49] Andrew Lawrence, "Tsilhqot'in Nation v British Columbia (2014): An Expansion of Title and Justification," Centre for Constitutional Studies, April 15, 2015, www.constitutionalstudies.ca/2015/04/tsilhqotin-nation-v-british-columbia-2014-an-expansion-of-title-and-justification/.
[50] See Cameron Ayn Carlson, "The Promised Land: The Re-affirmation of Tribal Lands in Oklahoma," *Journal of NAIITS* 19 (2022): 87-99; Rebecca Nagle, *By the Fire We Carry: The Generations-Long Fight for Justice on Native Land* (New York: Harper, 2024).
[51] *McGirt v. Oklahoma*, 1, 8.

life-giving, asset-based Turtle Island hermeneutics that reads Scripture with an eye toward thinking about how people groups such as the Israelites in the Hebrew Bible fought hard to acquire, preserve, and defend their promise and covenanted sovereignty to observe Creator's laws, ceremonies, and rituals in dignity, harmony, and peace.[52]

CONCLUSION: THE EUCHARIST, AN ADAPTED CEREMONY BY JESUS

Ceremonies and rituals are living embodiments of grace that change and develop over time. This possibility of adapting and experimenting with rituals is playfully illustrated in season two of *Reservation Dogs*. In the second episode, two of the teen "reservation dogs," Willie Jack and Cheese, are taken to a local river by Uncle Brownie (a pot-smoking elder, played by Gary Farmer) and Bucky (Brownie's estranged friend, played by Wes Studi) in order to lift a curse that Willie Jack perceives to be tearing her friends apart. In the first part of the cleansing ritual, Uncle Brownie and Bucky lead a "strong prayer" to Creator in which the two elders comedically reconcile over past grievances and seek to "out–medicine man" each other in their dueling prayers. "These elders have lived very complicated lives," Cheese mutters under his breath, responding to Willie Jack's exasperated confusion over what they just experienced. Leading the teens to the riverside, Uncle Brownie announces, "Now we sing a song." "An old song," Bucky adds, "and then the water will just take [the curse] away." Uncle Brownie then takes a bundle of items that embody the curse from Willie Jack, throws it into the river, and begins to sing: "She's a good girl, loves her mama." "Loves Jesus," Bucky harmonizes, "and America too."[53]

Suddenly, the Spirit Warrior William Knifeman appears. After critiquing the uncles for stumbling through the song, the Spirit joins in with them on the chorus of Tom Petty's famous ballad, "Free Fallin'." "It's not even that old of a song," Cheese complains. "It's like thirty years—that's old," Brownie rejoins. The Spirit Warrior then calls out: "Aho, old Warrior! Tell the little [fatherless children][54] . . . there that this most sacred of ceremonies is

---

[52]See Carlson, "Promised Land," 91-93.
[53]*Reservation Dogs*, episode 2, season 2, "Run," directed by Sterlin Harjo, August 3, 2022 on FX/Hulu.
[54]Again, our apologies to the show runners of *Reservation Dogs* for editing out their colorful language, but we must protect Danny's sweet ears and sensibilities.

complete. That in that red road, good way, cedar path, corn pollen way, that sun dance, stomp dance, smoke dance, long house, Episcopal way, that they, the little [rascals] . . . of the seventh generation have vanquished this most powerful of curses."[55] Writing in *Vulture* magazine, Roxanne Hadadi reflects on the power of scenes such as this one for Indigenous viewers: "Cultural traditions, teachings, and ceremony passed down from elders have power and strength wherever you encounter them. They don't have to be perfectly authentic—a Tom Petty song or a Star Wars–affiliated phrase can both work—but the affirmation they provide endures."[56] For us, this scene illustrates powerfully, however satirically, our hope that even in our imperfect attempts to live into, revitalize, and/or adapt our Indigenous ceremonies and practices, Christ in his generous love is present and hears our prayers, and that the things we do may shape us to be the people Creator wants us to be.

While some people may protest these adaptations, Indigenous cultures adapt and evolve; they always have. Indigenous cultures are not static and frozen in time.[57] They are living and dynamic, which is part of their beauty.

For a biblical model of what proper spiritual discernment might look like for adapting rituals, consider Luke's account of the Jerusalem Council in Acts 15:1-29. Here the apostles and elders practice deep listening as they give space for stories to be shared about the Spirit's presence in Paul's ministry, for theological concerns to be voiced, and for Scripture to be consulted. For the Torah-observant followers of Jesus who argue against Paul's ministry of not requiring Gentiles to be circumcised, their position is in effect, "The Bible says it, I believe it, that settles it!" However, the apostles and elders are not satisfied with this position, as it conflicts with how they intuited the Holy Spirit's activity among the testimonies of "signs and wonders" (Acts 15:12)

---

[55]*Reservation Dogs*, episode 2, season 2, "Run," directed by Sterlin Harjo, August 3, 2022 on FX/Hulu.

[56]Roxanne Hadadi, "*Reservation Dogs* Grew Up with the Help of Its Grown-Ups," *Vulture*, September 28, 2022, www.vulture.com/article/reservation-dogs-season-two-finale-analysis.html.

[57]We also want to acknowledge the reality that some Indigenous Christians specifically desire to preserve their cultural traditions with as little adaptation as possible. For instance, Paul Sneve notes that he and other Lakota participate fully in both Lakota ceremony and Christian ceremony but not blended together. While we as authors enjoy and lean into the blended and adaptive usage of ceremony, we respect the decision of others to resist this blending. See Sneve, "*Anamnesis* in the Lakota Language and Lakota Concepts of Time and Matter," *Anglican Theological Review* 95 (2013): 492.

experienced by the wider community. The council ultimately discerns the Spirit supporting the sovereignty of Gentiles to not participate in the Jewish ritual of circumcision. The resulting letter to the Gentile churches simultaneously seeks to recognize the works of God in their midst while honoring the Scriptures by asking the Gentiles to abide by certain restrictions drawn from Leviticus 17–18 to foster inclusiveness and belonging (Acts 15:28).[58]

We also suggest that the Lord's Supper provides Indigenous followers of Jesus today with an example of the contextual adaptation of a sacred tradition and ceremony. Certain components of the original Passover and its subsequent celebration were directly relevant to Jesus' life and teachings, but it was not a one-to-one alignment. Jesus added something new to a ceremony that his people had been observing for many generations, connecting new meaning to the meal observance that would now celebrate the new covenant, which was inaugurated in his sacrifice on the cross. As we move into the early church, this ceremonial meal also moved from a yearly occurrence to a weekly occurrence. In this adaptation, the original meaning and intent of Passover was not dismissed but was honored while also seen and understood in a new way. Many Indigenous followers of Jesus have likewise sought to honor their cultural traditions and bring them authentically into their lifeways and their communal ceremonies of thanksgiving.

The embodied and tangible act of Communion is Christ's final passion prediction, indicating the significance of his upcoming death and its ability to bring people into Creator's family. As Communion is now a ceremony in the Christian church, it should not be missed that the initiation of this ceremony integrated with, adapted, and added to a currently existing ceremony of the Jewish tradition. This new ceremonial feast became a common component of the church gathering since the earliest of times, with the ceremony itself changing from a regular practice of eating together the "love feast" (1 Cor 11:33; Jude 12) to modern expressions that vary in frequency, wording, form, understanding, and so on. And while some may contend that this was the prerogative of Jesus as the unique Son of God (something we certainly affirm), our contention is that the work of Jesus here also provides a model for his followers today as well.

---

[58]Richard Bauckham, "James and the Gentiles (Acts 15:13–21)," in *History, Literature, and Society in the Book of Acts*, ed. Ben Witherington III (Cambridge: Cambridge University Press, 1996), 154-84.

Despite the church's frequent denigration and denouncement of ceremonial practices, some Indigenous Christians have sought to follow Jesus the way God made them and with the culture they were born into, understanding Jesus to be a transformer of culture, not a denouncer of it. This encompasses both cultural ceremonies and practices, as well as Indigenous worldviews and ways of knowing, with the ultimate aim of articulating, valuing, and dignifying Indigenous contextual theologies and praxes.[59] The work of Indigenous followers of Jesus today to integrate their cultural practices, worldviews, and lifeways that these ceremonies are tied to finds resonance in the institution of the Lord's Supper.[60] Jesus celebrated and entered fully into the ceremony of his people, even while transforming it and imbuing it with a new meaning. Indigenous followers today follow Jesus' example in engaging their culture as the gospel imbues their practices with new meaning, whether smudging, sweat lodge, powwows, or pipe ceremonies.[61] Both of us have been and still are on the journey of cultural reclamation. As trained biblical scholars, a lot of this work has existed in the realm of the mind, wrestling with ideas and theologies. But we recognize that Christianity is an embodied faith, one that expresses itself not simply through shared beliefs but also through shared practices that express the reality of those beliefs in our individual and communal lives.

In resonance with the ceremonial invitation that is spoken over the Lord's Supper across Turtle Island, "Come as you are, this table is set for you," we invite Indigenous followers of Christ to reclaim and revitalize their ceremonies honoring the Creator: "Come and get your love." Come to think of it, this makes a good invitation to the Lord's table: come and get your love.

---

[59]See Church, *Holy Smoke*; Richard Twiss, *One Church, Many Tribes: Following Jesus the Way God Made You* (Bloomington, MN: Chosen Books, 2000); James Treat, ed., *Native and Christian: Indigenous Voices on Religious Identity in the United States and Canada* (New York: Routledge, 1996); Steven Charleston and Elaine A. Robinson, eds., *Coming Full Circle: Constructing Native Christian Theology* (Minneapolis: Fortress, 2015); Clara Sue Kidwell, Homer Noley, and George E. Tinker, *A Native American Theology* (Maryknoll, NY: Orbis Books, 2001).

[60]This is true also of John's baptism, which had connections with the purification ceremonies of Judaism while also changing the practice into something new.

[61]For discussion of contextual practices, see Church, *Holy Smoke*. Non-Indigenous readers should not appropriate these traditions without Indigenous participation and leadership.

Conclusion

THE CALL OF THE DRUM

An Invitation to the Circle of Turtle Island Hermeneutics

WE BEGAN THE FIRST CHAPTER WITH THE DANCE, and now we conclude by inviting you to join us around the big drum. The call of the drum is often used in ceremonies and gatherings to draw the people together. The beat of a powwow drum fills and reverberates. It aligns our heartbeats in sync with one another. It reminds us of our connection to our own origins in our mother's womb, as the heartbeat is the first instrument we hear. And this in turn reminds us of mother earth and of the good and sustaining gifts she continues to provide for us all. As we sit at the drum, one of us pulls out a tobacco pouch and makes a horizontal and vertical line on the drum. This makeshift medicine wheel brings with it the reminder of how Indigenous people see the world and the integrated balance of all things. Tobacco, one of the four sacred medicines, is a gift from Creator and from the land. In reciprocity, we offer it back in thanksgiving. Together around the drum, we place our hands on the drum and pray that our songs and prayers would connect with the hearts of those who hear and connect us with Creator. As followers of Jesus, we pray this in the name of Jesus. Seeing the cross pattern of tobacco, we take heart that Jesus is the Creator, full of grace and truth, and is present in our ceremony.

As we pick our sticks up, someone in the circle reminds us that this drum was made by someone we may know or have heard of. We share what song(s) will be sung and are reminded of their composers. And we are reminded that this strong, resounding drum was once a good buffalo. We will join our voice with other aspects of creation to make music to Creator in thanksgiving and prayer. As we sit around the drum and sing, there may be pauses for instruction. Those who are sitting around the drum for the first time may receive some teachings from those more experienced. It is a sacred time, but not so rigid that we don't laugh and enjoy ourselves. And, depending on your tradition, either there are women sitting around the drum with you or they are encircling the men around the drum, joining their voices and shaking their rattles. There is beauty and medicine in our ceremonies.

Intergenerational trauma haunts Indigenous peoples. But following our many elders and teachers, we believe that there is also intergenerational medicine that exists within the heart and blood of Native people. While sharing a meal at one of Uncle Casey Church's favorite Mexican restaurants in Albuquerque, New Mexico, Casey shared with Chris about Native acquaintances of his who did not grow up within their respective Indigenous cultures but, when they heard the drum at their first powwow, felt something deep within them reverberate. These Natives felt the call of the drum and, with tears in their eyes, knew they were home. Chris and Danny both had similar experiences of feeling whole and connected when invited to join the drum circle at the annual symposium of NAIITS: An Indigenous Learning Community. If our bodies and the neurological synapses within our brains can remember life at its worst for our ancestors, they can also remember life at its best.[1]

These deep ancestral experiences of joy and connection are being tapped into again as we live into the way Creator has made us. This is part of our healing. This is part of our flourishing. "When we bring back the things that were taken away from us," Uncle Casey reflects, "that's going to provide the greatest healing."[2] When our friend Karen Jolly (Cree), who is assistant professor of Indigenous studies at Providence University College in Manitoba, Canada, tells her story about what it was like to live into her Indigenous identity fully as a Christian, she describes it as becoming whole. "I used to hate my Indigenous identity and culture," Karen explained, "but now I feel 'whole' and healed by bringing my Cree ceremonial life together with my Christian identity."[3] We hope all people experience this sense of wholeness in their experience as followers of Jesus and that these stories and experiences will inform their engagement with the Scriptures.

---

[1] For an overview of trauma studies and intergenerational Indigenous studies, see Kris Clarke and Michael Yellowbird, "Postcolonial Trauma and Memory Work," in *Decolonizing Pathways Towards Integrative Healing in Social Work* (London: Routledge, 2020), 47-69.
[2] Casey Church, interview, August 7, 2023.
[3] Karen Jolly, interview, June 19, 2024.

In reading through this work, you will see that this has been no defense of the institutional Western church. We recognize that great harm has been done by the church. Followers of Jesus must own and speak truthfully about their history. But we also know, from our own lives, from the lives of the communities we are part of, and from the stories of those who have gone on before us, that Jesus is good medicine. He was and continues to be recognized as one who speaks the words of life and who calls us to manifest radical love. Ella Cara Deloria (Yankton Sioux; aunt of Vine Deloria Jr.) tells the story of Chief Gall of the Dakota:

> The masses of people accepted the church eagerly. But certain ones, like Chief Gall who lived a mile from the mission, took a long time to study out the gospel message with care and to appraise it critically. I am told that at the beginning Gall always came to church painted up as for a war council, looking austere and a little frightening. The young clergyman knew he was on trial, he and his message. Gall would sit by the door with his weapons . . . and would watch every move the minister made. . . . In the end, he made a great feast with the clergyman as his honored guest. When all had eaten and smoked the pipe together, he spoke to him in a public oration, calling him *misun*, "my younger brother"—a social kinship term. . . . [Gall spoke] "*Misun*, for many moons I have sat at your wihuta [the seat by the doorway; a term denoting the humblest space in a tipi] and listened with critical attention to all you say. And now I have some conclusions. What you tell us this man Jesus [pronounced Jeh-zoos] says we must do unto others, I already know. Be kind to your neighbor, feed him, be better to him than to yourself, he says. All are brothers, he says. But that's an old story to me. Of course! . . . If anyone wants you to escort him part way, take him to his very tipi door. If he asks for your shirt, by all means give him your blanket also, he says. Well, all that I have always done, and I know it is good. But now he also says, Love your enemies, for they are your brothers. And he says, if someone strikes one cheek, let him strike the other, too. That I have never done. That I have to learn, hard as it sounds. What is entirely new to me is that the Wakan is actually the Father of all men and so he loves even me and wants me to be safe. This man you talk about [Jesus] has made Wakan-tanka very plain to me, whom I only groped for once—in fear. Whereas I once looked about me on a mere level with my eyes and saw only my fellow man to do him good, now I know how to look up and see God, my Father, too." . . . And so Gall was baptized and confirmed; and all his days he received special

instruction from time to time, calling the missionary in to have things clarified ever and again. He was not just grabbing at externals. He was a student of Christ's teachings.[4]

The Scriptures testify to this man, Creator-made-flesh, whom death could not defeat. It is these Scriptures that nourished Jesus' soul and will nourish ours as well. The call of the drum calls us to ourselves, with all of the gifts and stories we bring. Not everyone is a great drummer, especially Chris.[5] But we come alongside one another, help each other get on beat. Sometimes to sing new songs, sometimes to sing old songs in a new way. And in case you are a bit dense like Danny and don't immediately catch on to metaphors—we are not just talking about music but our encounters with Scripture too.

We hope that this book is received as an invitation for Indigenous followers of Christ to read Scripture in light of their own ancestral wisdoms, stories, and ceremonies. To dance through the medicine wheel of Turtle Island hermeneutics and produce fresh readings that inspire them to follow Jesus in their own contexts. This book is not meant to be the last word on the topic—only a *good word*, one that invites compelling, localized readings among First Nations peoples that don't simply replicate the concerns, worldviews, politics, and even seminary educations of their surrounding non-Indigenous cultures. Together we have explored such broad questions as:

- What are broad principles that animate and frame Turtle Island hermeneutics?
- How might Indigenous ways of recognizing the agency, personhood, and dignity of "all our relations" be present in the Bible?
- How might Indigenous notions of harmony help us to reframe the stories we tell about how Jesus, the proclaimer of Jubilee, reconciles the world into harmony with Creator?
- How might Indigenous experiences of vision, dreams, and respect for ancestors invite the church to recognize and reclaim biblical ways of encountering and knowing the divine and honoring our ancestors?

---

[4]Ella Cara Deloria, *Speaking of Indians* (Lincoln: University of Nebraska Press, 1998), 92-93.
[5]For evidence, see this recording of his drumming at the 2024 NAIITS Annual Symposium before he delivered a closing plenary talk based on chapter four of this book: NAIITS: An Indigenous Learning Community, "21st Annual NAIITS Symposium: Dreaming Our World Home," YouTube, June 8, 2024, 1:49:15, www.youtube.com/watch?v=H_MH_T8f9ug.

- How can the Bible provide space for remembering and processing the trauma that Christian settlers have inflicted on Indigenous peoples (e.g., broken treaties, trails of tears, the Sixties Scoop, and Indian residential schools)?
- How does the Bible provide a vision for truth, reconciliation, and healing between Christian and Indigenous communities?
- How can the Bible support and celebrate First Nation peoples' return to their ancestral ceremonies and traditions in a good way?

We are *painfully* aware of the many topics and stories of Scripture we *did not* address in this book. For example, there certainly remains *a good word* that needs to be spoken into the tragic and persistent injustice of murdered and missing Indigenous women; into the sustained attempts by energy corporations to undermine federal Indian law and sovereignty (i.e., Indian Child Welfare Act, Indian Gambling Act); and into the related climate apocalypse that transnational corporations are leading us toward. There remains *a good word* to speak to the ongoing threat to Indigenous sovereignty, land claims, and laws and policies governing the adoption and raising of Indigenous children. Is it your *good word* that we need?

In one of Chris's first interviews at the outset of this project, Uncle Casey shared some wisdom that has haunted him since. "You know, Chris," Casey intoned, "this thing you are doing, gathering stories, it's not going to be complete in two years or however long you plan on listening to people. This is going to take a lifetime to complete." Indeed, a lifetime. Turtle Island hermeneutics is never complete; it is organic, diverse, and verdant as nature around us. It may have its seasons, it may rest and need to be awakened from time to time, but it's our hope that it blossoms and produces good fruit for the healing of our nations and for the healing of the Western church.

When Scripture reading is at its best on Turtle Island, it is like a drum circle. It engages the community of creation, protocol, tradition, humor, harmony, heart, and beauty. It is our prayer that something in this book has resonated with your heartbeat. Know that Creator is at home within the rich stories and experiences of your Indigenous heritage and lands, which have something special to contribute to the local and global church's interpretation of Scripture in following Jesus more faithfully. Hear the call of the drum. Bring your gifts and join in.

Prelude/Appendix

SMOKE SIGNALS FROM THE TRAIL

Honoring Our Elders Around the Council Fire

WELL, THIS IS AWKWARD. According to Indigenous protocol, it's important to acknowledge those who have gone before you at the outset. Where our protocol-acknowledgments at the front of the book are a brief attempt to name many whose relationships with us informed our work, they do not adequately convey our appreciation or celebrate each person's inspiring interpretations of Scripture and theological engagement. In Indigenous communities important discussions take place around the council fire. The elders' voices are given prominence in the discussion, sharing with their nieces and nephews their perspective and wisdom that have taken their lifetimes to harvest. Let us gather around to listen while the fire is still crackling.

When we first set out to interview Indigenous leaders and writers about how their own culture and heritage informs how they read the Bible, we were guided by the premise that a distinct way of reading and interpreting Scripture has been alive and well on Turtle Island since the first Indigenous encounter with Scripture. It's unfortunate that such encounters haven't been as well documented and made accessible as other contextualized readings of Scripture have. We understood that we needed to marinate in stories, experiences, teaching, and relationships with elders and the land before setting out to produce this work. And we also had to marinate in the good work that has been published by Indigenous scholars in the past and present.

While Indigenous interpretations of Scripture have been printed to some degree, they are often buried in broader volumes of collected essays or bound in texts not carried by libraries. In this section, we hope to provide readers with a resource we wish we had as students thinking about what difference our Indigenous identities could bring to our readings of Scripture.[1] In order to keep this prelude/appendix succinct, its style admittedly reads like Wikipedia entries of people and their contributions. This extended protocol-and-acknowledgment section, then, also functions as a brief reference guide that can be skimmed. While we seek to identify some helpful works in print, we recognize that Indigenous interpretation of Scripture is a way of life that manifests in pulpits, contemplative prayers, ceremony, group Bible studies, translation efforts, and quiet devotional reading. Indigenous interpretations of the Bible need not be published to be meaningful. Much Indigenous interpretations are oral, living commentaries within communities.

Here we celebrate many of the brilliant ideas and ways of interpreting Scripture that didn't make it into our other chapters. For those of our uncles and aunties who have been wondering when we might reference them more, we saved the best for last (in print), which has been in the forefront of our minds and hearts.[2]

RESCUING THE GOSPEL FROM THE COWBOYS

From the earliest encounters with missionaries, First Nations peoples on Turtle Island have interpreted the Bible through their own lenses. William Apess (Pequot; 1798–1839), a Methodist minister, was an early advocate for equality and the ordination of ministers of color. In his 1833 essay *An Indian's Looking-Glass for the White Man*, Apess asked: "Did you ever hear or read of Christ teaching his disciples that they ought to despise one because his skin

---

[1]See also Jace Weaver, "From I-Hermeneutics to We-Hermeneutics," in *Native American Religious Identity: Forgotten Gods*, ed. Jace Weaver (Maryknoll, NY: Orbis Books, 1998), 1-25. Weaver poignantly introduces Indigenous interpretations of Scripture and envisions a postcolonial Native hermeneutics in which expansive community—including "all our relations"—is both an interpretive tool and the goal of interpretation (22).

[2]Portions of this final chapter adapt and reuse parts of what we have written in other spaces, including T. Christopher Hoklotubbe and H. Daniel Zacharias, "Turtle Island Biblical Interpretation," in *The New Testament in Color: A Multiethnic Biblical Commentary*, ed. Esau McCauley, Jannette H. Ok, Osvaldo Padilla, and Amy L. B. Peeler (Downers Grove, IL: InterVarsity Press, 2024), 25-34; Hoklotubbe and Zacharias, "Indigenous North American/Turtle Island Hermeneutics," in *Handbook on Postconservative Theological Interpretation*, ed. Ronald T. Michener and Mark A. Lamport (Eugene, OR: Cascade, 2024).

was different from theirs? . . . Did not he who completed the plan of salvation complete it for the whites as well as for the Jews, and others?"[3] In *A Son of the Forest*, Apess went on to compare Native customs to Hebrew traditions, suggesting Natives were descendants of the lost tribes of Israel.[4] Similarly, Arthur Wellington Clah (Tsimshian; 1831–1916), a Methodist missionary, chronicled his reflections on Scripture and the Christian life in extensive diaries. Clah even dreamed about Scripture, recounting one dream where Christ gave him passages to read from Mark 1:1-8 concerning John the Baptist's announcement of the Messiah.[5] Donald B. Smith documented the work of eight nineteenth-century Ojibwe Methodist ministers who preached Christ while advocating for Native rights against colonial oppression.[6] Edward Andrews's *Native Apostles* highlights countless Native itinerant preachers who contextualized the gospel to their Indigenous communities.[7] Our project stands on the shoulders of these saints and countless others, honoring their legacy of faith and advocacy.

Vine Deloria Jr. Vine Deloria Jr. (Standing Rock Sioux) is a foundational figure in Native American theology and Indigenous biblical interpretation. His book *God Is Red* was a foundational guide for many Indigenous peoples to articulate and legitimize their ancestral traditions apart from Christian Euroamerican theology.[8] Descending from a lineage of Dakota Episcopal ministers and having earned a theological degree from the Lutheran School of Theology in Chicago, Deloria Jr. was primed to critique biblical interpretations from an Indigenous perspective. For example, in chapters such as "The Problem of Creation" and "Sacred Places and Moral Responsibility," he contrasts Western Christian views of creation as a fallen event with Indigenous perspectives of creation as an interconnected tapestry requiring

---

[3] William Apess, "An Indian's Looking-Glass for the White Man," in *The Experiences of Five Christian Indians of the Pequod Tribe* (Boston: James B. Dow, 1833), 57. See also his autobiography, *A Son of the Forest*, in *On Our Own Ground: The Complete Writings of William Apess, A Pequot*, ed. Barry O'Connell (Amherst: University of Massachusetts Press, 1992).

[4] See O'Connell, *On Our Own Ground*, 52-97, esp. 92-94.

[5] Peggy Brock, *The Many Voyages of Arthur Wellington Clah: A Tsimshian Man on the Pacific Northwest Coast* (Vancouver: UBC, 2011), 172.

[6] Donald B. Smith, *Mississauga Portraits: Ojibwe Voices from Nineteenth-Century Canada* (Toronto: University of Toronto Press, 2013).

[7] Edward E. Andrews, *Native Apostles: Black and Indian Missionaries in the British Atlantic World* (Cambridge, MA: Harvard University Press, 2013).

[8] Vine Deloria Jr., *God Is Red: A Native View of Religion*, 30th anniv. ed. (Golden, CO: Fulcrum, 2003).

harmony.⁹ Moreover, Deloria Jr. highlights Indigenous peoples' focus on space and place over Western culture's emphasis on time and individualism. Reflecting on the impact of *God Is Red*, Tink Tinker observes that the distinctions Deloria Jr. articulated are now foundational for understanding Native cultures and thought.¹⁰ Deloria's work continues to shape the study of Indigenous traditions and worldviews.

Homer Noley, Tink Tinker, Clara Sue Kidwell. One of the first significant resources Chris encountered on Native American contributions to biblical interpretation was *A Native American Theology*, coauthored by Clara Sue Kidwell (Choctaw, Ojibwe), Homer Noley (Choctaw), and George E. "Tink" Tinker (wazhazhe/Osage), with contributions from Jace Weaver (Cherokee). This work articulates a Native hermeneutic advocating for self-determination in interpreting Scripture and culture, rather than relying on settler perspectives.¹¹ Organized around traditional theological themes—hermeneutics, creation, Christology, and more—it also addresses distinct Indigenous topics such as the trickster and land. While the volume's chapter on hermeneutics briefly introduces Indigenous interpretations of the Bible, the book primarily focuses on Native histories, stories, and lifeways rather than on Scripture. This book remains a foundational resource for Indigenous Christians and a cornerstone of Turtle Island hermeneutics.

Tinker was an early inspiration for Indigenous hermeneutics, though he now distances himself from works blending Indigenous and Christian worldviews, viewing these cultures as fundamentally incompatible.¹² For Tinker, eurochristian frameworks often corrupt Native worldviews, replacing community-ism with individualism, spatiality with temporality, and egalitarianism with hierarchical systems. He critiques how eurochristian missionaries reinterpreted Indigenous rituals and cosmologies to fit their own values,

---

⁹Deloria, *God Is Red*, 77-96, esp. 87.

¹⁰Tink Tinker, "Foreword," in Deloria, *God Is Red*, xii.

¹¹Clara Sue Kidwell, Homer Noley, and George E. "Tink" Tinker, *A Native American Theology* (Maryknoll, NY: Orbis Books, 2001), 21-31.

¹²Tink Tinker, interview, November 18, 2022. For an overview and development of Tinker's thought and life, see Tinker, "jesus, the gospel, and Genocide," in *The Colonial Compromise: The Threat of the Gospel to the Indigenous Worldview*, ed. Miguel A. De La Torre (Lanham, MD: Lexington Books/Fortress Academic, 2020), 133-60; Tinker, "Why Is Distinguishing a Native American World View from a Eurochristian One Important," in *Indigenous Religious Traditions in Five Minutes*, ed. Molly H. Bassett and Natalie Avalos (Sheffield, UK: Equinox), 199-201.

often stripping these traditions of their original meaning. Tinker argues that even the concept of the Creator has been sanitized, erasing the diversity of creators in Indigenous stories, such as Coyote (California tribes), Sky Woman (Haudenosaunee), and Nanabozho (Algonquin).[13] Tinker laments, "Ultimately, we cannot really frame the gospel with our own heritage; all we can do is add banal, Indian-like window dressing."[14]

Nonetheless, Chris credits Tinker's earlier work with inspiring him to explore how Indigenous stories might contribute to Christian theology. Tinker's suggestion that Christ, as God's eternal *Logos*, could inspire ancestral stories such as that of Corn Mother challenged traditional atonement theories and invited more expansive theological reflection.[15] Today, Tinker writes in the vein of Vine Deloria Jr., articulating critical distinctions between Indigenous and eurochristian worldviews and providing invaluable insights for ongoing dialogue.[16]

The NAIITS matriarchs. NAIITS: An Indigenous Learning Community has been essential in shaping our approaches to interpreting Scripture in authentically Indigenous ways.[17] Without NAIITS, there would still be Danny and Chris, but we'd be far less interesting to read. Before discussing the founders of NAIITS, we first acknowledge its matriarchs, recognizing that many Indigenous communities, including some our friends belong to, are matrilineal societies. Even in non-matrilineal nations, Indigenous cultures value the sacred balance of male and female roles within communities. As in many churches worldwide, much of the support within faith communities is carried out by women, and NAIITS is no exception. Bev LeBlanc, Katherine Twiss, Elaine Aldred, and Edith Woodley were partners in the work alongside their husbands. They offered sacrificial gifts of wisdom,

---

[13]Tink Tinker, "Why I Do Not Believe in a Creator," in *Buffalo Shout, Salmon Cry: Conversations on Creation, Land Justice, and Life Together*, ed. Steve Heinrichs (Waterloo, ON: Herald, 2013), 167-79.

[14]Tink Tinker, "Weaponized christianity: missiology, jesus, the gospel, and Indigenous Genocide," in *T&T Clark Handbook on Intercultural Theology and Missiology*, ed. John Flett and Dorottya Nagy (London: T&T Clark, forthcoming).

[15]Kidwell, Noley, and Tinker, *Native American Theology*, 76-84.

[16]See Tinker, "jesus, the gospel, and Genocide." See also Tink Tinker, "What Are We Going to Do with White People?," The New Polis, December 17, 2019, https://thenewpolis.com/2019/12/17/what-are-we-going-to-do-with-white-people-tink-tinker-wazhazhe-osage-nation/.

[17]For an overview of NAIITS's history, see Wendy L. Peterson, "A Gifting of Sweetgrass: The Reclamation of Culture Movement and NAIITS: An Indigenous Learning Community" (PhD diss., Asbury Theological Seminary, 2018), 184-88.

presence, organization, and support, contributing to both the foreground and background of NAIITS.

Wendy Peterson (Red River Métis) and Cheryl Bear (Nadleh Whut'en, Bear Clan) were part of the NAIITS's founding members and made significant contributions through their teachings, essays, and leadership. Wendy, as editor for the first fifteen volumes of the *Journal of NAIITS*, shaped much of the community's thinking. Her legacy is part of NAIITS's DNA. Cheryl's writings and teachings have also been influential.[18] I (Danny) have a significant memory of how Cheryl's words and songs at a 2018 Canadian Baptist conference were good medicine in my journey, helping me reclaim my Indigenous heritage and recognize that colonization, though devastating, could not take everything from Indigenous peoples nor did it take everything from my family.

Later, Shari Russell joined NAIITS and became its director after Terry LeBlanc's retirement. Her story and scriptural interpretation are featured in chapter six, for which we are thankful. Crystal Porter, a former NAIITS student and now professor, chairs the board of Indigenous Pathways, NAIITS's parent organization. Matriarchs continue to lead and shape this vital community.

Richard Twiss. Richard Twiss (Sicangu Lakota/Rosebud Reservation) is often regarded as a patron saint of the Native-led contextualization movement from which Turtle Island hermeneutics emerges. Twiss pursued doctoral studies alongside leaders such as Cheryl Bear, Wendy Peterson, Terry LeBlanc, Randy Woodley, and Ray Aldred to gain a hearing among non-Indigenous Christian leaders. A charismatic and in-demand speaker, Twiss was known for his ability to communicate hard truths with conviction, bridging Indigenous and non-Indigenous audiences. While neither of us met him before his passing in 2013, we have experienced his presence through NAIITS, the organization he helped establish, and the many lives he touched by encouraging others to reclaim their cultural heritage as followers of Jesus.[19]

---

[18]Cheryl Bear-Barnetson, *Introduction to First Nations Ministry* (Cleveland, TN: Cherohala, 2013); Wendy Peterson, Cheryl Bear, and Linda M. Martin, "Ways of Knowing Self: Reclamation of Real Indigenous Identity," *Journal of NAIITS* 9 (2011): 31-57.

[19]Volume 11 of the *Journal of NAIITS* was a memorial issue dedicated to Richard Twiss, with five tributes published. See also Sue Martell, Ray Martell, and Richard Twiss, *Dreamcatching: Following in the Footsteps of Richard Twiss* (Cleveland, TN: Cherohala, 2017).

Twiss was instrumental in the Indigenous-led contextualization movement, co-organizing the World Christian Gathering of Indigenous Peoples, initiated by Monté (Ngati Pukenga, Ngaiterangi, Te Arawa-Māori) and Linda (Te Atiawa o Te Waka-a-Māui) Ohia, which held eight gatherings from 1996 to 2011.[20] This global effort supported Indigenous communities in following Jesus in culturally authentic ways. Twiss's legacy continues through his books, *One Church, Many Tribes* and *Rescuing the Gospel from the Cowboys*, which document the Native contextualization movement and inspire Indigenous believers and allies.[21]

Twiss's work wrestled with issues of culture, drawing on the New Testament's treatment of Jewish and Gentile relations. He challenged conventional narratives, particularly around syncretism, arguing that all Christian traditions, including European ones, involve cultural mixing. This opened discussions on worldview differences, emphasizing that colonization imposed not just Euroamerican culture but its worldview as well. Personally, I (Danny) was profoundly influenced by Twiss's assertion that Jesus was a tribal man, rooted in the history, community, and land of his people. This perspective was a revelation for me and has deeply shaped my understanding of Jesus and the Gospels, as reflected in this book and my commentary on Matthew from an Indigenous perspective.[22]

Adrian Jacobs. In *Aboriginal Christianity: The Way It Was Meant to Be*, our elder and uncle Adrian Jacobs (Cayuga of the Six Nations Haudenosaunee Confederacy) powerfully writes about how Scripture in dialogue with First Nations stories and traditions casts a compelling vision toward living and healing into a healthy Indigenous church. Speaking about Creator's design for diversity, Jacobs warns against a flat reading of the story of the tower of Babel (Gen 11:1-9) that interprets God's multiplication of languages to halt construction of the tower as suggesting that the diversity of cultures results from Creator's judgment. Diverse cultures, Jacobs contends,

---

[20]You can read a fuller narration on the World Christian Gathering of Indigenous Peoples in Peterson, "Gifting of Sweetgrass," 173-78.

[21]Richard Twiss, *One Church, Many Tribes: Following Jesus the Way God Made You* (Minneapolis: Chosen Books, 2000); Richard Twiss, *Rescuing the Gospel from the Cowboys: A Native American Expression of the Jesus Way* (Downers Grove, IL: InterVarsity Press, 2015).

[22]H. Daniel Zacharias, "Gospel of Matthew," in *The New Testament in Color: A Multiethnic Bible Commentary*, ed. Esau McCaulley, Janette H. Ok, Osvaldo Padilla, and Amy L. B. Peeler (Downers Grove, IL: IVP Academic, 2024), 43-94.

are a natural outgrowth of Creator's command to spread.[23] Ultimately, Jacobs is concerned about an all-too-common experience of missionaries who assume that their cultural expression of Christian sacraments is the only correct way of worshiping the Creator, either prohibiting or denigrating Indigenous attempts to honor Christ within the forms of their own ancestral ceremonies, feasts, and rites-of-passage rituals. Throughout *Aboriginal Christianity*, Jacobs catalogs Scripture passages and stories that illustrate the Creator's care for animals and plants, Creator's prophetic inspiration among and provisions for Gentile/Aboriginal peoples, and Creator's concern for upholding treaties and vision for healthy ecclesial decision-making processes that are in line with Indigenous values, stories, and traditions. *Aboriginal Christianity* and *Pagan Prophets and Heathen Believers* were early classics among many Indigenous Christian circles, empowering ministers and lay leaders to envision what church communities would look like if they were guided by their Indigenous cultures.[24] In addition to these works, Uncle Adrian's numerous articles in the *Journal of NAIITS* are testament to his keen insights, his poet's heart, and his prophetic challenge to the wider church.

Terry LeBlanc. Terry LeBlanc (Mi'kmaq, Acadian), like many NAIITS founders, has been ministering among Indigenous peoples since before Chris and Danny were born. Uncle Terry's work spans global community development and supporting Indigenous networks. His teachings have made significant contributions to missiology, theology, culture, mission history in Canada and Indigenous, trauma-informed care and counseling. His involvement in the World Christian Gathering of Indigenous Peoples alongside Richard Twiss, and his leadership in Canada's first Sacred Assembly and Reconciliation Proclamation, have laid vital groundwork for ongoing reconciliation efforts in the Canadian church.

Meeting Uncle Terry years ago sparked my (Danny's) journey of cultural reclamation and the integration of theology and biblical studies through an Indigenous lens. Much of my past decade's research and writing would not exist without this relationship. Uncle Terry and the other NAIITS founders

---

[23] Adrian Jacobs, *Aboriginal Christianity: The Way It Was Meant to Be* (Belleville, ON: self-published, 1998), 22.

[24] Adrian Jacobs, *Pagan Prophets and Heathen Believers* (Edmonton, AB: self-published, 1999).

have also gifted the community with shared language and concepts such as right-relationship, right-relatedness, and asset-based thinking, which feature prominently in this book. These ideas fuel the work of many within NAIITS, though their origins often blur over time, evolving from "Terry once said" to "the elders say" and even "like I often say." This is how wisdom and teaching infuses itself and perpetuates within a community that is truly communitarian.

This living, dynamic community, enriched by the contributions of its members and the cloud of witnesses around us, reflects a communal ethic that values shared wisdom over intellectual property. If that ever changes, Chris and Danny may face some amusing charges of copyright infringement. Nonetheless, Uncle Terry's legacy continues to shape and inspire the NAIITS community and the work of Indigenous followers of Jesus.

Randy Woodley. Randy Woodley (descendant of the United Keetoowah Band of Cherokee), another founding member of NAIITS, has worked with Indigenous peoples for decades.[25] His doctoral work laid the groundwork for his influential book *Shalom and the Community of Creation*, a work deeply meaningful for both of us, especially resonating in chapter three.[26] Danny had the pleasure of hosting Randy and Edith (Eastern Shoshone) at Acadia Divinity College for the Hayward Lectures, which led to another significant book, *Indigenous Theology and The Western Worldview: A Decolonized Approach to Christian Doctrine*.[27] Randy has made substantial contributions through his books, articles, and teaching career at Portland Seminary. Now, he and Edith co-sustain the Eloheh Indigenous Center for Earth Justice and have transitioned to writing screenplays.[28]

A particularly important contribution is Randy's discussion of the "four books"—creation, conscience, community, and Scriptures—that serve as teachers. This fourfold framework, explored in chapter six of *Mission and the*

---

[25] Read Woodley's retelling of his story and early work as a "missionary oppressor" in Randy S. Woodley, *Mission and the Cultural Other: A Closer Look* (Eugene, OR: Cascade, 2022). The founding members of NAIITS are Ray Aldred, Cheryl Bear, Cornelius Buller, Steve Cheramie-risingson, Adrian Jacobs, Terry LeBlanc, Wendy Peterson, Richard Twiss, and Randy Woodley.
[26] Randy S. Woodley, *Shalom and the Community of Creation: An Indigenous Vision*, Prophetic Christianity (Grand Rapids, MI: Eerdmans, 2012).
[27] Randy S. Woodley, *Indigenous Theology and the Western Worldview: A Decolonized Approach to Christian Doctrine*, Acadia Studies in Bible and Theology (Grand Rapids, MI: Baker Academic, 2022).
[28] See Randy Woodley and Edith Woodley, *Journey to Eloheh: How Indigenous Values Lead Us to Harmony and Well-Being* (Minneapolis: Broadleaf Books, 2024).

Cultural Other, helped to give birth to our Turtle Island hermeneutics medicine wheel approach, which is detailed in chapter one above.

Randy's legacy continues to shape Indigenous theology and practices. His willingness to challenge conventional academic norms while centering Indigenous wisdom has left a lasting impact, not only in scholarship but also in how Indigenous communities engage theology and creation care.

Ray Aldred. Ray Aldred (Cree), yet another founder of NAIITS, currently serves as the director of the Indigenous studies program at Vancouver School of Theology. Ray has decades of experience in ministry and has published significant work in Indigenous theology and biblical interpretation. In particular, his focus on story as foundational for Indigenous peoples and approaching Scripture as story has significantly shaped our present work.[29] Especially important for us is Uncle Ray's work on communal identity and its wider implications for theology. This work has helped us as we reflected and built our Turtle Island hermeneutics medicine wheel. As Ray has shown, an Indigenous identity is not only communal but is also inclusive of land.[30] His writing reminds us that land is not a commodity or resource but a place we belong to, a place that is part of our personal and communal identity. And in this book we show from the Scriptures that this was true of Jesus as well. This shows the interconnected nature of Indigenous identity, worldviews, and lifeways—an interconnectedness we embody and practice in our medicine wheel hermeneutical approach. Danny had the privilege of interviewing Uncle Ray in preparation for this work and to teach with him at Vancouver School of Theology's Indigenous studies summer school program. Chris made one unmemorable online appearance in Uncle Ray's New Testament course and hasn't been invited back.

As we complete our review of the NAIITS founders, we also acknowledge the two remaining founders of NAIITS that have not been highlighted above,

---

[29]Ray Aldred, "The Resurrection of Story," *Journal of NAIITS* 2 (2004): 5-14; Ray Aldred and Catherine Aldred-Shull, "First Peoples, Narrative, and Bible Translation," in *Reading In-Between: How Minoritized Cultural Communities Interpret the Bible in Canada*, ed. Néstor Medina, Alison Hari-Singh, and HyeRan Kim-Cragg (Eugene, OR: Wipf & Stock, 2019), 96-111. Focused more specifically on Romans but still with his storied approach, see Ray Aldred, "North American Indigenous Perspective," in *Preaching Romans from Here: Diverse Voices Engage Paul's Most Famous Letter*, ed. Joseph B. Modica, Lisa M. Bowens, and Scot McKnight (Eugene, OR: Wipf & Stock, 2023), 75-90.

[30]See Ray Aldred, "An Alternative Starting Place for an Indigenous Theology" (PhD diss., Toronto School of Theology, 2020); Aldred, "The Land, Treaty, and Spirituality: Communal Identity Inclusive of Land," *Journal of NAIITS* 18 (2019): 1-17.

Steve Cheramie (Houma-Biloxi Chitimacha) and Cornelius Buller (the only non-Indigenous founding member). These two men contributed to the early formulation of the NAIITS community before their passing.

Mark Wallace. We hope one day to have the pleasure of meeting Mark I. Wallace to thank him for his contributions to our thinking. In particular, Wallace's two works *Finding God in the Singing River* and *When God Was A Bird* have stirred in us a greater appreciation for the presence of God in creation and our ability to encounter God through creation.[31] Wallace's work, along with Mari Joerstad's *The Hebrew Bible and Environmental Ethics*, has also challenged the typically pejorative use of "animism" as a label for Indigenous worldviews, showing not only how scholars and Christians have wrongly misinterpreted the phenomenon but also how animism has much resonance with Christian theology and the Scriptures.[32]

Steven Charleston. Danny and Chris wish they could present this book as the first monograph on Native American interpretations of Scripture, but that honor belongs to retired Episcopal Bishop Steven Charleston (Choctaw) and his groundbreaking work, *The Four Vision Quests of Jesus*.[33] Its impact on our interpretation of Scripture cannot be overstated, as evidenced by how often we reference it. Charleston offers a close reading of the Gospel of Matthew, framing key events—such as John the Baptist's witness, Jesus' baptism, the transfiguration, Jesus' prayer on the Mount of Olives, and his crucifixion—through the lens of vision quests. He also interprets the ministries of John and Jesus within Indigenous frameworks of sacred clowns and tricksters, and juxtaposes biblical exodus stories with the Choctaw experience on the Trail of Tears, which Chris builds on in chapter five.[34] For Danny, Charleston's essay "The Old Testament of Native America" was an early and transformative influence during his theological education.[35]

---

[31]Mark I. Wallace, *Finding God in the Singing River: Christianity, Spirit, Nature* (Minneapolis: Fortress, 2005); Wallace, *When God Was a Bird: Christianity, Animism, and the Re-enchantment of the World*, Groundworks: Ecological Issues in Philosophy and Theology (New York: Fordham University Press, 2018).

[32]Mari Joerstad, *The Hebrew Bible and Environmental Ethics: Humans, Nonhumans, and the Living Landscape* (Cambridge: Cambridge University Press, 2019).

[33]Steven Charleston, *The Four Vision Quests of Jesus* (New York: Morehouse, 2015).

[34]See Charleston, *Four Vision Quests*, chap. 6.

[35]Steven Charleston, "The Old Testament of Native America," in *Lift Every Voice: Constructing Christian Theologies from the Underside*, rev. and expanded ed., ed. Susan Brooks Thistlethwaite and Mary Potter Engel (Maryknoll, NY: Orbis Books, 1990), 69-81.

Charleston, along with Elaine A. Robinson, also edited *Coming Full Circle: Constructing Native Christian Theology*, which provides a proactive approach to Christianity as a positive expression for Native people to claim and define on their own terms.[36] Similar to Noley, Tinker, and Kidwell's *Native American Theology*, this volume addresses traditional theological categories while engaging deeply with Native ceremonies, histories, and lifeways, rather than focusing on Scripture. One standout contribution is Marcus Briggs-Cloud's (Muscogee/Maskoke, Wind Clan) chapter on the biblical theme of new creation, which highlights the intentional Maskoke community *Ekvn-Yefolecv*.[37] This community embodies a vision of revitalizing Maskoke language, culture, and sovereignty—a new creation, indeed. Like *Native American Theology*, we highly recommend *Coming Full Circle* and hope our work complements these groundbreaking volumes.

Laura E. Donaldson. Laura E. Donaldson (Cherokee) was one of the first feminist Indigenous interpreters Chris encountered during his graduate studies.[38] In "The Sign of Orpah," Donaldson repositions Orpah as a symbol of resisting cultural assimilation and an aspirational model for Indigenous people. She interprets Ruth's story in light of how US politicians, including Thomas Jefferson, promoted intermarriage as a means of assimilating and civilizing Native Americans. Donaldson also highlights how Cherokee matrilineal customs—according to which husbands joined their wife's clan—were disrupted as Cherokee women married white men and assimilated into their husbands' culture. While Christian interpretation and Jewish midrash celebrate Ruth for her loving faithfulness (*ḥesed*) to Naomi, Orpah is castigated as the foil to Ruth's faithfulness for returning back to her "mother's house" (Ruth 1:8). However, Donaldson reframes Orpah as a symbol of hope for Cherokee women, representing loyalty to traditions and sacred ancestors.[39]

---

[36] Steven Charleston and Elaine A. Robinson, eds., *Coming Full Circle: Constructing Native Christian Theology* (Minneapolis: Fortress, 2015), viii.

[37] Marcus Briggs-Cloud, "Creation—the New Creation: A Maskoke Postcolonial Perspective"; Charleston and Robinson, *Coming Full Circle*, 89-118.

[38] See Laura E. Donaldson, "Native Women and Double Cross: Christology from the Contact Zone," *Semeia* 73 (2002): 96-117; Donaldson, "Theological Composting in Romans 8: An Indigenous Meditation on Paul's Rhetoric of Decay," in Heinrichs, *Buffalo Shout*, 142-48.

[39] Laura Donaldson, "The Sign of Orpah: Reading Ruth Through Native Eyes," in *Hope Abundant: Third World and Indigenous Women's Theology*, ed. Kwok Pui-lan (Maryknoll, NY: Orbis Books, 2010), 148.

Ruth, in contrast, is viewed as a mythologized "Pocahontas," valued only for aiding the dominant class. Where Ruth's journey to Judah "involves relinquishing of her ethnic and cultural identity," Orpah's decision to return to her indigenous mother's home then becomes "a courageous act of self and communal affirmation."[40]

Indigenous Anglican ministers and bishops. In Canada, former National Indigenous Anglican Bishop Mark MacDonald has been a force for change for many decades. Mark's work has crisscrossed him across the continent, strengthening Indigenous believers and confronting the wider church with hard questions in his gentle manner. Danny has been privileged to share time in ministry with Mark as part of Indigenous theological training of the Anglican church. In an interview, Mark stated:

> I find it helpful to ask myself: "How would an elder look at this passage? How would they understand it? In what way would it impact them? How would they read it?" Part of it has to do with circumstances of survival. Survival was a big issue, and when you survive for a long time you obviously were doing something right. You had insights into how things worked that are really important. The elders are critical to the identity of the whole community. Now Indigenous culture and identity are trying to go through a renaissance—a kind of recovery and restoration—and the elders are the key to that because they're the ones who have the wisdom and the values and the perspective. So I see elders as really critical.[41]

Another labor of love that deserves mention is the *First Peoples Theology Journal*, something done with a larger group of editors and contributors of Indigenous faith leaders from around the world. This group included Rev. Dr. Martin Brokenleg, whom Danny had the privilege of interviewing in preparation for this work. Brokenleg's life and work is inspirational, and we hope one day to see memoirs from Dr. Brokenleg in print. Danny was also privileged to spend time with Rev. Vincent Solomon in preparation for this work and benefited greatly from listening to the stories from the *Sacred Teachings* podcast hosted by Rev. Canon Ginny Doctor until her passing.

---

[40] Donaldson, "Sign of Orpah," 146, 149.
[41] Joey Royal, "Deep Faith: A Conversation with Bishop Mark MacDonald," *Covenant: TLC's Online Journal*, October 14, 2016, https://livingchurch.org/covenant/deep-faith-a-conversation-with-bishop-mark-macdonald.

ON COWBOYS AND CANAANITES

Robert Allen Warrior's (Osage) iconic essay, "Canaanites, Cowboys, and Indians," is often students' first introduction to Indigenous interpretations of Scripture.[42] Warrior questions whether the exodus story, foundational for many liberation theologies, can offer hope to Native Americans. His answer, to the surprise of many Christians, is no. The God of Israel who liberates also conquers, displaces, and kills the Indigenous peoples of Canaan. For Indigenous people, Warrior suggests, the clear identification is with the Canaanites. While scholars debate the historicity of the conquest narrative in the book of Joshua or whether the Canaanites assimilated into Israel, the story's destruction and dispossession of the Canaanites remain palpable.[43] Even assimilation, Warrior argues, erases Indigenous stories and perpetuates cultural loss. Warrior concludes that Native Americans seeking justice may need to look beyond Christianity, highlighting a deep tension between Indigenous identity and a faith marred by colonialism and genocide.[44] Warrior's essay reminds us that "while texts may not be fixed in meaning, they are not free-floating signifiers either. They are imbricated in histories of which they cannot easily be disentangled."[45]

In response, Jace Weaver (Cherokee) turns to the story of Zelophehad's daughters (Num 27; Josh 17). He suggests these daughters, whose names correspond to towns in northern Canaan and thus indicate they were probably Canaanites themselves, symbolize the vulnerable advocating for themselves while maintaining their cultural integrity as Canaanites among Hebrew settlers.[46] Mary Crist (Blackfeet) expands on Weaver's reading, stating that this story can be a model for Indigenous people on "how to go about sharing

---

[42]Robert Alan Warrior, "Canaanites, Cowboys, and Indians: Deliverance, Conquest, and Liberation Theology Today," in *Native and Christian: Indigenous Voices on Religious Identity in the United States and Canada*, ed. James Treat (New York: Routledge, 1996), 93-100.

[43]We recognize the many and layered discussions on Joshua and the conquest further complicate the narrative and discussion, as scholars debate the level to which this historical event can truly be understood as a military conquest or a slow spread and settlement into Canaan. A recent suggestion by Matthew Lynch is that the conquest should be seen as the completion of the exodus, with the military sites of Canaan historically being Egyptian-controlled city-states. See Matthew J. Lynch, *Flood and Fury: Old Testament Violence and the Shalom of God* (Downers Grove, IL: IVP Academic, 2023), chap. 11.

[44]Warrior, "Canaanites, Cowboys, and Indians," 100.

[45]Andrea Smith, "Decolonizing Theology," *Union Seminary Quarterly Review* 59 (2005): 78.

[46]Jace Weaver, "A Biblical Paradigm for Native Liberation," in Treat, *Native and Christian*, 104.

God with, and living in the middle of, a foreign people, yet preserve their own identity."[47]

William Baldridge (Cherokee) finds hope in the story of the Canaanite woman (Mt 15:21-28).[48] Despite Jesus' initial rebuff, calling her a "dog," she claims her voice and persuades Jesus to heal her daughter. For Baldridge, this symbolizes reconciliation, with Indigenous peoples being able to "change the heart of God" and achieve healing and harmony.[49]

James Treat (Muscogee/Creek) suggests this story reflects Jesus' overcoming his ethnocentric bias, recognizing the woman's "great faith" (Mt 15:28) on its own terms without requiring her to conform to Jewish traditions. The Canaanite woman becomes a model for Indigenous people seeking affirmation in Christian spaces, prompting "Jesus to recognize the validity and authenticity of her unique faith experience, even though at first it seemed strange, inferior, or even non-existent."[50]

For Mark Charles (Diné/Navajo), there doesn't seem to be any satisfying way to handwave Jesus' denigration of the Canaanite woman as a dog. Similar to Treat, Charles finds Jesus holding "the ethnocentric views of his time" and seeming to hold Gentiles at arm's length, including the centurion (Mt 8:5-13; Lk 7:1-10) and the man with the unclean spirit living among the tombs in the Gerasene region (Mk 5:1-20; Mt 8:28-34; Lk 8:26-39). For Charles, Natives as Gentiles find themselves written into the story only when Cornelius, the centurion, and his household receive the Holy Spirit and are baptized (Acts 10:1-48). Yet Charles highlights Jesus' charge to the healed Gerasene man (Lk 8:39) to return home and share what God has done as an invitation to contextualize faith within Indigenous traditions. This perspective has motivated Charles to explore Navajo creation stories alongside the Bible for what a reconciled relationship with Creator looks like.[51]

---

[47]Mary Crist, "Frybread in Canaan," *First People's Theology Journal* 1, no. 1 (2014): 12.
[48]William Baldridge, "Native American Theology: A Biblical Basis," in Treat, *Native and Christian*, 100.
[49]Baldridge, "Native American Theology," 101. New Testament scholar Richard Bauckham also interprets the Canaanite woman's words as having the power to change Jesus' mind. See Bauckham, *Gospel Women: Studies of the Named Women in the Gospels* (Louisville, KY: Westminster John Knox, 2021), 41-2.
[50]James Treat, "The Canaanite Problem," *Daughters of Sarah: The Magazine for Christian Feminists* 20 (1994): 24.
[51]Mark Charles, "Good Medicine Way 03/07/22 with Mark Charles," YouTube, March 8, 2022, 2:26:48, https://youtu.be/YfCf-mj5sWU?si=vuhrl2ElyDvQfEZh. Of course, the topic of how the

Returning to the Canaanite woman, we wonder whether Jesus plays the role of a "sacred clown," whose playful offense served to invite something magical from the Canaanite woman that might not have otherwise occurred. In Indigenous traditions, sacred clowns, which include *koshares* of the Pueblos in the Southwest and *heyokas* of the Sioux in the Plains, are notorious for saying and doing contrary, even offensive things in order to shock their audiences into new insights.[52] By calling the woman a "dog," Jesus provokes the determined mother's sassy *word* (*logos*) and declaration of faith, which holds a power that she may not have known she had but will now never forget.[53] This story challenges toxic ethnic hierarchies and centers the woman's voice as an agent of healing. In Creator's kin-dom, there are no more "dogs"; all children are welcomed to the table as heirs. It also invites theological reflection: Can our Christology hold a Jesus who grows in wisdom (Lk 2:52) and confronts his people's history of dispossessing others?

TRANSLATION IS INTERPRETATION

Entire monographs could be written on how the ceremonial lifeways, stories, and values of First Nations peoples have shaped Bible translations in their languages. These translation projects, historic and ongoing, represent rich moments of Turtle Island hermeneutics.[54] Ray Aldred and Catherine Aldred-Shull have written about the "hermeneutic of love," a dynamic of mutuality in which both a people and the biblical story are transformed through their encounter.[55] This approach envisions translations grounded in Indigenous

---

Gospels represent the value of Gentiles is more complicated. In Mt 1–2 alone, righteous Gentile women are identified in Christ's lineage (Mt 1:1-14), and the presence of the magi (Mt 2) further establishes the inclusion of the Gentiles in the Messiah's story. See also Randy Woodley's response: "Good Medicine Way 03/21/22 with Randy Woodley," YouTube, March 21, 2022, 2:16:02, https://youtu.be/8ei2_zgcHaU?si=lMdsWSTboQkHNAw_.

[52] Charleston, *Four Vision Quests*, 56-64.

[53] Chris credits this insightful reading to his friend Mitzi Smith, *Womanist Sass and Talk Back: Social (In)Justice, Intersectionality, and Biblical Interpretation* (Eugene, OR: Cascade, 2018), 28-45, esp. 41-45.

[54] For a very brief introduction to the history of Bible translation in Canada among First Nations peoples, see Aldred and Aldred-Shull, "First Peoples, Narrative, and Bible Translation," 101-7.

[55] Aldred and Aldred-Shull define a "hermeneutic of love" as "a dynamic of mutuality that takes place between a people and a biblical story: as a people encounter the gospel, its message changes because of the ethno-cultural identity and history of the people—but those people also change as a result of encountering the gospel. Neither the scripture nor the people become something they were not meant to be" ("First Peoples, Narrative, and Bible Translation," 98).

categories, theologies, and worldviews, reflecting their "heart language." For example, a First Nations translation of Jesus healing Bartimaeus (Mk 10:46-52) might emphasize how the story poetically begins and ends on "a path" (*hodos* in Greek), resonating with the First Nations' emphasis on place over time.[56]

In September 2024, Chris traveled to his ancestral lands of Choctaw, Mississippi, to meet with the Choctaw Bible Translation Committee. This team, composed of elders fluent in Choctaw, including Roseanna Tubby, is committed to updating the previous Choctaw version of the Bible such that it reflects more modern spoken Choctaw. Their sessions, filled with joy and spiritual presence, blend translation work with storytelling, passing cultural and linguistic knowledge to younger generations.

Terry Wildman (Ojibwe, Yaqui) is the lead translator of the *First Nations Version*, which he completed with an Indigenous translation council to renarrate biblical texts in the heart languages of English-speaking First Nations people.[57] Unique to this translation is its use of Native naming traditions, such as Jesus as Creator Sets Free, Mary as Bitter Tears, and Bethlehem as House of Bread. The style of the prose is inspired by the storytelling voice of elders such as Black Elk, whose teachings inspired Wildman and many other Indigenous people to revitalize their Indigenous cultures. While the *First Nations Version* has faced criticism, its reception among many Native American laypeople and congregations has been overwhelmingly positive, evidenced by heartfelt letters expressing gratitude for its resonance and impact. In October 2022, Chris observed a workshop led by Terry in which he guided college students in rewriting Psalm 15 to reflect their Native heritage. Students reflected on Scripture, identified names of sacred hills from their lands (Ps 15:1), and looked up questions on their phones that they never thought to ask, including whether their tribe lent money at interest (Ps 15:5)

---

[56]Aldred and Aldred-Shull, "First Peoples, Narrative, and Bible Translation," 108-9. This spatial interpretation comes from George E. "Tink" Tinker, *Spirit and Resistance: Political Theology and American Indian Liberation* (Minneapolis: Fortress Press, 2004), 95-96. Tinker notes that translations tend to translate the Greek word *hodos* differently as "roadside" (Mark 10:46) and "way" (Mark 10:52), thus leading English readers to miss identifying any significance to the repetition of the place in this passage.

[57]Terry M. Wildman, ed., *First Nations Version: An Indigenous Translation of the New Testament* (Downers Grove, IL: InterVarsity Press, 2021), ix. See also Wildman, *Sign Languages: A Look at the Historic and Prophetic Landscape of America* (Maricopa, AZ: Great Thunder, 2011), in which Wildman interprets Scripture in light of US policies toward Native Americans.

or how their elders metaphorically described morality. What was produced was nothing short of stunning and sacred. Terry and his wife, Darlene, who is a talented flutist, continue to invest in the spiritual development of Indigenous young adults through their nonprofit Rain Ministries and work with Native InterVarsity, modeling Indigenous interpretations of Scripture in their speaking engagements and workshops.

TURTLE ISLAND HERMENEUTICS IS FOR SETTLERS TOO

Our vision for Turtle Island hermeneutics has been deeply enriched by settler-allies who engage the Bible toward decolonization, healing, and harmony. Just as Euroamerican readings have shaped First Nations readers, Turtle Island hermeneutics also has something to share with settlers striving to live in right-relationships with all their kin. We are particularly grateful for allies who amplify Native American perspectives to bring attention to their stories.

For example, Daniel L. Smith-Christopher's engagement with the book of Daniel alongside Lakota traditionalists on the Rosebud Reservation informs his commentary's parallels between Jewish experiences of Babylonian imperialism and Indigenous experiences of US colonialism.[58] Similarly, L. Daniel Hawk's *Joshua in 3-D* deconstructs how interpretations of Joshua have justified US conquest and dispossession of Native peoples.[59]

Non-Indigenous scholars such as William Stolzman, Achiel Peelman, and Mark Clatterbuck have amplified Indigenous voices in works such as *The Pipe and Christ*, *Christ Is a Native American*, and *Crow Jesus*.[60] These books feature dialogues on how Indigenous Christians harmonize—or wrestle with—Christianity within their ceremonies, traditions, and values.

One poignant example from *Christ Is a Native American* is sister Eva Solomon (Ojibway), who connects Luke 24's Emmaus story to Indigenous traditions, arguing that First Nations peoples must reflect on their own sacred

---

[58] Daniel Smith-Christopher, "The Book of Daniel," in *New Interpreter's Bible* (Nashville: Abingdon, 1996), 7:17-152.
[59] L. Daniel Hawk, *Joshua in 3-D: A Commentary on Biblical Conquest and Manifest Destiny* (Eugene, OR: Cascade Books, 2010).
[60] William Stolzman, *The Pipe and Christ*, 7th ed. (Chamberlain, SD: St. Joseph's Indian School, 2007); Achiel Peelman, *Christ Is a Native American* (Eugene, OR: Wipf & Stock, 1995); Mark Clatterbuck, *Crow Jesus: Personal Stories of Native Religious Belonging* (Norman: University of Oklahoma Press, 2017).

histories, their own "Old Testament," to understand Christ.[61] Solomon sees this echoed in John 4, where Jesus asks the Samaritan woman, in Solomon's words, "[to] drink from the well of your ancestors." Reflecting on her own traditions at Spirit Mountain in Ontario, Solomon realized the gospel's new meaning for her: the Samaritan woman's story was her story, affirming that understanding her people's history deepens her understanding of God's presence in their journey.[62]

Steve Heinrichs. We appreciate the work of Steve Heinrichs, who has edited volumes advancing and celebrating Indigenous voices and values in biblical interpretation in *Buffalo Shout, Salmon Cry: Conversations on Creation, Land Justice, and Life Together* and *Unsettling the Word: Biblical Experiments in Decolonization.*[63] As made clear in his introductions and entries in each volume, Heinrichs has invested much of himself toward the task of decolonizing biblical interpretation and theology among white settlers to promote justice, ecological sustainability, reconciliation, and reparations. Both books are chock-full of so much goodness, ranging from challenging critiques and stories meant to make readers uncomfortable with the destructive commitments of modern cultures and consumer capitalism to short, experimental pieces of poetry and poetic renarrations of biblical stories. For example, in *Unsettling the Word*, our friend Cheryl Bear (Nadleh Whut'en, Bear Clan), an award-winning musician, writes her own sensual love/worship song riffing off Song of Songs 1:5. Bear closes her song, "our love is a cedar longhouse made only for us / i trust this man more than i trust anyone / there is no shame, no fear, only / deep and effortless love."[64]

Ched Myers and Elaine Enns. Ched Myers's contribution to *Unsettling the Word* exemplifies a decolonizing approach to biblical interpretation, inviting readers to renarrate biblical stories in light of their bioregions, native inhabitants, and sociopolitical contexts. Living on Chumash land in Oakview, California, Myers reimagines John the Baptist's introduction in Mark 1:1 9 with imagery native to his region:

---

[61]Peelman, *Christ Is a Native American*, 128.
[62]Peelman, *Christ Is a Native American*, 129.
[63]See Heinrichs, *Buffalo Shout*; Steve Heinrichs, ed., *Unsettling the Word: Biblical Experiments in Decolonization* (Maryknoll, NY: Orbis Books, 2018).
[64]Cheryl Bear, "No Fence Can Hold," in Heinrichs, *Unsettling the Word*, 125.

Chumash and others caught in the Mission system went out to Kitsepawit [John the Baptist, reimagined as a historic Chumash cultural informant]. They came from all over southern California. A few Settlers too, even all the way form the big pueblo of San Francisco. They came for his purification ceremony in Matilija Creek up in the mountains, washing the colonial civilization right off and out of them.[65]

Myers explains that Matilija Creek's location, tucked away in the mountain canyons, would have been ideal for secretive Native resistance gatherings—resonant with a counterimperial reading of John the Baptist's apocalyptic message against Rome. His approach encourages settler Christians to research local biomes and Indigenous histories to creatively retell Scripture, fostering curiosity and empathy while revealing new dimensions of biblical stories. We also recommend Myers's and Elaine Enns's *Healing Haunted Histories: A Settler Discipleship of Decolonization*, which offers nuanced interpretations of Scripture alongside guidance for settlers to explore their family histories, addressing both trauma and colonial legacies. This is an essential resource for settlers learning to walk gently toward justice and reconciliation with Indigenous neighbors.[66]

Damian Costello. Damian Costello, a Catholic scholar of Black Elk and director of postgraduate studies for NAIITS, has offered groundbreaking insights into ceremonial and sacramental theology within Scripture.[67] Costello identifies parallels between the symbolism of horns in ancient Hebrew tradition and their role in Plains Indigenous cultures, such as that of the Lakota.[68] In the Hebrew Bible, horns symbolize divine power, as seen in the phrase "the horn of my salvation" (Ps 18:2, NRSV), and represent mighty kings (Dan 7:7-8; Rev 5:6). When ancient Hebrews imagined and sought to depict divine power,

---

[65] Ched Myers, "A Shaman Appeared in Ventura," in Heinrichs, *Unsettling the Word*, 193.
[66] Elaine Enns and Ched Myers, *Healing Haunted Histories: A Settler Discipleship of Decolonization* (Eugene, OR: Cascade Books, 2021).
[67] See Damian Costello, *Black Elk: Colonialism and Lakota Catholicism* (Maryknoll, NY: Orbis Books, 2005); Costello, "With the Red Heifer Ceremony, God Purifies the People Through the Earth," Earthbeat, April 25, 2024, www.ncronline.org/earthbeat/viewpoints/red-heifer-ceremony-god-purifies-people-through-earth; Costello, "Black Elk, White Buffalo Woman and the Mystery of the Red Heifer Ceremony," Earthbeat, April 26, 2024, www.ncronline.org/earthbeat/viewpoints/black-elk-white-buffalo-woman-and-mystery-red-heifer-ceremony.
[68] Damian Costello, "In Vermont Parishes I Rediscovered the Power of Moses' Horns and an Ox's Sacrifice," Earthbeat, February 25, 2023, www.ncronline.org/earthbeat/viewpoints/vermont-parishes-i-rediscovered-power-moses-horns-and-oxs-sacrifice; Costello, "A Buffalo Skull Behind the Altar Harkens Back to the Horn of Salvation," Earthbeat, April 17, 2023, www.ncronline.org/earthbeat/viewpoints/buffalo-skull-behind-altar-harkens-back-horn-salvation.

the horns of the mighty auroch often came to mind, an intimidating ancestor of modern cattle. The ark of the covenant features horns (Ex 27:2, 1 Kings 1:51; Amos 3:14; Rev 9:13), and Numbers 23:22 compares God's power to the horns of wild oxen. Similarly, for Plains peoples, bison horns and skulls symbolize strength and divine power, often filled with sweetgrass and adorning medicine lodges and Native churches. While dismissed by some settlers as idolatrous, this iconography offers insights into how ancient Hebrews symbolized divine power.[69]

Costello also examines the New Testament's representation of Jesus as a sacrificial ox. The Gospels of Matthew, Mark, and Luke and Hebrews describe Jesus' blood as the "blood of the covenant" (Mt 26:28; Mk 14:24; Lk 22:20; Heb 9:20; 10:29), recalling Exodus 24, where Moses binds Israel to Creator through the sacrifice of oxen. The oxen's blood, splashed on both the altar and the people, creates a covenantal bond, making them blood relatives with Creator and the blood-red earth from which Adam ("earth") came.[70] Just as the oxen then provided a great feast for Israelites, so does Jesus' body provide sustenance for his followers in the Eucharist. Costello also notes the visual resemblance of Jesus on the cross to an ox or bison skull, connecting this imagery to Psalm 22, which Jesus references from the cross (Mk 15:34; Mt 27:46). The psalm describes Creator answering a cry for help "from the horns of the wild oxen" (Ps 22:21). Costello's work invites readers to reconsider the rich, overlapping symbolism of horns and sacrifice in biblical and Indigenous traditions, offering new depth to the phrase "the horn of our salvation."[71]

THE FUTURE IS INDIGENOUS

As we honor our uncles and aunties, we also celebrate the emerging voices of Indigenous scholars in biblical studies and theology. Many are just beginning to publish or are still earning credentials, yet their contributions are already

---

[69] As for other overlapping functions of horns, the ancient Hebrews used rams' horns to store sacred oil for anointing (Ps 92:10; 1 Sam 16:13; 1 Kings 1:39), similar to how Indigenous people used bison horns to store medicine.

[70] Damian Costello, "Through the Blood of Christ the Ox, the Eucharist Raises Us to 'Real Life,'" Earthbeat, July 9, 2024, www.ncronline.org/earthbeat/viewpoints/through-blood-christ-ox-eucharist-raises-us-real-life.

[71] See esp. Costello, "With the Red Heifer Ceremony"; Costello "Black Elk, White Buffalo Woman," where Costello shares the story of Black Elk's vision of Wanikiya, "a red spirit who transformed into a buffalo and sacred medicine so that the people may live," whom Black Elk identifies with Jesus or "He Who Makes Live"—further connecting Jesus with bison/red heifer within a Lakota theology.

shaping the field. Below we highlight several who inspire us and others in the NAIITS community.

Anna M. V. Bowden and Meredith Warren. Chris initially felt alone as a Choctaw biblical scholar until meeting Danny and later Anna M. V. Bowden (Choctaw), associate professor of New Testament at Louisville Seminary. Bowden's 2024 presentation at the Society of Biblical Literature, "Ganiodaiio, John of Patmos, and the Dangers of Assimilation," compares how Handsome Lake, a Seneca prophet, and John of Patmos both see a "bloodied Jesus" in their visions. Neither prophet, Bowden argues, wants their audience to forget that Jesus was brutally killed at the hands of imperial power or to forget others who have similarly been harmed by the empires that rule over them. Similarly, Meredith J. C. Warren (Métis), senior lecturer at the University of Sheffield, is working on apocalyptic themes in the Indigenous novel *Moon of the Crusted Snow* by Waubgeshig Rice (Anishinaabe). Stay tuned!

Kelly Sherman-Conroy and Lisa Dellinger. Kelly Sherman-Conroy (Lakota), pastor of All Nations Church in Minneapolis and the first Indigenous woman to earn a doctorate in Lutheran theology, reads John the Baptist as a *heyoka* (sacred clown) who disrupts norms to elicit deeper insight, echoing Steven Charleston's analysis.[72] "In Native theology," Charleston explains, "John's [contrarian] role is to paint the background so the figure in the foreground may stand out even more clearly. This is the work of the *heyoka* in traditional Native society."[73]

Lisa Dellinger (Chickasaw), trained under Tink Tinker, contributed a chapter on sin in *Coming Full Circle*.[74] Her work shows how settler Christian notions of sin imposed traumatic hierarchies on Native peoples, displacing Indigenous values of harmony. Dellinger envisions healing through centering the Holy Spirit as active in our Indigenous stories and theological anthropology.[75]

Amy N. Allan. Amy N. Allan (Choctaw, Cherokee, Tuscarora) is completing her dissertation with NAIITS, which juxtaposes Genesis with Indigenous

---

[72]Charleston, *Four Vision Quests*, 56-64.
[73]Charleston, *Four Vision Quests*, 83.
[74]Lisa A. Dellinger, "Sin—Ambiguity and Complexity and the Sin of Not Conforming," in Charleston and Robinson, *Coming Full Circle*, 119-32.
[75]Lisa A. Dellinger, "Reclaiming Indigenous and Christian Narrative Epistemologies: Refusing US Settler Colonialism's Theological Anthropology of Sin" (PhD diss., Garrett-Evangelical Theological Seminary, 2019).

stories to consider how each depicts the divine and how such characterizations shape how we relate with Creator, other humans, and our more-than-human kin.[76] In reading Genesis in conversation with the creation story associated with Sky Woman, as shared among the Haudenosaunee, Allan highlights shared values of gratitude, ecological respect, and sacrality of space.[77] Both stories challenge Western hierarchies that elevate humans over creation. Allan calls for solidarity with creation, pursuing the Cherokee value of *tohi*—harmony, reciprocity, respect, and calming peace.

Mackenzie Griffin. Mackenzie Griffin (Cree, Saulteaux) creatively retells the exodus story through a First Nations lens in a story submitted as a creative final project for a NAIITS course taught by Chris. Griffin frames the story of Moses, whom she names zhaabiiwose or "The One Who Walks through Waters" in Ojibwe/Saulteaux, within a larger narrative of an eight-year-old child recalling his grandmother's stories in an attempt to cope with his struggles in an Indian residential school in Canada. The child remembers his grandmother's story of zhaabiiwose, a child who, like himself, was scooped up from his First Nations family and raised by a family from the dominating culture. If Griffin's artful premise weren't fascinating enough, she provides an inspired retelling of Moses hitting the rock of Horeb (Ex 17; Num 20) that offers a compelling reason as to why God punishes Moses so harshly, prohibiting him from entering the Promised Land, for striking the rock twice.

> So, raising [his staff] in the air to silence the people, [zhaabiiwose] gets ready to speak, but they don't stop talking over one another. He gets frustrated, strikes the rock twice. Water pours out and the people drink. "That's good right?" I interject, still not quite sure where the story is going. "Oh yes, the people needed water. Just as I said, Kisemanito [the Creator] is kind, compassionate, always willing to listen to those complaining tribal people. But zhaabiiwose wasn't supposed to hit the rock. The rock was powerful, sacred. It contained all the water that would clench the people's thirst. When zhaabiiwose smashed the rock, he violated the people's treaty. The ancient treaty, between

---

[76] Amy N. Allan's publications include "Pursuit of Harmony with Nature: A Theological Reflection on Creation Based on Genesis 1–2 and the Native American Sky Woman Story," *Ex Auditu: An International Journal for the Theological Interpretation of Scripture* 37 (forthcoming). See also Allan, "Women Are Sacred: Indigenous Perspectives on the Bible and Women," in *The Bible and Women*, vol. 9.2, *The Contemporary Period: Current Trends*, ed. Lidia Rodríguez Fernández, Ilse Müllner, Arianna Rotondo, and Mary Ann Beavis (Atlanta: SBL Press, forthcoming).

[77] Allan, "Pursuit of Harmony with Nature."

Kisemanito and zhaabiiwose's ancestors. The one that demanded respect and generosity for all of creation. The one that said we would never abuse what had already been given to us freely."

Griffin's story suggests that Moses' shortcoming lies in violating an ancient treaty of respect with creation. While we may never know what the Hebrew scribes intended or how its earliest audiences understood this story, here is a beautiful example of Indigenous midrash or interpretative expansion of the Numbers story that celebrates Indigenous values and assumptions about our kinship with creation, which includes respect for the rocks.

SMOKE SIGNALS: DRIVING FORWARD, LOOKING BACKWARD

Well, one last awkward omission. We recognize that we missed an opportunity to reference the classic 1998 film *Smoke Signals*. The movie, based on Sherman Alexie's *The Lone Ranger and Tonto Fistfight in Heaven*, itself is a coming-of-age journey story following two young men, Thomas (played by Evan Adams) and Victor (played by Adam Beach), who set out on a road trip from their Coeur d'Alene Reservation in Idaho to retrieve the ashes of Victor's estranged father. In this dramedy, Thomas and Victor explore what it means to be Native, wrestle with the legacy of alcohol and abuse, and reconcile over their conflicting feelings over Victor's father, whom Victor resents and Thomas admires at the beginning of the film. It's also a sort of coming-of-age, rite-of-passage movie for Native youth today, with parents sitting their children down to watch this film or college students discovering it for the first time at their Native American student gatherings. Blurting out Thomas's iconic line *"Hey Victor!"* is enough to garner a smile from the most stoic among us.

That said, there is a scene that fits with the theme of this chapter. As Thomas and Victor make their way out of the reservation, walking along the highway, a car approaches them, driven by Lucy Goosey (played by Elaine Miles) with her friend. The girls barter a ride for a story from Thomas, who tells a story about Victor's dad, Arnold, who, to quote Danny's favorite line, "[during the sixties] was the perfect hippie, because all the hippies were trying to be Indians anyway." Of interest to us is the car, which can apparently only drive *in reverse*, with Lucy looking out the rearview mirror as she makes her way backward *going forward* to her destination. This scene brings a smile to our faces as it connects us to our elder and Uncle Terry LeBlanc—who too was once a "perfect hippie" and whose own customary signoff for emails, "smoke signals from the trail," inspired our chapter title. The car driving in reverse embodies Uncle Terry's understanding of Indigenous principles of progress, which involves walking into the future *backward*, with our focus on what has worked well in the past to guide us forward. It is in this spirit that we have focused on those who have done good work before us and who spent time with us during our research, as we invite readers to imagine new possible futures and directions to travel.

GENERAL INDEX

Acting Good, 103-4
Ahab and Jezebel, 106-8
Aldred, Cat, 206-7
Aldred, Ray, 19-20, 109, 196-97, 200, 206-7
Allan, Amy N., 212-13
ancestors, 2, 8-11, 20, 34, 37, 68, 79, 83-90, 102
Apess, William, 192-93
asset-based theology, 22-25, 160, 163-64
Augustine, 16
Augustine, Sarah, 129
Babylonian exile (as interpretive lens), 14, 68, 74, 113-16, 118-19, 120
Baldridge, William, 205
Bauckham, Richard, 35-36, 49, 75
Bear, Cheryl, 87, 176, 196, 209
Begay, Donnie, 59
Begay, Renee, 86
Black Elk, 8, 62-63, 92-95, 98, 101, 207, 210
boarding schools (U.S.), 132-38
Bowden, Anna M. V., 212
Brave Heart, Basil, 15, 135, 142, 150-51
Brett, Mark, 37
Bright Path/Harmony Way, 56-59, 65, 74
Brokenleg, Martin, 20, 84, 203
Buck, Allen, 125
buffalo and the Great Race (Lakota), 33-34
Canaanites and conquest narratives, 122-23, 128, 204
Catholic Church 2022 apology, 148-49
ceremony, 17, 21, 26, 28, 30, 58-59, 61-63, 65, 67, 76-78, 80, 83, 88, 100, 121, 125, 140, 150-51, 162-66, 168-77, 180-83
Charles, Mark, 149, 205
Charleston, Steven, 11-12, 59, 61-63, 68, 96-97, 99, 113, 201-2
Cherokee plant-medicine story, 55-56
Church, Casey, 15, 21, 58, 168, 186
Clah, Arthur Wellington, 107-8, 193
Clatterbuck, Mark, 26, 208
Colgan, Emily, 41

community of creation, 5-6, 10, 16, 19, 28, 34-35, 38-39, 44-50, 53-54, 56, 58, 74-75, 80
Corn Mother, 27, 63-64, 195
Crist, Mary, 204-5
cultural genocide, 6, 11, 22, 27-28, 133, 135, 151
Dawson, Christina, 176
decolonization/decolonizing biblical interpretation, 7, 11, 125, 129, 154, 208-9
Dellinger, Lisa, 59, 212
Deloria, Ella Cara, 187-88
Deloria Jr., Vine, 76, 79-80, 91, 97, 100, 104, 193-94
Doctrine of Discovery, 3-4, 6, 25, 125-26, 129
Donaldson, Laura E., 202-3
dreams and visions, 56, 84, 90-96, 98-102, 188
Eggie, Cameron, 155
Elijah, 50, 71-72, 89, 96, 107
Enns, Elaine, 47, 105-6, 209-10
Fools Crow, Frank, 63
Good Medicine Way, 15
Great Race (Lakota creation tale), 32-34, 55
Griffin, Mackenzie, 213-14
guilt, national vs. individual, 147
Harmony Way, 56-60, 92-93, 126, 128-30, 188-89
Hawk, L. Daniel, 208
He Sapa (Black Hills, South Dakota), 111-12
Heinrichs, Steve, 209
Hernandez, Ted, 169-71
Holy Spirit, 16-19, 21-22, 26-28, 31, 52-53, 60, 66, 90-91, 94, 97, 100-102, 158
Indian Act (1875), 149-50, 178-79
individualism, 35, 58, 84, 137, 194
intergenerational trauma, 87, 105, 134, 143, 186
Jackson, Kimberlee Medicine Horn, 15-16
Jacobs, Adrian, 110, 127, 197-98
Jennings, Willie James, 24, 146
Joerstad, Mari, 47, 201
Johnson, Elizabeth, 51, 65
Jolly, Karen, 180
jubilee, 57, 69-74, 77-78, 80

GENERAL INDEX

Kidwell, Clara Sue, 34, 194, 202
King, Thomas, 30
Kolia, Brian, 41
Krawec, Patty, 129, 151
Krischke, Megan Murdock, 157-58
Lajimodiere, Denise K., 141-44, 150
Land Back movement, 124-27
land, theology of, 36-39, 43, 45, 69-70, 72
language revitalization, 22, 28-29
LeBlanc, Matt, 22
LeBlanc, Terry, 22-23, 60, 87, 126, 164, 196, 198-99, 214-15
Leviathan, 10, 14, 40-41
liturgy (native hymnody), 113, 115-16, 120-21
Lomawaima, K. Tsianina, 154-55
MacDonald, Mark, 202
Manifest Destiny, 4, 154
Martin, Willard, 11, 136
McKay, Mabel, 94, 99
McKinney, Ron, 120-21
medicine wheel, 7-9, 19, 25, 28, 89, 91, 105, 163, 185, 188
missions/missionaries, 11, 15, 26-28, 58, 82, 104, 151, 160, 175, 192, 198
Montijo Fink, Kelly, 90
Moses, 50, 52, 65, 85, 89, 96, 100, 121, 132-33, 156, 167, 210-11, 213
Myers, Ched, 47, 105-6, 124-25, 209-10
Naboth's vineyard (land dispossession), 105-6
NAGPRA (Native American Graves Protection and Repatriation Act), 154
NAIITS (Indigenous Learning Community), xiv-xvi, 1, 22-23, 31, 87, 132, 152, 161-62, 186, 195-96
Nez Perce land return (Wallowa), 125
Noley, Homer, 34, 194, 202
numbered treaties (Canada), 107-12, 149, 178-79
Original Instructions (Original Testament), 12, 56-57, 59, 68, 83, 121
Paul, 3, 13, 22, 60, 63-66, 91, 96, 98-101, 157, 162-63, 165-66, 168, 172-77, 181
Peterson, Wendy, 162, 196
pipe ceremony, 21, 92, 150, 183
Porter, Crystal, 86-87, 196
Pretty On Top, Kenny, Jr., 67
Promised-land rhetoric in colonization, 4, 127-29, 146
Quintanilla, Christina, 87
Rachel's lament (mourning mothers), 151
Raheb, Mitri, 107
reconciliation, 148-52, 157-58, 205
reparations, 73, 106, 126-27, 130, 146-47, 158

Reservation Dogs, 82-3, 88, 180-81
residential schools (Canada), 132, 134-39, 144-46, 148-51, 155, 213
Robbins, Anna, 131, 147-48
round dance, 1-2, 28-29
Russell, Shari, 132-33, 196
salvation, 58, 60, 64, 68-69, 73-75, 80, 210
Scoops (60s, 80s, Millenium), 132-34, 136, 155, 189
Sky Woman, 2-3, 195
shalom (soteriology), 60-69
Sherman-Conroy, Kelly, 212
Shingoose, Dean, 91, 136
sin, 58-59, 62, 65
Sinclair, Raven, 133-34
Smith-Christopher, Daniel, 116, 152, 154, 156, 208
Smoke Signals, 214-15
Sneve, Paul, 67, 164, 181
Snow, Tony, 91, 136
sovereignty (religious and national), 177-80
Standing Bear, Luther, 139-40
Street-Stewart, Elona, 31
sun dance, 28, 61-63, 66, 177-78, 181
temptation narrative, 17, 51-53, 72, 75, 96-97
terra nullius, 4, 128
Three Stars, Lenore, 32, 35
time orientation, 38, 163-64
Tinker, Tink, 27-28, 34, 64, 164
Trail of Tears, 113-18, 179, 189, 201
Treat, James, 205
treaties, Peace and Friendship Treaties, 149
treaty-covenant theology, 107-12, 121-22, 127-30
Treaty of Dancing Rabbit Creek, 112-13, 117
Truth and Reconciliation Commission of Canada, 125-26, 135, 143, 145-46, 148-49
Twiss, Richard, 23, 89-90, 122, 160-61, 166, 177
vision quests, 17, 96-97, 201
Wabanaki/Abenaki creation story, 2-3
Wallace, Mark, 201
Warren, Meredith J. C., 212
Warrior, Robert, 128, 204
Weaver, Jace, 68, 192, 204-6
Wildman, Terry, 207-8
Wilson, David, 82
Wilson, Eugene, 28-29
Wilson, Larry, 20, 91
Woodley, Edith, 55, 195, 199
Woodley, Randy S., 31, 55-58, 79, 123, 199-200
World Christian Gathering of Indigenous Peoples, 197-98
Wovoka, 93
Yarholar, Clarence, 15, 58, 168

SCRIPTURE INDEX

APOCRYPHA

Tobit
4:17, *85*

Sirach
30:18, *85*

Epistle of Jeremiah
60-69, *174*

1 Maccabees
1:63, *141*
2:19, *86*
2:51, *86*

OLD TESTAMENT

Genesis
1, *21, 25, 34, 39, 40, 43, 45, 52, 163*
1–2, *13, 57, 213*
1–3, *37*
1:2, *52*
1:3, *44*
1:4, *44*
1:5, *44*
1:6, *44*
1:7, *44*
1:8, *44*
1:9, *44*
1:10, *44*
1:11, *44*
1:11-13, *45*
1:12, *44, 45*
1:14, *44*
1:16, *44*
1:17-18, *44*
1:18, *44*
1:20, *44*

1:20-21, *36*
1:21, *44*
1:22, *36, 40, 44, 45*
1:24, *36, 44, 45*
1:25, *44*
1:26, *44*
1:27, *25, 34, 44*
1:28, *27, 42, 45*
1:29-30, *45*
1:30, *36*
2, *36, 37*
2:1, *36*
2:4, *37, 72*
2:5-8, *39*
2:7, *36*
2:15, *38, 39, 78, 121*
2:18, *39*
2:21-24, *51*
3, *23, 25, 163*
3:8, *50*
4, *174*
4:10, *36, 130, 135*
4:12, *38*
6:17, *51*
8:20–9:17, *42*
9, *43*
9:1, *42*
9:1-17, *42*
9:5, *42*
9:5-17, *121*
9:6, *25*
11:1-9, *197*
12:4-9, *167*
13:18, *167*
14:22, *123*
15:18-21, *121*
17:1, *121*
17:1-22, *121*
17:9, *38*
18:1, *167*

18:10, *167*
18:18, *72*
21:22-24, *123*
21:25-34, *123*
23:4, *123*
23:7, *123*
23:12, *123*
32:22-31, *9, 105*
37:5-8, *95*
41:1-45, *95*

Exodus
2, *133*
2:12, *133*
2:13-14, *133*
3:1, *52*
3:4, *52*
3:5, *52*
12:17, *38*
12:25, *38*
13:10, *38*
15:20, *168*
16:28, *38*
17, *213*
21:28, *43*
24, *211*
24:3-8, *121*
24:4-8, *65*
27:2, *211*
30:1-6, *169*
30:34-36, *169*
31:13-16, *38*
34:11-12, *123*

Leviticus
16:29-34, *147*
17–18, *182*
19:26-31, *85*
25:3-6, *70*
25:8-55, *69*

SCRIPTURE INDEX

25:23, *106*
25:23-28, *106*
25:25, *106*
26:44, *121*

Numbers
10:10, *167*
12:6, *94*
20, *213*
22:22-35, *47*
23:22, *211*
27, *204*
28:11-15, *167*
36:7, *106*

Deuteronomy
4:31, *121*
6:10-11, *129*
6:10-12, *129*
7:9, *121*
7:12, *123*
18:9, *86*
18:9-14, *85, 86*
18:11, *86*
18:13-14, *86*
26:14, *85*

Joshua
9, *122*
17, *204*

Judges
2:1, *121*
2:2, *123*
4:4-5, *167*
19–21, *6*

Ruth
1:8, *202*

1 Samuel
3:2-15, *95*
16:13, *211*
28–29, *85*

2 Samuel
6:5, *168*
21:1, *122*
21:2, *122*
21:5, *122*
21:9, *122*
21:14, *122*

1 Kings
1:39, *211*
1:51, *211*
17:8-24, *71*
21, *105*
21:1-7, *106*
21:8-16, *107*
21:17-26, *107*
22:19-23, *95*

2 Kings
5:1-14, *71*
25, *114*
25:11-12, *114*

1 Chronicles
29:14, *129*
29:15, *129*

2 Chronicles
18:18-22, *95*
36:15-21, *74*
36:20-21, *74*

Ezra
7:9, *116*

Nehemiah
5:1-13, *74*
5:13, *74*

Job
5:22-23, *75*
7:7-10, *86*
12:7-8, *18*
12:7-10, *16, 42*
38–41, *10, 41*
38:8-11, *14*
40, *10*
41, *10, 41*
41:1-34, *14, 41*

Psalms
2, *68*
8:3, *17*
15, *207*
15:1, *207*
15:5, *207*
18:2, *210*
19:2, *45*
22, *211*
22:21, *211*
50:6, *45*
74:12-14, *14*
78:1-4, *85*
92:10, *211*
97:6, *45*
104, *40, 41, 45*
104:5-9, *40*
104:6-9, *14*
104:10-13, *40*
104:14-23, *40*
104:19-23, *40*
104:25-26, *40*
104:26, *14, 40, 41*
104:27-30, *41*
104:31, *45*
105:8-10, *121*
137, *114, 118, 119, 120*
137:1, *119*
137:2, *119*
137:9, *120*
139:7-10, *21*
148:3, *17*
150:4, *168*
150:6, *46*

Proverbs
6:6-11, *16*
10–31, *10*
22:17–23:11, *10*
22:28, *86*
26:4-5, *13*

Ecclesiastes
5:6-7, *95*

Song of Solomon
4, *41*

Isaiah
2:3-4, *57*
8:18-20, *86*
8:19, *86*
11:6-9, *57, 75*
21:1-10, *95*
24:1-20, *46*
32:15-20, *46*
33:7-9, *46*
40:5, *75*
47:8, *120*
51:9-12, *13*
54:10, *121*

61, *71*
66:22-24, *167*

Jeremiah
3:6, *167*
4:23-28, *46*
12:1-4, *46*
12:7-13, *46*
17:9, *22*
23:9-12, *46*
23:16, *95*
23:32, *95*
31:15, *120, 151*
31:33, *121*
32:40, *121*
52, *114*

Ezekiel
1:23-25, *49*
6, *43*
6:9, *43*
6:13, *167*
9:1-10, *95*
16:59-62, *121*
18, *148*
18:4, *148*
37, *157*
37:9-10, *158*
37:12, *158*
37:14, *158*
37:25-26, *121*

Daniel
1:2, *152*
1:4, *139*
1:7, *139*
1:8, *140*
1:12, *140*
2, *144*
3, *141, 144*
3:1-6, *141*
3:7-18, *142*
3:19-28, *142*
3:25, *143, 152*
3:28-29, *144*
3:30, *144*
4, *144*
4:28-37, *153*
5, *153*
5:1-2, *153*
5:6, *153*
5:17-22, *153*

5:23-25, *153*
5:25, *153*
6, *142, 144*
6:24, *144*
6:25-28, *144*
6:28, *144*
7, *93*
7:7-8, *210*
11:32, *150*

Hosea
4:1-3, *46*

Joel
1:5-20, *46*
2:28, *90*

Amos
1:2, *46*
3:14, *211*
8:1-2, *95*
9:7, *3, 72*

Zechariah
6:1-8, *95*

NEW TESTAMENT

Matthew
1–2, *206*
1:1-14, *206*
1:3-6, *72*
1:20-25, *96*
2, *206*
2:12, *96*
2:13, *96*
2:18, *151*
2:19-23, *96*
3:16, *97*
4:1-11, *96*
4:2, *97*
5:45, *72*
7:15-20, *18*
8:5-13, *205*
8:28-34, *205*
13:24-30, *18*
15:21-28, *205*
15:28, *205*
16:2-3, *18*
17, *46*
17:1-8, *89, 96*
17:25, *46*

19:16-30, *73, 124*
21:19-21, *18*
26:28, *122, 211*
26:36-46, *96*
27:19, *96*
27:32-55, *96*
27:46, *211*
28:19, *52*

Mark
1:1-8, *193*
1:1-9, *209*
1:12-13, *17*
1:13, *75*
1:14, *51*
3:34-35, *9*
4:30-32, *18*
5:1-20, *205*
8:22-25, *75*
9:2-8, *89*
10:17, *124*
10:17-31, *73, 124*
10:19, *124*
10:20, *124*
10:21, *124*
10:22, *124*
10:46, *207*
10:46-52, *207*
10:52, *207*
14:24, *122, 211*
15:34, *211*

Luke
1, *72*
1:8-10, *169*
1:8-23, *96*
1:26-38, *96*
1:28-30, *72*
1:51-53, *72*
1:80, *75*
2:8, *75*
2:8-14, *96*
2:36-38, *72*
2:52, *17, 206*
3:2-6, *75*
3:22, *52*
4, *70*
4:21, *71*
4:28-30, *71*
5:1-11, *77*
5:30, *73*
6:12-16, *73*

SCRIPTURE INDEX

7:1-10, *205*
7:11-12, *72*
7:34, *73*
7:41-42, *72*
8:2-3, *73*
8:4-8, *18*
8:26-39, *205*
8:39, *205*
8:48, *73*
9:28-36, *89, 96*
9:31, *89*
9:35, *89*
9:36, *89*
9:53, *89*
12:24-30, *18*
15, *67*
15:1-2, *73*
17:11-19, *73*
17:21, *79*
18:18-30, *73, 124*
19:1-10, *126*
19:8, *126*
19:8-9, *73*
21:1-4, *72*
22:20, *122, 211*
23:27, *73*
23:44-45, *75*
23:49, *73*
23:55-56, *73*
24, *208*
24:6-10, *73*

John
1:11, *54*
1:14, *51*
3:16, *53, 74*
4, *209*
10:22-23, *167*
19:14, *65*
19:36, *65*

Acts
2:17-18, *66*
2:42, *165*
2:46, *168*
3:1, *168*
5:19-21, *96*
5:20-22, *168*
8:26-40, *96*
9:1-9, *99*
9:10-19, *96*
9:11-12, *99*
9:20, *168*
10:1-6, *96*
10:1-48, *205*
10:10-20, *96*
12:7-10, *96*
13:5, *168*
13:14-15, *168*
15, *13*
15:1-29, *181*
15:12, *181*
15:13-21, *182*
15:28, *182*
16:6-10, *99*
17:26, *3*
18:9-11, *99*
18:26, *168*
19:8, *168*
21:26-30, *168*
22:6-11, *99*
22:17-21, *99*
22:21, *99*
26:12-18, *99*
26:16, *99*
26:18, *99*
27:23-24, *99*

Romans
3:9, *22*
3:10, *22*
3:10-18, *22*
3:23-24, *65*
3:25, *65*
4:25, *65*
5–6, *177*
5:9, *65*
5:10-11, *65*
6:6, *166*
7:23, *65*
8, *54, 202*
8:9-11, *66*
8:15-17, *9*
8:17, *68*
8:18-23, *54*
8:21, *54*
8:22, *54*
8:34, *65*
10:9, *60*
14:1, *177*
14:2-3, *177*
14:3, *177*
14:5-6, *168*

1 Corinthians
2:1, *98*
2:7, *98*
3:16, *22, 66*
4:1, *98*
5:7, *65*
6:19, *21*
6:20, *65*
11:23-34, *165*
11:25, *65*
11:26, *165*
11:33, *165, 182*
14:2, *98*
15:3-5, *98*
15:8, *98*
15:20-23, *166*
15:51, *98*
15:53-57, *65*

2 Corinthians
3, *100*
3:15-16, *100*
5, *157*
5:17, *162, 166*
5:18-19, *157*
6:17, *162, 166*
12:1-12, *99*
12:2-7, *98*
12:9, *99*

Galatians
1:6-9, *100*
1:11-12, *98, 173*
1:15-16, *98*
2, *13*
2:1-10, *176*
2:2-3, *98*
2:3-4, *176*
2:4, *176*
2:11-14, *173*
3:7, *9*
3:15-18, *173*
3:22, *174*
3:23, *174*
3:26, *98*
3:27, *67*
4, *173*
4:3, *173*
4:4-7, *9*
4:5, *172*
4:6-7, *66*
4:8, *175*

4:8-11, *162, 173*
4:21-31, *100*
5:1, *176*
5:11-12, *100*
5:12, *173*
5:13, *176*
5:16, *176*
5:22-23, *176*
6:13, *100*

Ephesians
1:9, *98*
3:3-4, *98*
4:22, *166*
6:19, *98*

Philippians
3:2, *100*
3:12, *80*
3:20, *79*

Colossians
1:15, *51*
1:15-20, *42, 74*
1:17, *50*
1:20, *3, 54*
1:24, *63*

1:26-27, *98*
2:2, *98*
2:16, *167*
3:9, *166*
3:12-15, *57*
4:3, *98*

1 Thessalonians
4, *93*

2 Timothy
3:16, *10*

Hebrews
2:7, *34*
7:19, *88*
7:22, *88*
8:6, *88*
9:14, *66*
9:20, *211*
9:23, *88*
10:29, *211*
10:32-34, *87*
11, *87*
11–12:12, *87*
11:35–12:3, *87*
12:1, *87*

2 Peter
1:4, *66*

1 John
3:24, *22*
4:13, *22*

Jude
12, *182*

Revelation
4–5, *1, 2, 49*
4:2-11, *48*
4:3, *48*
4:3-4, *48*
4:6-8, *49*
4:7, *49*
4:9, *50*
4:10, *50*
5:6, *210*
5:8-14, *50*
5:9, *1, 11*
9:13, *211*
21–22, *50*
21:5, *54*

www.ingramcontent.com/pod-product-compliance
Lightning Source LLC
Chambersburg PA
CBHW031426150426
43191CB00006B/408